D1616801

Tip of the Spear

A VOLUME IN THE SERIES

THE UNITED STATES IN THE WORLD

Edited by Benjamin A. Coates, Emily Conroy-Krutz,
Paul A. Kramer, and Judy Tzu-Chun Wu
Founding Series Editors: Mark Philip Bradley and Paul A. Kramer

A list of titles in this series is available at cornellpress.cornell.edu.

Tip of the Spear

Land, Labor, and US Settler Militarism
in Guåhan, 1944-1962

Alfred Peredo Flores

Cornell University Press
Ithaca and London

First published 2023 by Cornell University Press

Library of Congress Cataloging-in-Publication Data

Names: Flores, Alfred Peredo, 1980– author.
Title: Tip of the spear: land, labor, and US settler militarism
    in Guåhan, 1944–1962 / Alfred Peredo Flores.
Description: Ithaca: Cornell University Press, 2023. | Series: The
    United States in the world | Includes bibliographical references
    and index. |
Identifiers: LCCN 2022055136 (print) | LCCN 2022055137 (ebook) |
    ISBN 9781501771347 (hardcover) | ISBN 9781501771354 (pdf) |
    ISBN 9781501771361 (epub)
Subjects: LCSH: Militarism—Guam—History—20th century. |
    Guam—Politics and government—20th century. |
    Guam—History—20th century. | United States—Armed
    Forces—Guam.
Classification: LCC DU647 .F56 2023 (print) | LCC DU647 (ebook) |
    DDC 355.02/1309967—dc23/eng/20221122
LC record available at https://lccn.loc.gov/2022055136
LC ebook record available at https://lccn.loc.gov/2022055137

Dedicated to my parents and ancestors

Contents

Acknowledgments   ix

Note on Language   xv

Abbreviations   xvii

Introduction: Becoming the Tip of America's Spear   1

1. CHamoru Land Stewardship and Military Land Taking   16

2. The Remaking of Guåhan   41

3. The Civilian Military Workers of Guåhan   61

4. Militarized Intimacies   87

5. From Breadbasket to Naval Air Station   114

Conclusion   133

Notes   137

Bibliography   173

Index   199

Acknowledgments

The support I received from colleagues, family members, mentors, and friends was instrumental in the making of this book. I would first like to express my gratitude to the *manåmko'* (elders) who allowed me to interview them. Much of the knowledge I have obtained has come from the people who graciously trusted me with their stories and to the family and friends who have passed on. They have taught me life lessons that will live on through me and in the generations that follow.

This book took root while I was a graduate student at the University of California, Riverside. Thank you to Lucille Chia, Rebecca "Monte" Kugel, Robert Perez, Dylan Rodríguez, and Clifford Trafzer for your guidance. Special thanks go to Monte for encouraging me to apply to PhD programs that could support my research aspirations and to Robert for introducing me to Native Studies. In particular, Robert's mentorship put me on the path that has led me to the publishing of this book.

As a doctoral student at the University of California, Los Angeles (UCLA), I was supported by a community of classmates, faculty mentors, friends, and staff members in writing my dissertation. Thank you to Milo Alvarez, Juliann Anesi, Victor Bascara, Ellen-Rae Cachola, Miguel Chavez, Jolie Chea, Chris Chin, Jean-Paul deGuzman, Melany Delacruz-Viesca, Gabe Flores, Elizabeth González Cárdenas, Carlos Hernandez, Kelly Lytle Hernández, Lauren Hirshberg, Kris Kaupalolo, Dahlia Morrone, Hadley Porter, Brandon Reilly, Christen Sasaki, Charlie Sepulveda, José Luis Serrano Nájera, Eboni Shaw, Michael Slaughter, Meg Thornton, Kēhaulani Vaughn, Pualani Warren, and David Yoo. A special shout-out to Brandon, Charlie, Christen, Gabe, Jean-Paul, Juliann, Kēhaulani, and Pualani for their continued support. I also want to acknowledge Keith L. Camacho, Robin Derby, Toby Higbie, and Valerie Matsumoto, who served on my dissertation committee. Keith and Valerie deserve recognition for reading several drafts of my dissertation, writing dozens of recommendation letters, and sharing every ounce of knowledge they have with me. For these and other acts of generosity, I am indebted to Keith and Valerie for positively influencing my development as a scholar, teacher, and mentor. I strive to support my students the way you have and still do for me today.

In regard to research support, I would like to acknowledge the staff at the Humanities Guåhan (formerly the Guam Humanities Council); *Leatherneck* magazine; US National Archives and Records Administration in College Park, Maryland, and in San Bruno, California; the Nieves M. Flores Memorial Library; the Richard F. Taitano Micronesian Area Research Center at the University of Guam; the Guam Preservation Trust; and the Hamilton Library at the University of Hawai'i at Mānoa. Special thanks goes to Stuart Dawrs, Patty Everett, Robert Glass, Terry Kennimer, Kimberlee Kihleng, Marisa Louie, Lourdes Nededog, Perry Pangelinan, Nathaniel Patch, Sandra Stanley, Monique Storie, and Charles Wheeler. The funding to support the research for this book has come from the following institutions: UC Center for New Racial Studies; UCLA American Indian Studies Center; UCLA Asian American Studies Center; UCLA Department of History; UCLA Graduate Division; UCLA Institute of American Cultures; and the Western History Association. Portions of chapter 3 first appeared as "No Walk in the Park: US Empire and the Racialization of Civilian Military Labor in Guam, 1944–1962," *American Quarterly* 67, no. 3 (September 2015): 813–835, copyright © 2015 The American Studies Association.

I am also fortunate to have had the support of people who have shared their knowledge of Guåhan history and CHamoru culture with me. *Saina ma'åse* to Jesi Lujan Bennett, Michael Lujan Bevacqua, Mar-Vic Cagurangan, Jacob Camacho, Leevin Camacho, Michael Clement, Hope Cristobal, Vivian Dames, Micki Davis, Tina DeLisle, Vince Diaz, James Farley, Ann Hattori, William Hernandez, Frankie Laanan, Victoria-Lola Leon Guerrero, David Lujan, Fran Lujan, Hope Cristobal Lujan, Kelly Marsh, Antoinette Charfauros McDaniel, Jolene Mendiola, Laurel Monnig, Shannon Murphy, Tiara Na'puti, Leiana Naholowa'a, Lisa Natividad, Kristin Oberiano, Josephine Ong, Craig Perez, Michael Perez, Heidi Quenga, Joey Quenga, Joe

Quinata, Sett Quinata, Carmen Quintinalla, Olivia Quintanilla, Raymond Ramirez, Jenna Sablan, the late Joe T. San Agustin, Bernie Schumann, Jessica Solis-Bado, Christine Tenorio, Michael Tuncap, Robert Underwood, and James Perez Viernes.

At the Claremont Colleges, I thank my colleagues for their support and kindness: Sefa Aina, Jennifer Alanis, Bill Alves, Claudia Arteaga, Aimee Bahng, Isabel Balseiro, Jih-Fei Cheng, Wendy Cheng, David Cubek, Ambereen Dadabhoy, Marianne de Laet, Stacey Doan, Erika Dyson, Gary Evans, Ken Fandell, Anup Gampa, Madeline Gosiaco, Sharon Goto, Jeff Groves, Vivien Hamilton, Todd Honma, Charles Kamm, Zayn Kassam, Debbie Laird, Linda Lam, Warren Liu, Joyce Lu, Julia Lum, Mike Manalo-Pedro, Rachel Mayeri, April Mayes, Jane Mi, Sarah Lynn Miralles, Lynne Miyake, M. Bilal Nasir, Gladys Nubla, Giovanni Ortega, Sal Plascencia, JoAnna Poblete, Tomás Sandoval, David Seitz, Paul Steinberg, Lisa Sullivan, Asena Taione-Filihia, Hung Thai, Tamara Venit-Shelton, Darryl Wright, Linus Yamane, and Kathy Yep.

I am also grateful for another group of individuals who have supported me in a variety of ways. Thanks go to Crystal Baik, Rick Baldoz, Dan Borses, Connie Chen, Patrick Chung, Augusto Espiritu, Becka Garrison, Anna Gonzalez, Rudy Guevarra, Christine Hong, Jane Hong, Monica Kim, Lon Kurashige, Shelley Sang-Hee Lee, the late Paul Lyons, Erica Morales, Madelsar Ngiraingas, Fuifuilupe Niumeitolu, Kiri Sailiata, Dean Saranillio, Paul Spickard, Amy Sueyoshi, Ty Tengan, Victor Thompson, Susie Woo, Kristi Woods, Erin Kahunawaika'ala Wright, Grace Wu, and Judy Tzu-Chun Wu. In particular, Judy deserves special recognition for her continued mentorship and support.

My book has also greatly benefited from the opportunities to circulate earlier versions of it with several groups of scholars. At the Claremont Colleges, I participated in a writing group with Jih-Fei Cheng, Todd Honma, and Gladys Nubla that was supported through a Claremont Colleges 2019–2020 professional development network grant. Their feedback was integral in helping me draft a book proposal that I eventually submitted to Cornell University Press. Todd deserves additional acknowledgment for organizing us and writing the grant that we were funded with. Then, in February 2020, I held a book manuscript workshop with scholars Maile Arvin, Wendy Cheng, Todd Honma, Jana Lipman, David Seitz, and Judy Tzu-Chun Wu. Their comments drastically improved the book. Todd deserves my additional recognition for organizing the workshop. Finally, in April 2022, I circulated two chapters from my book with faculty and students at UCLA.

I want to thank Olivia Anderson, Juliann Anesi, Lance Bello, Keith L. Camacho, Jolie Chea, Evyn Lê Espiritu Gandhi, Gabrielle Lupola, Valerie Matsumoto, Henrietta McNeill, Adam Moore, Josephine Ong, Jessica Schwartz, and Avory Wyatt for providing me with insightful feedback on the conceptual framework for the book. Their support and collegiality helped move me forward in the revision process. Special thanks goes to Adam for commenting on an additional chapter.

I also want to thank the entire Cornell University Press team. Special appreciation goes to Sarah Grossman, Michael McGandy, and Jackie Teoh for their prompt responses to all of my inquiries and for their patience as I navigate the book-publishing world for the first time. I would also like to recognize The United States in the World series editors, Benjamin A. Coates, Emily Conroy-Krutz, Paul A. Kramer, and Judy Tzu-Chun Wu. I am grateful to have their guidance and support of this book. Finally, I want to thank the two anonymous readers whose comments have tremendously improved my manuscript, David Martinez for serving as my indexer, and production and copy editors Michelle Asakawa, Mary Kate Murphy, and Mary C. Ribesky.

The completion of this book has only been possible through the care and love I have received from my family and close friends. I also want to thank Jacob Camacho, Tanya and Victor Cho, Beatrice Contreras, Anthony Dornfeld, Amber Hanson-Iñiguez, Abby and Mark Juhasz, Hoang Le, Levi Martinez, Jay Mirseyedi, Jimmy Placentia, Jecsy Ranilla, Armando Rimada, Ajay Sanathara, Erin Soo-Hoo, and Chris Stout for their moral support.

Finally, I would like to thank my family in Guåhan, South Korea, and the United States for their care and unconditional love. Saina ma'åse to Barbara and Juan Camacho, Frank Flores, Joe Flores, Marie Flores, Sandy and Pete Flores, Rodney Flores, Lou Flores-Quitugua, Niki Galvan, Debbie Peredo Lujan, Arlene Pangelinan, George Quitugua, Joe and Lola Sablan Santos, and Nenita Santos. I also want to thank all of my cousins, especially Melissa and Vince Quitugua for connecting me to interviewees in Guåhan. My brother-in-law Nam Nguyen and his wife, Nicole Nguyen, also deserve my thanks for their care. To my brother-in-law Josh, thank you for your support. My deepest gratitude goes to my parents-in-law Huong and Son Nguyen for the home-cooked meals and your help in raising Matua and Tasi. Thank you to my nephews Antoinee and Takai and my niece Jastin for the laughter and smiles that have made my life more joyous. Words cannot describe the credit my sister Queen Flores Little deserves for always supporting me. This book would not be possible without her. To my mother, Min U, and my father, Alfred, your life lessons, love, and sacrifice has allowed me to pursue my passion for teaching and research. Finally, my children, Matua and Tasi, and my partner, MyLinh, deserve the final acknowledgment. Matua, inspired me to finish this book as quickly as possible so he and I could attend to pressing matters such as playing Mario Kart 8. Tasi reminded me that it was important for me to take breaks from revising the book so I could serve as her prop as she learned how to walk. All joking aside, my children motivate me every day to be a better person. To my partner, MyLinh, thank you for always listening and supporting me. Your labor and love have made this book come to fruition.

Note on Language

CHamoru is a living language. Throughout this book, I have used the spelling of CHamoru words that I believe is the most reflective of CHamoru survival and cultural regeneration. Much of this information is derived from the Commission on CHamoru Language and the Teaching of the History and Culture of the Indigenous People of Guåhan. For example, I use "CHamoru" instead of "Chamoru" or "Chamorro." The latter two are the most common versions found in historical sources and contemporary writings. I also attempt to foreground survival through the Indigenous spelling of villages and place names. For example, I use "Guåhan" even though "Guam" is the most common spelling and pronunciation. However, at times, I do use "Chamoru," "Chamorro," and "Guam" if I am quoting a primary or secondary source or if an interviewee has communicated to me that is their preference. This will also be evident in my use of "Guam" in relation to institutions such as the "Government of Guam." As such, there will be shifts in the spelling of CHamoru words throughout this book to reflect how the making of history is a living and ongoing process. It is also important to note that CHamorus are from and reside in other parts of the Mariana Islands. If any reference is made to CHamorus outside of Guåhan, it is done so in reference with the name of the specific island they come from. For example, I will use the phrase "CHamorus of Sa'ipan (Saipan)."

There are other challenges when writing about Native/Indigenous histories and colonialism. Words such as "Pacific Islands," "Micronesia," and "Micronesian" are all problematic for various reasons. With that said, I utilize

"Oceania," "Pacific Islands," and the "Pacific" interchangeably. For CHamorus and other Pacific Islanders, these words are most commonly used to describe the land and ocean of the region. I also acknowledge that words such as "American" and the term "white Americans" to describe people from the United States are problematic as well. However, I have chosen to use these words to help demarcate among the several different racial, ethnic, and national communities that are written about in this book.

Abbreviations

AFL-CIO	American Federation of Labor–Congress of Industrial Workers
APRO	Asia and Pacific Regional Organization
BMP	Brown-Pacific-Maxon
DPRK	Democratic People's Republic of Korea
FCG	Filipino Community of Guam
FLSA	Fair Labor Standards Act
GLCC	Guam Land and Claims Commission
ICFTU	International Confederation of Free Trade Unions
ILO	International Labor Organization
LUSTEVECO	Luzon Stevedoring Corporation
MASDELCO	Marianas Stevedoring Corporation
NAS	Naval Air Station
ONI	Office of Naval Intelligence
PCLU	Philippine Consolidated Labor Union
POEA	Philippine Overseas Employment Administration
POW	prisoner of war
PTA	Parent-Teacher Association
PTUC	Philippine Trade Unions Council
TPD	territorial post differential

Tip of the Spear

Introduction

Becoming the Tip of America's Spear

Throughout the late 1980s and early 1990s, I spent many childhood weekends in the city of Perris, California. My paternal grandparents, Pedro Martinez Flores (*familian Kabesa*) and Soledad Chargualaf Flores (*familian Kulo*), had purchased approximately five acres of rural land in this Southern California city, which is located seventy miles southeast of Los Angeles. What they did with this land was extraordinary. Specifically, they built a five-acre *lāncho* (ranch) that included many of the sights, smells, and sounds that you would find in the Mariana Islands.[1] For example, their lāncho had animals such as chickens, goats, pigs, and pigeons. My experiences in observing these animals taught me life lessons such as not to bother mother hens and their chicks and the reproductive practices of pigs.

My grandparents' lāncho contained memorable makeshift structures that included a *kusinan sanhiyong* (outdoor kitchen) that had a restaurant-size grill used for cooking chicken and pork ribs marinated in soy sauce and vinegar, *champulado* (chocolate rice pudding), *fina'denne'* (spicy sauce), *hineksa' aga'ga'* (red rice), chicken *kelaguen* (chicken salad), and shrimp patties (fritters).[2] They also had a *såla sanhiyong* (outdoor living room) where family and friends ate food and socialized under the stars during special occasions such as fiestas, holiday parties, and rosaries.

My grandparents' lāncho had a profound impact on my life because it was the foundation for my understanding of CHamoru culture.[3] My grandparents demonstrated *inåfa'maolek* (to make good) which meant their decisions and actions were geared toward helping family, friends, and even acquaintances. This was frequently done through the hosting of people who needed a place to stay temporarily or long term. It was common for me to meet "new" aunties and uncles almost every time I visited. Although these people were not legally related to me, they were part of our family through an Indigenous understanding of kinship that includes people who are not related to you through lineage or as in-laws. It is these memories that influence the writing of this book, which is centered on the relationships between people and the land.

The stakes and urgency in writing this book serve as a way to understand how contemporary geopolitics and US empire have affected Guåhan and its people. In 2017 US president Donald J. Trump announced that the Democratic People's Republic of Korea (DPRK) would "face fire and fury like the world has never seen" in response to US intelligence reports that North Korea (as it is commonly referred to) had developed nuclear warheads.[4] North Korea responded by stating it was "carefully examining the operational plan for making an enveloping fire at the areas around Guam."[5] Later that year, the DPRK declared, "We have already warned several times that we will take counteractions for self-defense, including a salvo of missiles into the waters near the US territory of Guam."[6] This international incident was significant because North Korea's threat reminded the world of Guåhan's strategic importance as being part of the "Greater United States."[7] In addition, the provocations that the United States and the DPRK governments made toward each other had a lasting effect that not only created fear in Guåhan but also reverberated throughout Oceania.[8] For example, many people believed that North Korea had launched an attack on Hawai'i during the 2018 false missile emergency alert that lasted more than thirty minutes and sent thousands of people frantically running and hiding for shelter.[9] Ultimately, the political tensions between the United States and North Korea are part of a Cold War legacy that continues to bring the threat of elimination to the people of Guåhan and other places in Oceania.

Though Guåhan is a modern-day US colony, US control of the island has never been predicated on resource extraction. Rather, Guåhan serves to maintain, expand, and secure US capitalist interests throughout Asia.[10] This colonial strategy dates back to the late nineteenth century, when US naval officer and historian Alfred Thayer Mahan wrote that a modern nation needed a powerful navy and colonies to "facilitate and enlarge the operations of shipping," which were integral to international trade and commerce.[11] Although the technology of warfare has changed, Mahan's overall argument still rings true today through US policies such as the "Pivot to Asia."[12]

Guåhan also serves as a place to wage war. This is highlighted by the fact that the island is commonly referred to as the "tip of America's Spear" for its strategic military location.[13] Currently, the 212-square miles of Guåhan hosts two major military bases: Andersen Air Force Base and Naval Base Guam, which house "nuclear attack submarines, aircraft carriers, F-15s, F-22 stealth fighters, Global Hawk surveillance drones, and B-1, B-2, and B-52 bombers.[14] These bases facilitate power projection and training exercises such as Operation Valiant Shield,[15] a biennial exercise that brings together approximately twenty thousand military personnel from the US Air Force, Army, Navy, and Marine Corps to participate in "war games" that have been taking place in the Mariana Islands[16] region since 2006. As such, military bases in Guåhan have never functioned in isolation from other bases in the region but rather are an integral part of US empire in Asia and Oceania.[17] This contemporary reality of perpetual warfare and elimination has led me to the central questions of this book: When and how did Guåhan become of the tip of America's spear? What effect did it have on the lives of those who lived on the island? How have CHamorus survived US settler militarism?

The history of the US militarization of Guåhan demonstrates the island's significance in Oceania. Yet this story cannot be fully comprehended without examining the linkages between militarization and settler colonialism. Here I find the concept of *settler militarism* helpful. As historian Juliet Nebolon argues, settler militarism illustrates how "settler colonialism and militarization have simultaneously perpetuated, legitimated, and concealed one another."[18] This process also includes how the US government has justified settler colonialism through militarization. In the case of Guåhan, the construction and maintenance of military bases during World War II and after was predicated on the confiscation of privately owned land. However, in 1962 settler militarism in Guåhan shifted due to the Vietnam War and Executive Order 11045, which ended the US Navy's authority in regulating the travel of all civilians to and from this island. This change in military policy led to the rise of a tourist economy that modified how settler militarism functioned on the island. Thus, 1944 and 1962 serve as important bookends that tell the story of how Guåhan became the tip of America's spear.

My primary argument is that the US military occupation of Guåhan was based on a co-constitutive process that included CHamoru land dispossession, discursive justifications for the remaking of the island, the racialization of civilian military labor, and the military's policing of interracial intimacies. The cohering of these ideas, policies, and people comprise the infrastructure of empire that was integral to how Guåhan's military bases came into existence and were maintained.[19] Following anthropologist David Vine, I incorporate an expansive definition of bases as a way to unmask the interconnections across a variety of military sites such as airfields, civilian military labor camps, communication stations, firing ranges, military hospitals, ordnance annexes, recreational facilities, roads, war memorials, and anything else associated with the military.[20] Unlike other places in Oceania such as Aotearoa (New Zealand), Australia, and Hawai'i, Guåhan provides a unique case study because it demonstrates that settler colonialism does not require the presence of a settler majority. In fact, bases in Guåhan were able to maintain themselves through a small but constant influx of settlers that included laborers, military dependents, and soldiers. In turn, these bases served in the vital projection of the United States as a Cold War hegemon in the western Pacific.[21]

My secondary argument utilizes the conceptual framework of Native survivance/survival to examine how CHamorus have endured settler militarism.[22] According to Native scholar Gerald Vizenor, Native survivance is "unmistakable in native stories, natural reason, remembrance, traditions, and customs and is clearly observable in narrative resistance and personal attributes, such as the native humanistic tease, vital irony, spirit, cast of mind, and moral courage."[23] CHamorus and their allies have continuously petitioned the US Congress, filed court cases, issued public critiques that denounced the military, and, in some cases, openly violated military policies.[24] Juxtaposing these forms of Indigenous resistance against settler militarism exposes how militarization and settler colonialism are overlapping structures of power. My emphasis on survivance also underscores CHamoru cultural continuity through Indigenous land stewardship and *kostumbren CHamoru* (CHamoru custom and culture). CHamoru survival is especially poignant given the fact that settler militarism requires the participation of CHamorus, People of Color, and white Americans, which enables these structures of power to operate.[25] In other words, settler militarism has impacted the lives of all people residing in Guåhan, not just CHamorus.[26] Ultimately, my choice to highlight these voices of resistance does not suggest that CHamorus (and others) were not complacent or complicit; rather, it is an attempt to underscore how they have survived US military occupation.

The lands that US military bases were constructed upon during or immediately following World War II were largely acquired through the Guam

Land and Claims Commission and declarations of taking. This legal mechanism, coupled with the passing of the Guam Organic Act of 1950 (which conferred US citizenship to CHamorus), concealed the coercive measures that the military used to condemn land throughout the island. In turn, American periodicals continued to obscure the confiscation of privately owned land through articles that credited the military for the modernization and improvement of Guåhan's infrastructure. These newly acquired lands were then converted into bases through the labor of approximately 28,000 civilians, mostly men from the Philippines and a smaller number of white American southerners who provided the bulk of the workforce. Their recruitment was justified through a narrative that CHamorus were unskilled to fill the jobs that needed to be completed and that Filipino and white American workers had contributed to the rehabilitation of Guåhan. In actuality, this narrative was rooted in a hierarchical labor system that was based on race and nationality. This capitalist cost-saving strategy provided greater control and regulatory power over the workforce. The mass migration of workers to Guåhan also produced a variety of "militarized intimacies" that were amicable, contentious, and violent.[27] In response, the military created laws that were fused in the policing of radical organizing and interracial encounters among CHamorus, Filipinos, and white Americans. For the military, regulating these interracial intimacies was instrumental in upholding the US government's reputation as a moral nation and reducing the possibility of these incidents generating anti-US military sentiment.

Militarization and Settler Colonialism

Tip of the Spear contributes to the scholarship on militarization and settler colonialism with an emphasis in Guåhan. The work of J. Kēhaulani Kauanui, Haunani-Kay Trask, Patrick Wolfe, and others has foregrounded how settler societies seek to "eliminate"[28] or "suppress"[29] Native people in order to replace them[30] using violence, which is a central feature of settler colonialism.[31] This informs how I analyze military bases and the process of militarization as an extension of settler colonialism. According to feminist scholar Cynthia Enloe, "Militarization is a step-by-step process by which a person or thing gradually comes to be controlled by the military or comes to depend for its well-being on militaristic ideas."[32] Military bases control communities through a variety of strategies such as economic dependency, law, war, and violence (epistemological, physical, and structural). As such, military bases are the physical manifestation of militarization and settler colonialism as structures of power. The violence that military bases produce becomes more visible when juxtaposed with an Indigenous understanding of land.

Pacific Islander studies serves as a way to center the epistemologies of Indigenous People of Oceania. For example, CHamorus believe their bodies are an extension of the land, ocean, and sky. This belief is integral to how they trace and perpetuate Indigenous knowledge and genealogy, which is essential to their cosmology and epistemology (which I discuss in detail in chapter 1). Thus, military bases in Guåhan are founded on the elimination of both CHamoru bodies and the land, which includes the desecration and concealment of ancestral burial grounds, the home of spirits who inhabit the island, Indigenous flora and fauna, and even entire villages such as Sumai (Sumay).

The construction of military bases in Guåhan is also predicated on another feature of settler colonialism: Indigenous and imported labor. Throughout Oceania, nations such as Australia, France, the United Kingdom, and the United States have all relied on a racialized workforce to advance their capitalist endeavors. Examples include the "blackbirding" (coercion or kidnapping) of Pacific Islanders in Australia and the importation of indentured South Asian laborers in Fiji, the use of Asian plantation labor in Hawai'i, and the recruitment of Filipino military workers in Guåhan. Workers from Asia have been preferred due to their proximity to the Pacific Islands and their exploitable status as foreign laborers. As a result, previous scholarship has focused on how Asian workers in Oceania have become associated with settler colonialism. As scholars Candace Fujikane and Jonathan Okamura argue, Asian settlers are defined as people who "support the structure of the settler state."[33] In the case of Guåhan, the US military and its construction contractors recruited several thousand men from the Philippines in the 1950s and 1960s to work as military laborers. At times, their presence was justified through a settler colonial narrative that their labor was necessary to rehabilitate the island after World War II and reconstruct Guåhan after natural disasters such as Typhoon Karen in 1962. But the vast majority of these workers primarily helped to expand the US military's presence throughout the island. At the same time, these workers were subjects of US colonialism and hegemony. Militarization, as scholars Setsu Shigematsu and Keith L. Camacho argue, is a "structuring force of (im)migrations, displacement, and diasporas."[34] Specifically, the US government's pre–World War II colonization of the Philippines produced the conditions in which Filipinos migrated to the island to work as military laborers. This context is instrumental in understanding the motives for why some Filipinos accepted jobs as military workers. But as historian JoAnna Poblete has argued in her work on Filipino plantation labor in Hawai'i, their status as "US colonials" made them exploitable since they were not granted the same wages and labor rights as white Americans.[35]

As scholars Jodi Byrd, Iyko Day, and Dean Saranillio argue, historical context and "one's relationship to a system of settler colonialism"[36] should be taken into account when defining who is a settler, and terms such as "aliens"[37] or "arrivants"[38] are helpful categories to differentiate various racial and ethnic groups from one another. Though I agree with Day and Saranillio, my use of *settler* throughout this book does not suggest that a particular individual or group of people supports military occupation or the settler state.[39] Rather, I have chosen to foreground a Native perspective that defines a settler as any person who does not have an Indigenous genealogical connection or ancestry to the land they are living upon.[40] This also means that Native people can be settlers on the lands of other Native people if they, too, do not have an Indigenous connection to that particular place. Furthermore, my analysis of how military bases are a function of settler colonialism is an attempt to underscore their shared similarities to other settler sites such as the California mission system, American Indian boarding schools in North America, prisoner of war camps, and even detention centers and prisons, which have all undertaken the project of Native elimination and suppression.[41]

Bases, Forts, and Settler Militarism in Guåhan

In 1565 Miguel Lopez de Legazpi claimed ownership over Guåhan for the Spanish Crown, which used the island as a site to resupply galleons that transported gold, silver, and trade goods between Acapulco and Manila. It was not until 1672 that Spain decided to establish its first settlement with the construction of a fort in the village of Hagåtña (Agaña). This outpost was under the leadership of Jesuit priest Diego Luis San Vitores, whose primary objective was to convert CHamorus to Catholicism. The Spanish used the colonial strategy of *reducción*, which they developed in the Western Hemisphere, to force converted CHamorus to relocate to barrios or communities that were organized around a church.[42] This policy made Spanish surveillance and conversion easier since they consolidated scattered CHamoru populations into a small number of communities.[43] Thus, the fort at Hagåtña (and the several other forts that were later established)[44] was a crucial site in the subordination of CHamorus as subjects of the Spanish Crown.[45] Spain's establishment of a settlement in Guåhan also allowed it to protect its claims against its "inter-imperial" European rivals.[46] As colonial subjects, CHamorus were obligated to provide labor, pay taxes, and support Spain's trade galleons that traversed Oceania.

The Spanish-American War and the Treaty of Paris (1898) brought a new colonial power to Guåhan. The US government's stated justification for occupying Guåhan was based on benevolent assimilation, centered on the establishment of colonial order through education, governance, law, infrastructure, policing, and Western medicine. Yet its primary interest was Guåhan's strategic location in the western Pacific, which facilitated trade with Asia.[47] Shortly after the end of the Spanish-American War, the US Navy seized Spanish colonial sites in the island including Apapa (Apra) Harbor, the governor's residence in Hagåtña, and Plaza de España.[48] For the rest of the pre–World War II era, the US government did little to invest in the militarization of the island. Instead, it used Guåhan as a coaling station to resupply American ships that traveled between Asia and the United States.

World War II was the crucial event that transformed Guåhan into a critical node in the United States' globe-spanning military empire. Immediately following the bombing of Pearl Harbor, the Imperial Japanese Army captured Guåhan, occupying the island from 1941 to 1944. In the summer of 1944 the US military "liberated" Guåhan from Japanese occupation. Subsequently, the liberation of the island disguised the fact that the US military used the same bases that the Japanese had built at places such as Sumai and Tiyan.[49] The war also ushered in an intensified era of militarization that resulted in the construction of new military bases including Andersen Air Force Base in northern Guåhan. For the remainder of the war, Guåhan was utilized as a staging ground to support US military operations throughout the western Pacific. Most notably, components for the atomic bombs that were dropped on Hiroshima and Nagasaki were first transported to Guåhan and then transferred to Tini'an (Tinian).[50] By the end of the war, the US military occupied approximately 58 percent of the entire island.[51] In essence, the liberation of Guåhan helped produce an accelerated era of militarization predicated on the displacement and, in some instances, permanent removal of CHamorus from their lands.

As shown in figures 0.1 and 0.2, the Cold War and the continued militarization of Guåhan brought the potential for mass elimination to Oceania. During the Korean War, Guåhan was designated as a Strategic Air Command base that housed, resupplied, and transported vehicles, weapons, and soldiers throughout Asia and the Mariana Islands.[52] This included the US

Figure 0.1. Two-hundred-and-sixty-pound fragmentation bombs stored in an open revetment, 1954. Source: US National Archives and Records Administration.

military's allocation of fifteen nuclear bombs to the island and the storage of nuclear warheads at Andersen Air Force Base and Fena Naval Magazine.[53] Guåhan was now home to US nuclear weapons that were capable of bringing mass elimination to people living in Asia and Oceania.

During the Vietnam War, Guåhan occupied an undisputed role as the tip of America's spear in the Pacific. The island served as a staging ground for Operations Arc Light and Linebacker II, which resulted in the dropping of hundreds of thousands of bombs across Cambodia, Laos, and Vietnam. In addition, the military used Guåhan to launch Operation Ranch Hand, which resulted in the spraying of approximately twenty million gallons of Agent Orange, a dangerous herbicide, for an entire decade. Flights from Guåhan were also used to scatter land mines throughout Vietnam that resulted in the deaths or injuries of approximately 100,000 Vietnamese.[54] US military bases in Guåhan now brought mass extermination to the people of Southeast Asia. Finally, Operation New Life involved the processing and relocation of over 100,000 Vietnamese refugees to Guåhan, most of whom had been

Figure 0.2. Hundreds of four-thousand-pound bombs lined up at an ammunition depot near Andersen Air Force Base, 1954. Source: US National Archives and Records Administration.

displaced by the war.[55] In many ways, the US government's use of Guåhan to "save" Vietnamese refugees shrouded the fact that these bases were all constructed upon land confiscated from CHamorus.[56] Operation New Life culminated with one of the most politically contentious issues among American politicians at the time, when 1,500 Vietnamese refugees were put on a merchant ship that returned them to Vietnam.[57] In the early 1970s the US military attempted to acquire additional land, including Sella Bay in southern Guåhan, which was consigned for use as an ammunition wharf. However, CHamoru activists, environmentalists, and legislators were successful in delaying the project, forcing the navy to give up its objective. As CHamoru scholars Tiara R. Na'puti and Michael Lujan Bevacqua have written, by the end of the war, Guåhan had become a "place where the hammer of American power is remarkably visible, and the network of violence through which its force and interests around the world are protected."[58]

The US government's post-9/11 war on terror and the hunt for "weapons of mass destruction" has been used to justify additional attempted land grabs in Guåhan. In 2011 the US military attempted to acquire the ancient village of Pågat to use as a firing range.[59] Similar to Sella Bay, this was met with resistance from activists, community members, environmentalists, and politicians, and the acquisition was ultimately blocked by an international and interracial coalition. Instead, the military has begun the process of converting land that it already occupies in Litekyan (Ritidian), which is located on the northernmost point of Guåhan.[60] As of 2022, the US military occupies nearly one-third of the island, and its demand for more land has increased the cost of living while displacing CHamorus from their Indigenous lands and increasing the possibility of their mass elimination through war.[61]

Research Methodology

As a historian, I have utilized archives to trace US settler militarism in Guåhan. This included archival research at the US Naval History and Heritage Command in Washington, DC, and the US National Archives and Records Administration in College Park, Maryland; San Bruno, California; and Washington, DC. This research was illuminating because the documents I obtained via the Freedom of Information Act gave me insight into the intricate and complicated ways that settler militarism functions. This process required additional bureaucratic review that reminded me of the precarious nature of studying the US military. However, at times, the archives gave me the opportunity to read for Native survival through CHamoru protest and resistance to militarization.[62]

In addition, I made use of oral histories that reveal the experiences of people who had firsthand accounts of the impact that militarization had in Guåhan and on its people. As historian Valerie J. Matsumoto notes, it is difficult to document "the experiences of those less likely to leave extensive written records: women, ethnic minorities, and the working class."[63] This includes Native/Indigenous communities who come from societies where oral tradition or "talking story" are at the center of their epistemological practices.[64] At the heart of this study are thirty oral history interviews that I conducted with CHamorus, Filipinos, and white Americans.[65] Though I did not use all of the interviews for this book, the stories that were shared with me have informed my research in various ways. Interviewees ranged in age from fifty-five to eighty years, and, sadly, some have since passed on. *Manåmko'* (elders) provided me with stories of survival that highlight their experiences as land stewards and workers living in Guåhan after World War II.

For example, some of the manåmko' I spoke with are descendants of land-owners from the pre–World War II era; the historical experiences they con-veyed allowed me to trace how CHamorus valued land, then and now. Other interviewees were Filipinos who worked for the military and/or its contrac-tors. Their stories helped me understand the complex labor system that shaped their experiences. These interviews illustrate settler militarism through the lived experiences of people that cut against the colonial archive. They also further my commitment to promoting Native survival through the preser-vation of CHamoru stories for future generations. This process included my attempt to provide copies of each interview I have conducted to my partici-pants or their descendants, when possible. Not everyone will have the op-portunity or resources to preserve their family stories, so I have tried my best to support them by recording and returning their histories.

Besides oral history interviews, I conducted archival research in Guåhan. I found various examples of Native survival in court cases, government rec-ords, local newspaper articles, and photographs that provided additional insight into how CHamorus and other island residents perceived US mili-tarization. The archives I visited included the Humanities Guåhan, the Nieves M. Flores Memorial Library, and the University of Guam's Rich-ard F. Taitano Micronesian Area Research Center. Some of these sources have never been used in academic studies, and they help give additional clarity into the lives of CHamorus living under US military occupation during and immediately after World War II. Unraveling settler militarism in Guåhan also connected this research with military occupations throughout Asia, the Pacific, and the continental United States.

Because Filipinos have made up the largest civilian military labor force in Guåhan, I decided to also conduct archival research in the Republic of the Philippines. The various forms of public transportation infrastructure (jeepneys, railways, taxis, and tricycles) I used to visit archives at Ateneo de Manila University's American Historical Collection, the Lopez Museum and Library, the Department of Foreign Affairs, the Department of Labor and Employment, the National Archives, and the University of the Philippines Diliman served as a reminder of the labyrinth that writing about US mili-tary bases can feel like. At these archives, I unearthed government docu-ments, labor union correspondence, and popular periodicals that detailed the experiences of Filipino civilian workers in Guåhan. My most unexpected discovery was two vertical files at the Lopez Museum and Library that in-clude dozens of newspaper articles on Filipinos who traveled to Guåhan to work for the US military and its contractors. I also visited the Hamilton Library at the University of Hawai'i at Mānoa and the National Labor College in Silver Spring, Maryland, to search for government and labor records related to the US military occupation of Guåhan.

Outline of the Book

This book investigates how Guåhan became the tip of America's spear in the western Pacific and how the island connected people across geographic and political borders in Asia, Oceania, and the continental United States. My story begins in World War II when Japan—and later, the United States—occupied the island and transformed it into a major military site. It concludes in the early 1960s, when several major changes altered how settler militarism functioned in Guåhan, mainly via out-migration, suburbanization, and tourism.

Chapter 1 begins with an exploration of CHamoru land stewardship and the låncho (ranch) system that persisted through the Spanish period, the pre–World War II era, and the Japanese occupation of the island during World War II. Following this I detail how settler militarism functioned through the Guam Land and Claims Commission, which was the primary institution that facilitated the confiscation of CHamoru-owned lands. Mapping this process exposes how the military used fear to coerce CHamorus into selling their lands or accepting the cash settlements they were offered. This systematic condemnation of privately owned property throughout the island contradicts the liberation of Guåhan narrative used by the military. Addressing these injustices, many CHamorus and a small number of white Americans publicly criticized the military's occupation of lands that had been condemned.

Chapter 2 examines the discursive and material representations of Guåhan's pre- and postwar infrastructure through newspaper articles, magazines, personal journals, and other forms of popular culture. I show how the US military justified its occupation of the island through colonial notions of benevolence, modernity, and philanthropy, and I juxtapose these colonial representations with the militarization of harbors, homes, and roads as the construction of Guåhan's infrastructure primarily functioned to facilitate military activities and operations on the island and throughout the region. Thus, it was during this era that Guåhan was depicted as a burgeoning military site, an island paradise, and a modern suburb that was suitable for the temporary or permanent settling of US soldiers and their families.

Chapter 3 analyzes the creation of a civilian military labor system that was legitimized through a narrative of "reconstruction and rehabilitation." Now that the US military was occupying large tracts of land, it needed a sizeable labor force that could be disciplined and controlled. By the late 1940s the military and its contractors had hired several thousand civilian military workers to construct bases, buildings, homes, and roads throughout the island. These workers were mostly men who had migrated to Guåhan, with approximately 28,000 of them coming from the Philippines and 7,000 from the United States.[66] CHamorus also served as civilian military laborers, but they only numbered 5,831.[67] The military labor system created a hierarchical social and work experience based on racial and national categories. Additionally, the US government's relationship with private industry and its colonial endeavors linked Guåhan and the Philippines. In order to illustrate the experiences of these laborers, I utilize a working class labor analysis that focuses not only on what was constructed for the US military but also on workers' experiences and relations across groups. Finally, I discuss how the military and its contractors attempted to exploit the workers of Guåhan through proposed legislation like the Guam Wage Bill of 1956. This bill sought to make the island exempt from the US federal minimum wage and the Fair Labor Standards Act of 1938. The postwar permanent settlement of these workers resulted in demographic changes to Guåhan's racial and ethnic composition. Thus, the racializing of CHamorus, Filipinos, and white Americans shifted within the context of World War II and the Cold War.

Chapter 4 examines the militarized intimacies that occurred throughout the island. The rapid militarization of the island precipitated social and racial changes that permanently altered the island's demography, with CHamorus, Filipinos, and white Americans comprising the three largest racial groups. Interracial encounters could be amicable or, at times, violent. The US military was greatly concerned with these interracial relationships because the potential for cross-racial labor organizing, political solidarity (as discussed in chapters 1 and 3), and pervasive violence threatened the militarization of the island. In order to control these interracial intimacies, the military created local ordinances and immigration laws that provided them with the legal apparatus to police social relations in public spaces such as bars, clubs, dances, restaurants, roads, and villages. These laws fueled interracial antagonism and violence, thereby racializing CHamorus, Filipinos, and white Americans as loyal or subversive.

Chapter 5 brings together the major themes of the book and reveals what it was like to live near a US military base in the 1950s. In the immediate postwar era, NAS Hagåtña was one of Guåhan's three major military bases and the epitome of a settler site. Before World War II, NAS Hagåtña was composed of lånchos for families living in Hagåtña and other neighboring villages. During World War II, CHamorus were forced to provide the labor to convert the area into an airfield for the Imperial Japanese Army, and by summer of 1944 it became a US naval air base. As a naval air station, it was the primary site at which military personnel, their dependents, and civilian military workers entered the island. It also became the place where political tensions, the possibility of death, and violence occurred in and around the base. These overlapping narratives demonstrate the complex history of Tiyan and NAS Hagåtña as a settler colonial site but also a symbol of Indigenous memory that persisted beyond the existence of the base.

In the conclusion, I revisit my family's story within the historical context of the early 1960s. In 1962 two major events happened on the island. In August, President John F. Kennedy lifted the US Navy's security clearance program that allowed it to regulate the travel of all civilians to and from the island. This meant CHamorus and all island residents could travel freely. In November 1962, Typhoon Karen struck the island, resulting in the widespread destruction of residential homes, commercial businesses, and government buildings.[68] These events, coupled with the island's economic dependency on the military and the rising cost of land associated with militarization, produced an exodus of CHamorus who left the island to escape US military occupation. My grandparents were part of this CHamoru mass out-migration. Finally, the US military's entrance into the Vietnam War marked another important event. CHamorus enlisted in the US military to fight in the war. Their enlistment rates were significant enough that they experienced the highest casualty rate per capita of any ethnic group while also leading CHamorus to settle in the continental United States after leaving the military.

Chapter 1

CHamoru Land Stewardship and Military Land Taking

The conflicts were finally resolved, and I could look with unalloyed pride as the Americans landed and took off from what we Chamorros had won with so much sweat and pain. But to this day, I cannot arrive at the international airport or depart from it and not remember the agony that went into its original creation.
—Ben Blaz, *Bisita Guam: Let Us Remember Nihi Ta Hasso*

Ben Blaz was a CHamoru who was forced to work for the Japanese military during its occupation of Guåhan in World War II.[1] Blaz wrote a book about his time working at Tiyan, where he and hundreds of other CHamorus cleared vegetation, uprooted trees, and pulled huge rocks for the construction of a Japanese airfield.[2] After the US military's "liberation" of Guåhan in 1944, this airfield became the property of the US government and was transformed into US Naval Air Station Hagåtña (NAS Hagåtña)—and later, the site for Guåhan's international airport.[3] Blaz's recollection reveals how the island's present-day airport, NAS Hagåtña, and the Japanese airfield were built on a site where CHamorus were forced to labor, and where some perished.

In this chapter, I argue that the US military concealed and justified the coercive tactics it used to confiscate privately owned land through the "liberation of Guåhan" narrative, the Guam Land and Claims Commission (GLCC), and the Organic Act of 1950. The liberation of Guåhan is the notion that CHamorus willingly gifted their lands to the US military as an act of reciprocity for its role in ending Japanese military occupation.[4] The US military promoted this narrative as a way to disguise the coercive strategies it used to condemn privately owned land. The GLCC served as the institution that facilitated the condemning of land through declarations of taking, which was the legal mechanism that forced landowners to accept cash payments. This structure of Western land law was further cemented through the passing of the Guam Organic Act of 1950. Whereas CHamorus believed US citizenship would give them full political inclusion, the Organic Act instead codified the military's land takings since CHamorus were now legally beholden to US federal law, which included eminent domain. In the following sections I will first provide a historical overview that traces how CHamoru land stewardship persisted up until World War II. Next, I will expose how the narrative of Guåhan's liberation and the GLCC advanced US settler militarism. I will then subsequently discuss CHamoru survival, discontent, and the Organic Act. Ultimately, the military's systematic confiscation of privately owned land was integral to the infrastructure of empire that led to the rapid militarization of the island.

CHamoru Land Stewardship and Spanish Colonialism

For CHamorus, land (and, by extension, the ocean and sky) is the source of ancestral lineage, cultural perpetuation, and subsistence. CHamoru attorney and cultural preservationist Michael F. Phillips writes, "Land on Guam is literally the base of our culture. It incorporates special relationships: of clan, family, religion, and beliefs."[5] This was no more evident than in the pre–European contact era. Before the arrival of Spanish settlers, land in Guåhan was vested in the control of hereditary clans, which were spread throughout several villages on the island.[6] The rank and class of each clan determined the land or lands they had exclusive or shared access over.[7] Even though they did not conceive of land as individual private property, they protected their land against other clans and understood the importance of exclusive communal stewardship. Additionally, this control over communal resources was based on the extended family and was predicated on matrilineal descent, later resulting in the stewardship of specific areas of land and ocean.[8] Thus, an individual's access to the resources that came from the land or ocean was based on their maternal lineage, which gave women considerable power since their status played a major factor in determining their children's position in

CHamoru society.⁹ However, CHamorus did not simply view the land as a source for subsistence or ancestral lineage.

CHamorus viewed (and still do today) the human body as an extension of the land, ocean, and sky. This belief is grounded in the creation story of *Pontan* and *Fo'na,* brother and sister gods who sacrificed their bodies to create the island of Guåhan and its people. In this story, Pontan's eyes were used to create the sun and the moon while Fo'na's body was used to create *Lasso' Fu'a* (Fouha Rock), where CHamorus believe the first human beings emerged. CHamorus also had other ways to demonstrate the connection between their bodies and the land. As CHamoru historian Christine Taitano DeLisle notes, CHamoru *pattera* (midwives) would bury a baby's "placenta and the [umbilical] cord under the stairs of the house or near the house" to protect the child from injury or evil spirits as they grew older.¹⁰ Furthermore, several villages and places in Guåhan are named after body parts, such as the village of Barigåda (Barrigada), which means "side or flank"; Tiyan, which means "belly" or "stomach"; and the village of Hagåtña, whose name is related to the word *håga'*, meaning "blood."¹¹ These are just three examples that illustrate the spiritual and material ways CHamorus view their bodies as being an extension of the land. Thus, protecting the land and ocean was at the center of their cosmology and epistemology. However, the Spanish colonization of Guåhan altered CHamoru land tenure.

During the period of Spanish colonization, the låncho, or ranch, emerged as a space that reflected both older and newer forms of land tenure and stewardship. Beginning in the eighteenth century, the Spanish Crown introduced the concept of royal and individual land ownership. Under this system, the largest tracts of land were placed in the ownership of Spain and among the new *principalia* class, a small group of elite CHamoru families that intermarried with Spaniards.¹² Though most CHamorus lost access to large communal lands, many of them were able to obtain smaller plots of land for farming and ranching. CHamoru farmer Connie Snipes recalled, "My great-great grandfather was born in 1861. Before the [Spanish-American War] they [he and his family] homesteaded the Tiyan property. It was approximately sixty-six acres that they homesteaded. It was around that time they acquired it."¹³ Snipes's ancestors were part of the generation of CHamorus who were forced to transition into land stewardship that was centered on the låncho. Typically, lånchos were plots of land that were located away from residential neighborhoods and church locales established by the Spanish colonial government. The låncho system allowed many CHamorus to continue their agrarian and fishing lifestyles without being directly monitored by Spanish authorities.[14] As Joe E. Quinata, chief program officer for Guam's Historic Preservation Trust, recalls, "On the weekends, Friday night, you start packing yourself to go to the ranch and then the transformation occurs. You come to the ranch and you become total naked CHamoru."[15] CHamorus were permitted to live and work on their lånchos, provided that they return to their village homes to attend church functions. Furthermore, lånchos served as a safe haven for CHamoru clans to interact with each other.[16] CHamorus also continued to practice other forms of Indigenous land tenure. According to John S. Unpingco, former chief judge of the US District Court of Guam, "It's one of those things that is passed down but with no documents. People would say 'my father planted a lemon tree there.' The landmarks are the old ones used; 'that coconut tree to that coconut tree.'"[17] CHamorus maintained notions of Indigenous communal landownership and rejected its commodification since they did not adopt practices of enclosure and exclusion. Ultimately, the låncho system became the primary form of land stewardship during Spanish occupation that continued into the twentieth century.

US Military Occupation during the Prewar Era

In the pre–World War II era, the US government enacted strict laws that altered landownership in Guåhan.[18] Specifically, the Treaty of Paris allowed the US government to acquire 36,000 acres of Spanish Crown land (out of roughly 134,000 acres of total land in Guåhan).[19] Unsure of how to administer the island, President William McKinley gave administrative authority to the US Department of the Navy. In turn, the navy empowered the island's naval commander to also serve as the civilian governor.[20] This authority meant that naval governors could enact laws and pass general orders without the consent of the CHamoru people, Congress, or the president of the United States. For example, on January 30, 1899, Captain Edward D. Taussig issued a general order stating that "all public lands, recently the property of the Spanish Government, bordering on the port of San Luis d'Apra," now belonged to the US government.[21] Implemented without consultation of any CHamoru representatives, Taussig's order was the first major act of land confiscation that consolidated US naval control over the port area. Besides monopolizing control over the land and ocean of Apapa Harbor, the US Navy also managed all land transactions on the island.

On August 10, 1899, Guåhan's first official naval governor, Richard Leary, issued a law that forced CHamorus to obtain permission from the navy to engage in land exchanges. He declared that "all public lands and property and all rights and privileges, on shore or in the contiguous waters of the island, that belonged to Spain at the time of the surrender, now belong to the United States, and all persons are warned against attempting to purchase, appropriate or dispose of any of the aforesaid properties, rights or privileges without the consent of the United States Government."[22] In addition to dictating landownership, the US military sought to change CHamoru land stewardship out of a belief that subsistence farming stymied the creation of a wage labor economy.

US military officials urged CHamorus to use their lånchos to cultivate crops and raise livestock for market sale instead of relying on the land for farming, harvesting, and ranching to feed their families and to barter for other goods.[23] CHamorus grew a variety of crops, such as corn, rice, cassava, arrowroot, taro, yams, and vegetables including beans, melons, tomatoes, and pumpkins.[24] They also harvested fruits such as breadfruit, mangoes, papayas, avocados, bananas, lemons, oranges, and pineapples.[25] In addition, CHamorus raised cattle, chickens, and pigs. For CHamorus, land—and most vitally the låncho—provided the sustenance necessary for the survival of their families. In essence, being a steward of the land was more important than being a laborer in a wage economy. An unknown naval officer observed, for example, that the CHamoru farmer "walks to and from his ranch—unless he is the fortunate possessor of a bull cart—and works in the hot sun, not steadily, it is true, but enough to produce the food he and his family need; seldom does he produce a surplus for sale."[26] Even though some CHamoru men had jobs in the prewar period, the money they earned was used to pay taxes and to purchase goods imported from the United States. Moreover, the låncho system continued to provide the space necessary for the perpetuation and maintenance of extended family relationships in the prewar era, as it did under the Spanish colonial period. CHamorus spent a significant portion of their week at the låncho, and still do, giving them an opportunity to socialize with their kin, prepare food, sing and make music, and share gossip.[27] Thus, the låncho is an integral part of the CHamoru social fabric, supplying both physical and spiritual subsistence. CHamorus who did not have a låncho were able to continue the practice of land cultivation and stewardship through guålos (smaller plots) or gardens.[28] However, Japanese occupation altered CHamoru land stewardship during World War II.

Japanese Military Occupation and the "Liberation" of Guåhan

The Japanese military's invasion of Guåhan on December 8, 1941, and its subsequent occupation of the island was integral to the making of the liberation of Guåhan narrative. By December 10, the US military and the Guam Insular Force had surrendered.[29] The Japanese bombardment of the island forced many CHamorus to flee their homes and seek refuge at their lånchos, in caves, or in other villages. Within a matter of days, Japanese forces overran the island and occupied the most populated villages.[30] According to the late historian Dirk Ballendorf, "Soldiers also looted stores and homes, strutted, paraded, menaced, and hit the Guamanians. All 2,000 Guamanian residents of Sumay on Orote Peninsula were forced from their homes . . . and never again permitted to return except to pick up a few personal possessions."[31] For CHamorus, the experience of being forcibly removed from their homes generated discontent that would later serve the US military's projection of itself as the liberator of Guåhan, which was additionally cultivated through the implementation of other Japanese colonial policies.

Japan aimed to create "loyal" subjects through a colonial education system that sought to assimilate CHamorus.[32] Rosa Roberto Carter, for example, studied under both the American and Japanese colonial schools. According to Carter, the Japanese teachers "set out to indoctrinate us into the Japanese way of life and above all to be loyal to anything that was Japanese. Each day started with the assembly of everyone in school. We formed perfect lines, faced north, and bowed our heads in prayer and homage to the Emperor of Japan."[33] The Japanese military sought to remake CHamorus into docile and loyal subjects of Japan in order to exploit their labor. CHamorus came to despise the Japanese military for forcing them to be laborers.[34] However, Japan's attempt to assimilate CHamoru students backfired because these harsh educational experiences, which were intensified by their mandated roles as civilian military workers, would later inform their perceptions of the United States as their liberators from Japan.

By 1943 the Japanese military accelerated the construction of airfields and fortifications, as well as the production of agriculture throughout the western Pacific, due to the US military's impending invasion of the island. Places such as Inalåhan (Inarajan), Orote Peninsula,[35] and Tiyan became sites of intense manual labor.[36] Many CHamorus were forced to work long grueling days, clearing fields, dragging large rocks, and planting rice,[37] all while being exposed to extreme heat (average temperature of 88 degrees Fahrenheit), humidity (average of 65–85 percent), and rain (98 inches per year).[38] Some

CHamorus were placed in supervisory roles; for example, John Pangelinan was a section leader who was accountable for his group's daily production.[39] Pangelinan would be held responsible if his section did not produce enough food or complete a project in time. Furthermore, CHamorus from the northern island of Sa'ipan were conscripted to work as interpreters for the Japanese military, which produced postwar hostilities and contempt between the CHamorus of Guåhan and Sa'ipan.[40] Japanese soldiers also put CHamorus at risk by using their labor to create traps for American forces. Specifically, the Japanese military ordered CHamorus to lay coconut tree trunks or large rocks across roads and along the beaches to block and destroy American vehicles.[41] For these CHamoru children and adults, their relationship to the land was no longer simply based on stewardship and ancestral lineage; rather, their labor for the Japanese military linked their blood, sweat, pain, and, for some, death to the land. Additionally, for those who survived laboring for the Japanese military, their lives were forever impacted by their memories as coerced labor and of the other CHamorus who perished due to the brutal working conditions. For CHamorus, places such as Manenggon and Malesso' (Merizo)[42] became sites of death and haunting.[43]

CHamorus were murdered at various sites and villages throughout the island. For example, Maria Efe witnessed the execution of three CHamoru men at Manenggon. She recalled:

> Right there that evening after work we are called to assemble and if we didn't come to see there would be some punishment for us. The poor three men were there standing or kneeling in front of their graves that had already been dug for them. Ton Terlaje and Salas . . . got their heads cut off early and it just went right into their graves, and then one of the Japanese kicked their bodies into their graves, but that Tun Juan, who was a little fatter, had to be hit two times before his head was down in his grave.[44]

Efe's observations are similar to hundreds of other incidents in which Japanese soldiers beat, killed, and/or sexually assaulted CHamoru civilians. For some CHamorus, their deaths had permanently connected them to places such as Manenggon and Malesso'. Their traumatic link to the land has also played an important role in the US military's liberation of Guåhan narrative that has endured since World War II. Even today, ceremonies such as the "March to Manenggon" and the "Liberation Day" Parade annually commemorate those who were killed by the Japanese military and celebrate the US military's reinvasion of Guåhan in July 1944. As shown in figures 1.1 and 1.2,

Figure 1.1. Soldiers raise the US flag on a beach in Guåhan, 1944. Source: US National Archives and Records Administration.

this narrative was also reified in photographs that celebrated the US military's retaking of Guåhan. In turn, military officials believed that CHamorus owed the military their lands because the island had been "paid for in American blood."[45]

The GLCC

The US government's policy of containment[46] and its overseas "border control"[47] in Asia and the Pacific Islands was predicated on a US "military base network"[48] that legitimized the taking and occupation of privately owned land throughout Guåhan. Initially, this was a quick process, especially since the majority of CHamorus had been displaced from their homes during the Japanese invasion in 1941 and during the combat between Japan and the United States in 1944. As demonstrated in figures 1.3 and 1.4, the bombing of Guåhan resulted in the large-scale devastation of entire villages such as Hagåtña. By

Figure 1.2. Two US Marines hold up a sign that celebrates the military's reinvasion of Guåhan, 1944. Source: US National Archives and Records Administration.

August 1945, the US government occupied approximately 75 percent of all privately owned land on Guåhan "without formal recognition."[49] The largest areas of military-occupied land in the immediate postwar period included Barigåda, Sumai, Tamuneng (Tamuning), Tiyan, and Yigu (Yigo).[50] Parts of Barigåda became a naval radio station, while Sumai became a naval

Figure 1.3. Several buildings destroyed due to military bombardment in the village of Hagåtña, October 1944. Source: US National Archives and Records Administration.

base; Tamuneng, Tiyan, and Yigu were developed as airfields. The US Navy had acquired these sites once it defeated the Japanese military. Instead of returning the lands to their respective owners, the navy continued to occupy many of these properties using the justification of national security. In order to resolve this and other war- and territorial-related issues, the US Congress passed several public laws, including the Meritorious Claim Act of 1945. Once again granted administrative authority over the island, the US Navy then created the GLCC in April 1945.

The GLCC was the primary institution that obscured the military's coercive tactics in the confiscation of land legalized through Western law and premised on eminent domain.[51] Specifically, the GLCC had the power to determine privately owned property boundaries, provide compensation for property damage and/or loss, appraise property values, and offer settlements for injuries or deaths.[52] Only commission officials dictated the terms for land appraisal, evaluation, and acquisition. Additionally, the naval governor had the authority to appoint naval officers to act as members of the commission.

Figure 1.4. The complete destruction of a factory in Hagåtña due to military bombardment, October 1944. Source: US National Archives and Records Administration.

This power created an inherent conflict of interest since the naval governor typically assigned commission officials who were also naval officers. Thus, commission officials, for the most part, acted in the interest of the military and not for the people of Guåhan. The GLCC had several functions along these lines.

On January 8, 1950, for example, Chief Justice of Guam John C. Fischer issued a statement to the US Department of Navy Assistant Secretary John T. Koehler. In his memo, Fischer described how the military confiscated privately owned land:

> The landowner is talked to in the presence of the Village Commissioner who often acts as interpreter for the Chamorro speaking landowner and the government land negotiator. In most cases a Guamanian official of the government also accompanies the appraiser and negotiator. The procedure for notifying the owners that their lands have been taken is to send out an appraiser and negotiator who advises the owner of the value of his land insofar as the government is concerned and offers to settle on that basis.[53]

Military officials knew that many landowners were not linguistically or ed-ucationally equipped to understand the complex legal protocol involved with the taking of their land, let alone construe such negotiations as out-right theft.[54] Though some CHamorus actively aided the commission by serving as interpreters, it is unknown what motivated them to participate in this process. It is possible that they were coerced to serve as interpreters or received monetary compensation. Regardless, some landowners most likely found these interactions intimidating, especially since the people of Guåhan had just survived colonial rule under Japan. However, the commission was not a benign legal institution that simply evaluated boundaries and provided monetary compensation: it was the driving mechanism that disguised the military's coercive strategies in acquiring land in Guåhan.

The GLCC provided the navy with an institution that legalized the ac-quisition of privately owned land through US law. If a landowner refused to sell his or her property to the military, commission officials exercised the power of eminent domain by filing a declaration of taking with the Supe-rior Court of Guam.[55] This was followed by the depositing of money with the court based on the appraised value of the land, which finalized the trans-fer.[56] These officers acted with the belief and intent that landowners had no recourse in resisting the condemnation of land because they were colonial subjects. GLCC senior member Louis J. Rauber stated, "The power of a sov-ereign to appropriate for a public use such lands as are necessary is inherent in the sovereign and cannot be questioned."[57] The US military viewed cash settlements as legitimate compensation regardless if CHamorus disagreed or objected. Additionally, the function of the GLCC paralleled other institu-tions that the US government created to deal with Native people and their lands, such as the Indian Claims Commission, formed in 1946 to provide cash settlements to Native communities in the continental United States. In an attempt to better understand the impact of the military's land condem-nations, Secretary of the Navy James V. Forrestal requested a civilian com-mittee to evaluate the naval administrations of Guåhan and American Sāmoa that became known as the Hopkins Report.[58]

In 1947 Ernest M. Hopkins, former president of Dartmouth College, chaired the civilian committee, which found that the navy's land condem-nation policy should be reformed and be more inclusive of the CHamoru people. However, the committee also supported and legitimated the contin-ued military occupation of Guåhan and the usurpation of privately owned land as long as such acts were based on national security.[59] The committee report noted, "Only if such land is actually essential to the national defense should the ousting of the local residents even be considered."[60] The committee's evaluation thus supported military land takings as long as they were justified through national security. Furthermore, the findings of the committee were contradictory and not critical of the military or of government officials. The Hopkins Report stated:

> In considerable number they [CHamorus] are dispossessed of home and lands which have been destroyed or taken from them and they are without adequate understanding of the processes by which to secure replacement or compensation for these. This statement is not in disparagement of government officials stationed there who are bending every effort to bring order out of chaos, or of any government department, bureau or agency.[61]

While the committee's findings acknowledged that CHamorus were inadequately informed and unprepared to engage the military, the Hopkins Report failed to identify the navy as being responsible for unethically displacing families. Instead, the committee exonerated military and government officials even though they comprised the GLCC and were the primary agents in the confiscation of land. Therefore, the Hopkins Report validated military land takings as necessary to US national security, while simultaneously excusing the government from any wrongdoing and depriving numerous CHamorus of their lands. As a result, by 1949 the GLCC had displaced nearly six thousand CHamorus from their properties.[62] These CHamorus were relocated to other villages, such as Hågat (Agat), Dédidu (Dededo), and Sånta Rita, which disconnected them from their ancestral lands.

Coercion and Fear

As discussed earlier, the US government's liberation of Guåhan from Japan was one of the ways that allowed the US military to confiscate privately owned land without formal resistance. Another part of the liberation narrative was the notion that CHamorus willingly gifted their lands to the US military for being freed from Japanese rule.[63] As CHamoru historian Anne Perez Hattori writes, while some CHamorus may have been willing to give or loan their lands to the US military, "the arbitrary way in which lands were selected for condemnation and the inadequate compensation granted to dispossessed landowners stimulated Chamorro dissatisfaction both with the management of the land issue and with the hegemony exercised by the military government in general."[64] As Hattori points out, CHamorus quickly became disillusioned and outraged by the military's confiscation of their lands. Their frustration paralleled community discontent in other areas governed by the US military, as in Vieques, Puerto Rico.

In the post–World War II era, the navy confiscated land on both islands for use in building military installations. For Puerto Ricans, the loss of their lands fueled outrage. As sociologist Cesar J. Ayala and historian Jose L. Bolivar argue, "What is at stake is not whether property owners received some compensation, but the element of compulsion in the sale."[65] In Guåhan, "compulsion" meant coercion and fear, which was justified through US law that dismissed Indigenous CHamoru rights while simultaneously legitimizing the condemning of privately owned land in exchange for cash settlements (regardless of whether the landowner accepted the payment or not).

Many CHamorus feared US military and government officials. The late Carlos P. Taitano was a former Guam congressman and US military officer who was born on Guåhan in 1917. Taitano recalled what it was like to live under US naval governance. He stated, "CHamorus were afraid of the military. We were actually scared of them."[66] For CHamorus, the sights and sounds of American soldiers fighting in World War II were still fresh on their minds. This was only amplified by the large presence of military personnel in military uniforms, carrying guns, and driving vehicles such as tanks and jeeps.

In November 1949, for example, the US Sub-Committee on Public Lands held a hearing in Guåhan to address various political and social issues. The sub-committee members expressed surprise that CHamorus feared the island's military officials. Representative William Lemke said, "There has been intimation here on the floor and a lot of information privately given to us, that these Guamanians are afraid to oppose the Government—that they are afraid even to speak up here and give their honest convictions."[67] For Lemke and other US officials, the idea that CHamorus were afraid of the US government was a foreign concept that challenged their perception of the US military as liberators. However, for the people of Guåhan this was a reality. According to former Guam senator and attorney Joaquin A. Perez, "In Guam the people had been trained by years of military occupation to respect and revere military men and other officers of the law. A request from the military was equivalent to a command, and no respectable Guamanian would think of denying anything the military asked for."[68] Perez's congressional statement unmasks the liberation of Guåhan narrative and highlights the prevailing sentiment that CHamorus still feared the US military in the postwar era. For CHamorus, the reality of having lived under colonial rule for three centuries influenced how they perceived the military. This fear of authority translated into an advantage for GLCC officials when it came to land acquisition.

GLCC officials utilized various strategies to coerce property owners into selling their land, including deceit. Felicita Santos San Nicolas, who owned land in the village of Dédidu, recalled her interaction with land and claims officials:

> Sometime later another military representative came to visit me and said that the military had reconsidered the issue and now only wanted to lease the land. This was satisfactory to me because I knew that one day I would get my land back once again and would be able to farm it for the benefit of my family. What I didn't know, however, because I couldn't read English, was that the papers I was signing were for the sale of the property. Only later did I find out the horrible mistake.[69]

San Nicolas was not the only person tricked into selling their lands. Delfina Cruz discussed the loss of her land in the village of Hågat. As Cruz stated,

> He [her husband, Juan Cruz] knew the property was worth much more than $940.00, and so he refused to sign. Then he was told that there had been some misunderstanding and that the $940.00 was just for the rent. My husband was satisfied with this arrangement because he knew we would get our land back if it was just a lease so he signed the papers. As it turned out, the papers were for sale but my husband could not know this because he has little education and didn't understand the language in the documents. He had to take the authorities' word on faith.[70]

The memories of Cruz and San Nicolas help expose US settler militarism. First, commission officials did not always have interpreters present at their meetings with landowners. In several other federal land taking questionnaires, distributed by lawyers, some landowners mentioned that naval officials approached them without CHamoru interpreters. Second, commission officials relied on the fact that CHamorus did not have sufficient language or reading skills to understand the complex legal documents they were signing. Other CHamorus also echoed the experiences of Cruz and San Nicolas. Former Guam senator Joe T. San Agustin remembers working as a researcher for the land surveyor's office. San Agustin recalled:

They [GLCC officials] would go to a family that owned the property and they would persuade them to sign the document because Uncle Sam needs it. They would say, "don't worry, the Americans need your land but as soon as the war was over it would be returned to you." But this was never documented. The people didn't realize because they are not lawyers they signed documents that literally gave away their property they agreed for condemnation and they agreed for settlement.[71]

San Agustin's recollection underscores the military's use of deceptive and egregious practices used to usurp privately owned land. Besides these strategies, commission officials also used other measures to force CHamorus to comply with their requests.

In some instances, GLCC officials used the threat of incarceration or deportation to force CHamorus to sell their lands to the military. Antonio Artero Sablan remembers when military officials would visit his mother in an attempt to pressure her to sell their family's land in the village of Dédidu. Sablan recalled, "She was saying that the military officer at the time was telling her that if she doesn't sign the paperwork to give up her land, they are going to take my grandfather. I remember a number of times my mom would cry, and she was just really being intimated by them constantly coming to our house."[72] While Sablan is unsure if his mother signed away the land due to the threat of incarceration or if the military acquired it via declaration of taking, it is certain that the pressure military officials applied on landowners to sign away their lands was suffocating. Other landowners, such as Ciriaco C. Sanchez, had a similar experience. Sanchez recalled his father's negative encounter with commission officials in regard to their land in Hagåtña and Dédidu: "When my father still continued to refuse, Mr. Kamminga [a CHamoru commission official] threatened that my father could be court martialed. As my father was in the Navy Reserve at the time he became quite afraid because he didn't know how to protect himself and he didn't want to be thrown in jail and suffer disgrace."[73] Overwhelmed by the threat of incarceration, Sanchez's father felt that he had little choice but to agree to the settlement. Francisco S. Santos, a boatswain mate in the navy, endured a similar fate. When commission officials approached him regarding his land in Barigåda, Santos recalled, "I was told that the Navy was going to condemn my land and that I should sign the papers so I could get paid. I wasn't given any alternatives. . . . I really didn't know what do to because I was on duty at the time and really didn't feel I could disobey the Navy. I decided to sign because I was afraid of getting into trouble."[74] Like Sanchez's father, Santos feared being punished, which played a major role in his decision to sell his land. A further example of coercion is that of Urelia Anderson Francisco's husband. Francisco and her husband owned land in Barigåda, and she attested that "they would come out to my husband at his job at the Navy Golf course and take him away from his work. They threatened to take him to court and told him that the Navy could put him in jail for refusing to sell. These threats simply became too much and so my husband agreed to sign the papers for sale."[75] Naval governor of Guam C. A. Pownall wrote a letter that corroborates the harassment that Francisco's husband experienced. Pownall noted, "Some of the contacts [meetings with landowners] are brief, taking only a few minutes, while others may be hours long. Most of the investigations occur during the normal working day." He continued, "The Guamanian workers will be contacted at work or taken to other places as required by the Land and Claims Commission."[76] Pownall's letter, coupled with the experiences of displacement noted here, expose the unethical strategies and harassment that commission officials used to acquire land. Landowners who were employed or enlisted by the navy faced the threat of incarceration and the loss of wages used to provide for their families. The experiences of these CHamorus also counter the military's liberation of Guåhan narrative that claimed CHamorus had willingly gifted their land to the US government as an act of gratitude. In addition, these personal accounts demonstrate that some CHamorus worked for the GLCC and played a role in displacing other CHamorus from their lands. While it is unclear what motivated these CHamorus to be complicit in this process, CHamoru scholar Keith L. Camacho contends "Chamorro collaboration" with various military forces is complex because of the unknown circumstances surrounding the factors for their participation.[77]

It is unknown if CHamorus were coerced, hired, volunteered, or if it was a combination of all three factors that convinced them to work as GLCC officials. As this chapter has discussed, military officials used coercion as a tactic to manipulate landowners. This could have been the case for those CHamorus who worked for the GLCC. The GLCC also provided CHamorus with employment opportunities, which was important since many of them had to depend on wage labor for subsistence. Finally, some CHamorus may have volunteered to work as GLCC officials because they believed they could better serve their community as translators. Regardless of the factors for their participation, settler militarism in Guåhan required CHamoru participation to dispossess landowners from their properties. Thus, the experience of land loss was a deeply painful experience that recent generations of CHamorus are still coping with.

CHamoru Survival and the Organic Act of 1950

For many landowners, the military's condemnation of their lands proved more severe than financial losses. The late CHamoru rights activist and former leader of *Nasion* (Nation) Chamoru Ed Benavente discussed the loss of his mother's låncho in Tiyan. Benavente said, "My mother always talked story about the memories she had of farming and having family gatherings there. It was very emotional for her, especially when we would drive by the airport and she talked about the memories of her family's låncho."[78] Benavente's statement illustrates CHamoru survival through the emotional connection his mother had to their family's land in Tiyan. This link was rooted in the memories of family gatherings and ancestral lineage centered on the låncho. Cultural preservationist Joe E. Quinata states, "Land is an inheritance from your ancestors. It is not from your grandfather or your great grandfather; it is from your ancestors from way back when, passed down from generation to generation."[79] CHamoru farmer Connie Snipes echoes a similar sentiment about farming. She recalls, "Going out there and taking care of the land, I picture my great-great grandfather and great-great grandmother. I'm sixty-five years old and I still do it [farm]. It's in my blood. When you finish in the evening, it's wow, what a blessing. I can imagine what it was like for my great-great grandfather."[80] Memories such as these exemplify that for CHamorus, land provides the basis for Indigenous survival through the connection between ancestors, families, and identity. This spirituality is also embedded in the land, transcending generations and connecting ancestors through time and space. Thus, when the military displaced CHamorus from their lands, the military altered their reliance on it for self-subsistence while also disrupting, for some, their genealogical ties to specific villages.

By the 1960s, the US military had returned approximately 25 percent of Guåhan's land to its prewar owners or to the government of Guam. These lands were largely returned because the military no longer needed them and because the military still occupied approximately 25 to 30 percent of the entire island. However, the return of one's land did not guarantee permanent ownership. For example, Jose P. De Leon owned a home in the village of Barigåda, which the US military had confiscated during the American reinvasion of Guåhan. In 1946 De Leon requested that the governor of Guam return his home, which was being occupied by dependents of a naval officer.[81] Naval officers responded that De Leon was in his right to obtain ownership of his home. They also noted, "It is expected that within a few days authorization will be received for the acquisition of the land on which the house is located[;] it is recommended that Mr. De Leon be notified of the facts and urged not to press his claim."[82] The military's overriding authority to confiscate De Leon's land dwarfed his short-lived victory in regaining ownership of his home. Furthermore, landowners in the village of Yo'ña encountered a similar problem in dealing with the military.

In some cases, CHamorus who had their land returned to them found that formerly "fertile farmlands were returned as abandoned airfields, concrete pads, or as asphalt runways."[83] Take, for instance, the village of Yo'ña, where the military returned lands to CHamoru families in 1947. A memorandum written by director Harold Schwartz of the US Department of Agriculture and Fisheries described the process:

> From time to time various lands have been formally released to the respective Guamanian owners, but in actuality the owners are not always free to enter on to those lands, clear them preparatory to agricultural uses, and otherwise manage those lands as their own for the reason that Government-owned buildings and other improvements, abandoned materials, etc. have not been completely removed. [There are also] thousands of tent decks, and other abandoned materials. To a limited extent, Marine personnel is continuing to salvage materials in the subject area. So long as this practice continues[,] the native peoples are going to be hesitant to enter on their released lands and begin clearing away tent frames, old canvas, etc. for fear of inviting criticism from the cognizant military organization.[84]

Even when the US military returned land to CHamorus, the military did not guarantee them access to their property. Sometimes returned property was littered with materials that obstructed agriculture and made the construction of residences difficult to complete. Schwartz's comments also corroborated the notion that some CHamorus feared confronting the military regarding land issues. Thus, the return of land did not ensure that it could be used for farming, thereby devaluing its agricultural significance. With that said, some CHamorus whose property had been confiscated preferred to exchange their lands for other pieces of property.

CHamorus attempted to maintain their Indigenous practice of land stewardship even though the US military commodified land through the cash settlements they offered them via declarations of taking. Discussing how his farm in Barigåda was confiscated, CHamoru landowner Galo Lujan Salas asserted, "I found out that there was no way to keep the navy from taking the land, but I felt that I should at least get a comparable piece of property in exchange. As I understand it, Paulting [Salas's attorney] tried to negotiate for this, but he was told arrangements for substitute land could not be made."[85] Other CHamorus also preferred land exchanges. According to former Guam assemblyman Frank D. Perez, CHamoru landowners "would rather have another piece of land commensurate with the value of their land either in size or value, for an exchange of government land."[86] Perez's testimony exemplifies that CHamorus in the immediate postwar years preferred to rely on their lands for physical and cultural subsistence rather than sell it for money. In the same hearing, attorney Frank Leon Guerrero's comments reflects a similar sentiment: "In the Agat land cases I was the defense counsel for property owners. None of my clients wanted any monetary consideration. . . . Everybody asked for an exchange in kind." He continued, "That is the way our people look upon the value of land."[87] While land remained an important foundation for subsistence agriculture and familial bonds, it increasingly became a commodity that could be sold or purchased. Even though fear, deception, and coercion influenced CHamorus to accept land settlements in the immediate postwar period, some land takings were egregious enough to provoke small-scale CHamoru opposition.

CHamoru resistance to military land taking also spanned multiple generations within families. Joaquin Pangelinan Perez, the late senior policy advisor for former governor of Guam Madeline Bordallo, remembered the stories his grandmother told him about their family land in the village of Sumai. Perez recalled,

> My grandparents, the Pangelinan family, owned a large portion of Sumay. And my grandmother after the war told her kids and grandkids not to accept any money that was put aside by the courts for the condemnation. Not to accept any of that money because that was blood money. She had no intention to sell the land. As far as I know to this day that money is still in the bank.[88]

Perez's grandmother's position as family matriarch was powerful enough that her indignation lived on through her children and grandchildren. One of the most poignant and early examples of CHamoru opposition came as a result of the military's attempt to make Tomhom (Tumon) Beach into an exclusive military recreation area in the late 1940s.[89]

On May 10, 1948, the Guam Congress, composed of locally elected leaders, issued a letter to the governor of Guam that stated, "It is felt by the members of the Guam Congress that all beaches and seas of Guam should be declared public property and that all persons should have free access to any of these areas either for recreation or for fishing purposes."[90] The letter also noted, "The Guam Congress went on record in the May session as protesting the action of the military in proposing to appropriate the Tomhom Bay area for their exclusive control."[91] The issue of Tomhom Beach also caught the attention of white Americans who were sympathetic to the social and political issues affecting CHamorus. White American journalist Doloris Coulter wrote, "If there is any significance in the Tumon Beach story it lies in the fact that this is one of the few times when Guamanians strongly have protested an act either accomplished or contemplated by their Government."[92] CHamorus became increasingly frustrated with the military's acquisition and misuse of land.[93] Moreover, the military's inconsistent practice of loaning confiscated land for corporate use also generated CHamoru anger.

In a letter to the US secretary of defense, Secretary of the Navy John T. Koehler wrote that "the assertions against the government of having used land acquired by condemnation, for purposes other than public, are to some extent true. . . . There were instances of individuals and firms entering upon and using condemned land without any formal right of occupancy."[94] For example, the US naval government allowed the Commercial Corporation and Bamboo Enterprises to occupy privately owned land because they had "extensive investments in stocks and improvements."[95] This was problematic since military-condemned land was supposed to be used for national security or public good. Therefore, the corporate use of land that was acquired through eminent domain was questionable, as were the land condemnations premised on military expansion and the liberation of Guåhan narrative. However, CHamoru politicians and landowners were not the only people that the military attempted to displace.

Non-CHamoru landowners were also subjected to military land condemnations, as in the case of James Holland Underwood, a white American marine who settled on Guåhan in 1902. His grandson Robert A. Underwood, a former US Congress delegate and former president of the University of Guam, recalled, "His land was taken away, too. His land is still taken.

Near the fuel tanks down there near Piti."[96] James Underwood's experience illustrates that being white, a US citizen, and a former marine did not exempt him from having his private lot of land taken. Other non-CHamorus, such as Bernardo Delmundo Punzalan, a Filipino immigrant who owned several plots of land in Tiyan, had their land condemned. Punzalan's granddaughter, CHamoru rights activist Catherine Punzalan Flores McCollum, remembered,

> My grandfather's properties were taken three times. . . . He had four houses
> at the time. . . . They chased him out of two houses. He also had a business
> and was told to move. So he moved and then he was told to move again. And
> then they told him to get out again. So that's when he showed them his
> gun and said, "I'm not moving from this place, you guys move or I will
> shoot you where you stand."[97]

Though Bernardo Punzalan was able to keep the last portion of his property, he still lost the majority of his land to the military.[98] Underwood's and Punzalan's experiences reveal that racial background or US citizenship did not protect landowners from having their lands confiscated. Consequently, the military's taking of land from non-CHamorus such as Underwood and Punzalan created opportunities for solidarity between CHamorus and non-CHamoru landowners. The US military's continued taking of land in Guåhan generated criticism from white American civilians who became involved in challenging the military.

The most well-known American critic of the US military in Guåhan was John Collier, a former commissioner of the Bureau of Indian Affairs (1933–1945). In 1945 he and anthropologist Laura M. Thompson (Collier's wife from 1943 to 1955) founded the Institute of Ethnic Affairs, a nonprofit organization that was committed to finding solutions to problems "between white and colored races, cultural minority groups, and dependent peoples at home and abroad."[99] Collier openly criticized the US military's mismanagement of land in Guåhan. In 1946 he noted, "The fact[s] revelatory of Navy misrule on Guam are derived directly and currently from Guamanians who know their own situation and from recently demobilized naval officer personnel and not from a few of these but from many."[100] His statement discloses that naval misrule was rampant and that many people, both Americans and CHamorus alike, could attest to the negative circumstances confronting the people and the island. Then, in 1947, with the help of journalist Doloris

Coulter, Collier and Thompson founded the newsletter the *Guam Echo*, which reported on issues related to CHamoru political self-determination, Guåhan's economic development, and US military land confiscation.[101]

While marginal in its circulation, the *Guam Echo* critiqued the military's and the media's portrayal of the liberation of Guåhan. For example, in 1947 Coulter wrote an article based on CHamoru reports of naval misrule. She reported, "The people of Guam are sick and tired of being wards under the thumb of the United States Navy. . . . The 80th Congress will meet this month to find the 23,000 'nationals' of this island in the Pacific ready to fight for citizenship and an organic act."[102] Within the first few months, nearly fifty CHamorus who had become frustrated with the military's governance of Guåhan signed up to support the Institute of Ethnic Affairs through their paid memberships and the reporting of information to the *Guam Echo*.[103] But before Collier became an advocate for CHamorus, he was most known for creating the Indian Reorganization Act of 1934.[104] His actions and speeches in regard to Japanese Americans and Native Americans in the continental United States expose a contradiction in his political views of Indigenous and Asian American people. On one hand, Collier supported the US naturalization of CHamorus, but on the other hand, he had condoned the incarceration of Japanese Americans during World War II.[105] Moreover, Collier's involvement in working with both CHamorus and Native Americans demonstrates that these Indigenous people were linked through federal policies that included assimilation, militarization, sovereignty, and self-determination for Native people. Other Americans who preferred to remain anonymous were also critical of the US military's management of land. A journalist for the *New York Times* wrote, "Six months after the end of the war in the Pacific, the people of Guam are living in squalor. They are discouraged even from raising temporary shelters on land they own because the Navy may need that area later for military installations."[106] Collier, Coulter, and Thompson played a crucial role in trying to educate the US public in the continent about the social and political conditions of the island. Additionally, their work was instrumental in debunking the liberation of Guåhan narrative for liberal audiences in the continental United States. However, this white liberal discourse believed that US citizenship would resolve the economic and political issues that plagued Guåhan. In actuality, greater political inclusion through the Organic Act of 1950 only legitimized military land takings.

On March 5, 1949, the Guam Congress, which was comprised mostly of CHamorus, walked out of its session in protest against the naval government.[107] Specifically, CHamoru congressional members advocated for US citizenship and the implementation of a civilian government, since the island had reverted back to naval rule in 1944. This request for greater clarity of their political status had dated back to the early twentieth century, when the US government had initially taken control of Guåhan.[108] The members who participated in the protest and CHamorus throughout the island believed US citizenship and American democracy would protect them from naval rule.[109] And while the Organic Act did give the people of Guåhan civilian self-rule through the establishment of the government of Guam, the island and all of its residents were still subjected to military land condemnations, which continued after 1950, demonstrating that American notions of democracy and citizenship did not (and do not) guarantee full protection from the federal government.

On the surface, the Organic Act provided CHamorus with greater political rights and opportunities for self-government through guaranteed US citizenship and the establishment of a civilian government. In reality, this law codified the military's land condemnations and hardened the relationship between the island's political status to military interests and US national security policy. As historian Kristin Oberiano argues, "The Organic Act contained provisions [sections 28 and 33] that gave the President of the United States overall and complete control of the island."[110] Specifically, the Organic Act had clauses that allowed the president to designate lands that were vital for military use. This new law, coupled with the fact that CHamorus were now US citizens, cemented their vulnerability to land taking by the military.

The continued condemning of property, the growing practice in the commodification of land, and the increasing reliance on wage labor altered how some CHamorus perceived the cultural, economic, and political value of private military properties and of the låncho system more generally. Under the Spanish regime, CHamoru communal land ownership devolved into plots of private family land. After the United States took over the occupation of Guåhan, CHamorus were allowed to continue the practice of farming as their primary source of subsistence, but the period also marked the beginning of large-scale military land taking. The most significant event in the changing of land stewardship was World War II and the postwar era. The military's narrative of Guåhan's liberation, the GLCC, and the Organic Act of 1950 were integral to US settler militarism and constituted the most significant component of the infrastructure of empire that resulted in the massive confiscation of privately owned land. Though some CHamorus adopted the principle of land as a commodity, many aspects of CHamoru land steward-ship persisted. For example, CHamorus continued to rely on the land as a point of reference for genealogical and ancestral lineage. CHamorus with lånchos or guålos did and still do utilize their lands to host family gather-ings and to grow fruits and vegetables to supplement their wage labor. Yet the military's seizure of land in Guåhan resulted in the creation of the is-land's postwar settler society through the recruitment of military workers from the Philippines and the continental United States, a subject to which I will discuss in chapter 3.

Chapter 2

The Remaking of Guåhan

Cats and Macks and bulldozers puffed and backed and hacked, shaving away the jungle growth. Guam became alive and bustling with roads and road builders. The peanut-shaped piece of land, a thousand ocean miles from anywhere, began to glitter at night like a continental metropolis. What the U.S. wanted in the Western Pacific was a strategic site big enough for a good military base.

—*Life*, July, 2, 1945

For Americans living in the continental United States, *Life* magazine and other popular American periodicals provided a small window through which they learned about the island of Guåhan and its people. Together with military correspondences, nonfiction books, and travelogues, these publications proved instrumental in shaping the discourse on the US militarization of Guåhan.[1] The resulting narrative advanced US settler militarism through the modernization of the island's infrastructure while also making military expansion synonymous with modernity. Although this process was not unique to Guåhan, it was a significant component in establishing the US military's infrastructure that connected ideas, people, and places throughout the western Pacific Ocean.

In this chapter, I argue that American periodicals helped to justify the militarization of Guåhan (which included land confiscation) through a discourse of Western modernity and benevolence that was centered on the island's infrastructure. This discourse was an integral part of the militarization of Guåhan because it served to obscure the process in which the land that these bases had occupied was obtained. As Pohnpeian/Filipino scholar Vicente M. Diaz and CHamoru historian Christine Taitano DeLisle argue, roads and other forms of infrastructure "solidified modern American and colonial ideas about development and the assimilation of Indigenous CHamorus through notions of cleanliness and order that were also heavily racialized, gendered and sexualized."[2] A focus on the "material and symbolic" manifestation of infrastructure exposes how militarization and modernity went hand in hand in the physical remaking of postwar Guåhan.[3] In the prewar era, these depictions emphasized the island as an undeveloped tropical paradise that would later serve as justification for modernization.[4] In the postwar era, these depictions became heavily racialized and gendered. Moreover, American optics fostered a projection of Guåhan as a modern suburb that potentially attracted and appeased US soldiers and their families who were stationed on the island. In many ways, parts of postwar Guåhan were remade into an "America town" that included all of the images, sites, and sounds you would find in a continental US suburb.[5]

My use of "modernization" refers to the US military's development of the island's infrastructure using Western methods, supplies, and tools in the belief that such infrastructure would be "unquestionably favorable or desirable."[6] For American civilians reading about Guåhan from the vantage point of the continental United States, the transformation of the island's infrastructure symbolized the US military might and benevolence that was evident through its victory over the Axis Powers in World War II. Though the military had engaged in modernization projects in the prewar era, the end of World War II marked a significant shift in which the military heavily invested in the expansion of Guåhan's infrastructure.[7] Thus, the development of the island's infrastructure primarily aided the military's administration of Guåhan while simultaneously obscuring the desecration of Indigenous landscapes throughout the island. In turn, military officials and the media characterized US military expansion as benevolent to audiences in Guåhan and the continental United States.[8] To provide a larger context, I first discuss the prewar discourse on infrastructure projects such as Apapa Harbor, homes, and roads. I then examine how the US military and various periodicals perceived Japan's military occupation of Guåhan through infrastructure projects. The final section of the chapter focuses on the infrastructure of Cold War suburban life in US military bases.

Prewar Discourse on Guåhan's Infrastructure

In the prewar era, US settler militarism primarily functioned through education and health policies aimed at assimilating CHamorus rather than developing the infrastructure of Guåhan.[9] As CHamoru historian Anne Perez Hattori argues, this prewar discourse was grounded in the notion that American benevolence was necessary to acculturate CHamorus in regard to education and health.[10] Although the development of the island's infrastructure was also included in this plan, the military allocated the majority of its federally granted funds to support programs that forced CHamorus to adopt Western forms of education and health practices.[11] However, the one site that did capture the military's attention was Apapa Harbor.[12]

Located on the western coast of Guåhan, Apapa Harbor became the focal point for American commercial and military activity in the early twentieth century.[13] US military officer Henry Beers in 1898 described the port as "the best natural harbor in this entire area of the Pacific."[14] He continued, "Yet it is not a good harbor, for the exposure to the west permits strong ocean swells to enter, and it was and still is encumbered with banks and coral reefs, particularly in its eastern and southeastern parts, necessitating ships to anchor in the western portion of the harbor."[15] Beers's comments demonstrate that the US military was interested in the development of the harbor early in the twentieth century but that the harbor was not sufficiently developed to house ships. His insights foreshadow the US military's dredging of Apapa Harbor during World War II to make it suitable for commercial and military ships.[16] The military's prewar appraisal of the harbor was similar to its observation of Pu'uloa—better known as Pearl Harbor—in Hawai'i, as military officials there had also observed it to be integral to US naval power in the Pacific Ocean.[17]

Guåhan's roads were also characterized as being undeveloped and rural. Before the war, many of its roads were little more than dirt paths covered by overhanging jungle. Visiting Guåhan in the late nineteenth century, whaler J. F. Beane described "the branches of the bread fruit trees and fan topped palms, interlacing overhead, forming a magnificent archway of darkest green, through which the sunshine struggled, making golden lines across the broad plantain and banana leaves which drooped toward the center of the roadway."[18] Other visitors recalled similar memories. American missionary Mary Augusta Channell, who traveled to Guåhan in 1902, remembered, "Other towns are reached by bullock paths through the jungle; wild, with luxuriant, tropical foliage, immense palms and ferns, and unfamiliar shrubs bearing red, yellow or white flowers; vines hiding the pathway; and numberless parasites, all of which would delight the heart of a botanist."[19] Beane and Channell describe Guåhan's roads and jungles as being idyllic sights that were untouched by Western modernity.

In 1908 the US military paved and began to maintain the road that connected the village of Hagåtña with the villages of Piti and Sumai.[20] This roadway was important to the military because it linked the administrative capital of Hagåtña with Apapa Harbor and the commercial village of Sumai, both of which were integral in the transporting of food, livestock, mail, and supplies.[21] Approximately ten miles in length, the macadamized road was constructed using a common prewar method that utilized layers of crushed stone.[22] A US naval report from 1926 noted, "The military rebuilt the road from Piti to Agat to join with the road from Agat to Sumay," which connected "the naval reservation at Piti," indicating that it was a vital conduit for military purposes.[23] And while the navy encouraged CHamorus to use the road to expand commercial and economic activities related to the selling of farming produce, the road primarily served the US military.[24]

Guåhan's residential structures also eventually came under the military microscope of modernization. For the most part, Americans viewed prewar CHamoru dwellings as rudimentary and primitive symbols of Guåhan's landscape. Before World War II, the majority of homes were made of poles or thatch, and a few were constructed of wood and tin.[25] American Elizabeth Fairbanks in the early twentieth century described CHamoru homes as "wooden shacks, built on poles three or four feet above the ground, the space below being utilized by the pigs, dogs and chickens owned by the family. Houses made with these types of materials came into sharp contrast with modern Craftsman or Bungalow homes in the United States that were built with concrete footings or reinforced cement foundations."[26] While CHamoru houses may have appeared as primitive to outsiders, there were practical reasons as to why they were constructed in this manner.

As shown in figure 2.1, CHamorus relied on tree or grass materials such as bamboo and palm as primary materials for their houses because it provided good ventilation, which was important since the island's weather is extremely humid.[27] In addition, having a raised floor guarded against insects and other animals entering the home unexpectedly, while small openings in the bamboo walls made the sweeping of food and any other dirt or debris easy since it would fall to the ground below the house.[28] Having a

Figure 2.1. CHamoru women thatching palm fronds to be used in the construction of residential homes in the village of Hågat, November 1944. Source: US National Archives and Records Administration.

raised floor was especially important for CHamorus who lived near waterways that were subject to flooding from typhoons. Moreover, a thatched roof made of tightly overlapping coconut leaves or palm fronds enabled houses to withstand rainstorms.[29] Most importantly, the use of these abundantly available materials made sustainability and repair easier. CHamoru families and friends also typically participated in the repair of each other's homes, which reflected their cultural notions of identity and place.[30]

The island-wide construction of pole/thatched homes gradually diminished after World War II. The use of wood and tin also fell out of favor by the early 1960s, marking the island's increasing dependency on concrete-built homes and illustrating the preferred dwellings for Americans.[31] These and other postwar infrastructure projects were predicated on racialized and gendered notions of Western modernity that were partly connected to the "liberation" of Guåhan from Japan.

Gender, Race, and Infrastructure

Gender and race were used in the cultivation of a wartime racial discourse that was evident in the description of military infrastructure projects.[32] In 1945, *Life* magazine reported:

> The machine age came to Guam in a sudden rush when the Americans re-conquered the island. In the past ten months Army and Marine engineers and Seabees have made more physical changes on the island than the Japs had made in three years and other Americans [prewar naval administration] in the 43 years before. More than anything else, Guam is a monument to the energy of the Seabees. A "battalion" of Seabees build a 1,500 bed hospital there in 57 days. Natives are impressed by the big men in their big machines who can lay a road right past a village in an afternoon.[33]

As this article demonstrates, infrastructure projects were described with both racial and gendered overtones. American writers frequently applauded the US military's ability to conquer and transform the island while simultaneously criticizing Japanese soldiers and administrators as being incompetent.[34] This was punctuated through gendered portrayals of Seabee masculinity as well as, in the article quoted here, the implication that CHamorus were small in comparison to the "big men."[35] These claims of US military gender and racial superiority were similar to other US construction projects such as the building of the Panama Canal, which also received similar praise.[36]

As shown in figure 2.2, seabees were also credited for their work in the expansion of Guåhan's primary harbor, underscoring the island's rapid militarization. *Life* magazine described of Apapa Harbor, "Only Antwerp [Belgium] during the climax of the European campaign surpassed it in daily tonnage of cargo handled. Apra, Guam's harbor, which was once just a marshy inlet, has been deepened, widened and improved by the Seabees so that now it provides the Navy with anchorage, docks, fuel-supply, [and] repair facilities comparable to Pearl Harbor's."[37]

This article indicates that the expansion of the harbor was primarily for military operations. Additionally, the article credited Seabees for their labor while disregarding the fact that many of the families who lived in the neighboring villages of Piti and Sumai had been displaced for its expansion.

Returning to the subject of Guåhan's roads, in 1946 US Major General Henry L. Larson stated:

Figure 2.2. US military vehicle hauls a thirty-ton boulder that will be used in the construction of a giant seawall at Apapa Harbor, circa 1944. Source: US National Archives and Records Administration.

When we returned to Guam it was the monsoon season and heavy rains had turned the few dirt roads into a quagmire. . . . The physical rebuilding of the island was started by the Seabees. Their first roadbed was washed out by a torrential rain. Two semi-paved, two lane highways of poor construction and several negligible bull cart trails was the extent of the roadways when the island was taken. Today there are 150 miles of roads, more than 40 miles paved, including a four-lane express military highway.[38]

Larson's recollection obscured the militarization of Guåhan through his use of "rebuilding the island" to describe the military's construction of roadways.

In actuality, Larson's subtle reference to "military highway" unveils that roads, like Apapa Harbor, were modernized for the use of military purposes and not for the betterment of the island's civilian infrastructure. All in all, the modernization of Guahan and the racial and gendered depictions that characterized Seabee labor were integral to the US government's Cold War projection as a hegemonic power.

Military Benevolence and the Making of Infrastructure

The US military used benevolent paternalism to justify the militarization of Guåhan's infrastructure.[39] An anonymous writer for the military's public relations newsletter wrote in 1949, "The service of the navy to the nation does not stop there, it extends into the everyday lives of millions of our citizens and works for the welfare of all. . . . Every naval activity can serve the nation well in peace as in war."[40] Thus, the notion of benevolence served as a way for the military to conceal its intentions, which was to modernize the island's infrastructure for its use.

The primary goal of the US military in Guåhan was to develop the island into a forward base that could be used to launch future military operations. In a 1945 interview with the *New York Times*, General Larsen stated, "Thousands of marines, Seabees, Army engineers and natives are working twenty-four hours a day on the harbor, airfields and other installations."[41] He continued, "Obviously a lot of this work is of a nature that will be valuable in the post-war era."[42] Larsen's comments reveal that the modernization of the island's infrastructure went hand in hand with militarization, which would transform the island into a strategic location. This process was done in concert with the expansion of other US bases throughout the Asia-Pacific region, including Kwajalein in the Marshall Islands, which demonstrated the US government's investment in expanding a postwar militaristic policy throughout Micronesia.[43] However, at times, the legitimization of US militarism was not always monolithic.

The observations of American journalists sometimes ruptured settler militarism in ways that made US military occupation banal. In 1947, *Saturday Evening Post* writer Harold H. Martin reported, "But so far the job has been to transform, as fast as possible with money short and labor scarce, this 206 square miles of coral and volcanic rock into the great advance base of the Western Pacific[,] an outpost from which ships and planes may strike if and when the necessity comes."[44] Martin's comments illustrated the growing pro-

pensity for Americans to understand the expansion of Guåhan's infrastructure to be synonymous with militarization. Military periodicals echoed a
similar message. Also in 1947, the newly created US Air Force described the
expansion of the infrastructure as a process: "Determined to start anew to
build a better and more modern Guam, the Army and Navy moved fast to
exploit our victory in the Marianas to the fullest. Airfields had to be rushed
to completion. In the hillsides great coral pits were gouged and blasted. Com-
munications lines hastily went into operation. Hospitals mushroomed."[45]
Perceptions such as these were integral to the obscuring of the island's infrastructure as being projects of militarization.

Postwar Development of Guåhan's Infrastructure

American discourse on postwar road construction in Guåhan focused on
technological ingenuity. Describing the island, the *New York Times* stated,
"A vast, interlocking network of highways has been cut through the jungle-
covered hills."[46] The creation of these "highways" resulted in the military
creating 120 miles of hard-surfaced roads and 240 miles of secondary roads.[47]
As shown in figures 2.3 and 2.4, the rapid expansion of Guåhan's roadways
was viewed as an exceptional feat since the US military had only reoccupied
the island for approximately one year. The idea that Guåhan's jungles needed
to be subdued for the expansion of modern roads is reminiscent to similar
arguments made by nineteenth-century proponents of manifest destiny,
who believed that expansion would bring "progress" and "protection" to
the American West.[48] In the case of Guåhan, the US military subscribed to
this notion as well. Jungles and typhoons posed a frequent threat to the
maintenance of roads, and so the military felt it had to conquer and over-
come the natural landscape and weather of the island.[49] However, the paving of Guåhan's roads resulted in the desecration of landscapes that were
integral to CHamoru identity since many of them were displaced from
lands that were their home for multiple generations and for the loss of non-
human life that was destroyed. For the American public, the construction of
paved roadways concealed US militarism through notions of Western progress and the so-called liberation of Guåhan. No road better exemplified
this perception than the construction of Marine Corps Drive (also known
as Highway 1), then considered a symbol of modernity.

Marine Corps Drive was a marker of technological and military ingenuity.
As historian David Hanlon discerns, US military and civilian leaders addressed

Figure 2.3. Seabees plough, haul, and remove dirt from a mountain in preparation to pave a road, circa 1944. Source: US National Archives and Records Administration.

"certain humanitarian concerns about progress and betterment while at the same time ensuring Micronesia would be remade in ways that served the strategic interests of the larger American state."[50] While both the Spanish and American regimes disguised the development of this particular road to benefit CHamorus, the reality was that they maintained it for the use of

Figure 2.4. Asphalt plant used in the paving of roads and airstrips, 1944. Source: US National Archives and Records Administration.

their militaries. The Spanish initially cleared this road in the eighteenth century; the US Navy continued to expand it during the prewar era.

In 1945, General Larson named the road "Marine Drive" to honor the US Marines who "liberated" the island from Japan during World War II. It was further expanded and paved using modern materials to provide rapid military transportation that linked Apapa Harbor to various airfields and naval installations such as Harmon Airfield, Naval Air Station, Northwest Airfield, and North Airfield (also known as Andersen Air Force Base).[51] In order to transport supplies and cargo that came into Guåhan via Apapa Harbor, a roadway that connected these installations was needed. Some of these supplies included ammunition and bombs: CHamoru historian, the late Tony Ramirez recalls that as a child he saw a semi-truck crash "on Marine Corps Drive [as it was later renamed] with bomb shells scattered all over the road."[52] The military utilized this road to transport artillery and vehicles that were dangerous to the public. This was problematic because this was and still is the primary highway that most people use to travel on the western and northern

sides of the island. For CHamorus and other people who lived on the coastline in Hagåtña, the construction of Marine Drive destroyed their homes and
desecrated their lands and ancestral connections to a specific place. The US
military condemned the land of these homeowners, who were forced to
move to other places in Hagåtña or other villages such as Barigåda or To'to.
As CHamoru scholar Keith L. Camacho argues, CHamoru public memories of the war have developed in distinct and often divergent ways because
of a complex past premised on American and Japanese colonial histories."[53]
This was evident when in 2004, the government of Guam, led by CHamoru
governor Felix Camacho, renamed the road "Marine Corps Drive" to ensure that all visitors and future generations of Guåhan's residents would remember the US military's liberation of the island from Japan. The naming
and subsequent renaming of the road made infrastructure projects in Guåhan
synonymous with militarization. It also highlights how US settler militarism
from World War II has persisted, which is evident in how some CHamorus
support the military's occupation of the island. Following the war, the US
military was credited for constructing homes in Guåhan using concrete and
designs that were considered modern. One of the earliest housing projects
occurred in the village of Hågat in 1946. The US Navy reported:

> The homes, designed by Navy Commander Allan T. Squire, officer-in-
> charge of the City Planning commission, take into consideration the needs
> of the people and the climatic conditions. Designs represent a permanent
> type of wood or concrete block construction and are meant only for Agat.
> Dwellings designed for Agaña are expected to be larger. The designs for
> the homes are not intended to be in any way restricted to the three sug-
> gested types. All homes built in new Agat however will be required to fol-
> low a building code and zoning law as established by the City Planning
> commission, planning board and the Island Commander.[54]

During World War II, the villages of Hågat and Sumai sustained high levels
of damage due to US military bombardment. The military attempted to obscure the destruction of Hågat and the condemning of the entire village of
Sumai through the construction of new tract-style homes in Hågat and in
the neighboring village of Sånta Rita (which did not exist before World War
II) to compensate those families who were displaced from their ancestral
homes due to the construction of US Naval Base Guam. They then directed
the CHamorus who had been dispossessed to live in these new homes and
villages. These new homes were especially important because the US Navy

had no intention of returning the land to the prewar families who lived in Sumai.[55]

In postwar Hagåtña, the US military redrew the village's boundaries and redistributed smaller land allotments to mirror Western-style suburban tract homes. This was only possible because in World War II, the US military bombarded the entire village to drive out Japanese forces. In the process, Hagåtña was destroyed and the military was credited for rebuilding the entire village in a modern fashion that relied on Western forms of architecture, city planning, and materials. An American travelogue written in the late 1950s described Hagåtña as

> arisen from its own ashes to become a western Pacific metropolis. Situated between towering cliffs and a glistening green bay, the city is the business and governmental center of the Territory. Stores and specialty shops line its four-lane bayside highway, Marine Drive. [The most] historic spot in town is the restored Plaza de España with its modern government buildings and crumbling Spanish ruins.[56]

As in the case of Sumai, many of the prewar residents of Hagåtña who lived near the coastline were removed because the military had confiscated their lands to build Marine Corps Drive and other structures such as government buildings and shopping plazas. For many CHamoru families, the postwar reorganization of Hagåtña complicated land ownership and the construction of new homes due to the reduction of land allotments. In some cases, the military left CHamorus to fend for themselves when it came to restoring their postwar homes.

In the immediate postwar period, some CHamorus had to rebuild their homes without military or government assistance. The late anthropologist Laura M. Thompson, who spent several years in Guåhan, took note of these events. As she observed, "They [CHamorus] are living now, some in pre-fabricated dwellings, some in Quonset huts, and some in temporary houses they have built themselves out of surplus war materials."[57]

The US government also justified its militarization of the island through its construction of suburban style homes for US servicemen and their families who settled on the island either temporarily or permanently.[58] According to *New York Times* writer Walter Sullivan,

> The construction of permanent housing is probably the biggest job under way here. Typhoon proof homes for service men and their families are being

built. Their cost is such that even at present levels a large mansion could be built for the same price in the United States. Meandering rows of houses, all alike, are springing up, reminiscent of housing developments in suburban America except for their design. The roofs of slab concrete and the heavy shutters are built to resist winds that seldom blow across Nassau and Westchester Counties.[59]

This process was similar in other parts of Micronesia. As historian Lauren Hirshberg notes, the US military recruited the nation's top scientists and engineers to Kwajalein to construct "small town suburban luxuries."[60] The construction of modern homes also occurred at Andersen Air Force Base. On October 26, 1958, the *Territorial Sun* reported: "The new homes will be typhoon proof of a style resembling a modified ranch type. . . . At this stage of construction, homes will seemingly pop-up overnight."[61] Black Construction Company was hired to complete this housing tract project, which included approximately one thousand homes in Andersen Air Force Base. As in other instances, these homes were built for the sole purpose of housing American servicemen and their dependents, rather than housing CHamorus and other civilian residents. In many ways, this relationship between construction contractors and the US military represented the military industrial complex that linked corporations, federal spending, and the military. Moreover, as in the case of life on other military bases in Guåhan, these houses reinforced the idea of American suburban living through ranch-style tract homes. Other Americans indirectly reported that suburban homes were only intended for Americans. American writer Stuart Udall described postwar Guåhan: "Modern buildings, fine highways, busy stores, electricity, running water, sewer systems, theaters, service stations, radio and television, and other contemporary Western services and facilities are common. In the villages, however, many homes are frame buildings with open windows and high porches, with stilts used as supports rather than concrete foundations."[62] As Udall revealed, the military remade parts of Guåhan into what architect Mark L. Gillem refers to as "America towns" or modern suburbs that served to attract and appease US servicemen and their families.[63]

In rare moments, American writers did not have a monolithic view of the military's construction of homes and openly criticized them for CHamorus' postwar poverty and landlessness. For example, *New York Times* journalist Robert Trumbull noted, "They [CHamorus] live in squalor and must continue so until Congress appropriates funds to restore what was theirs until the American fleet opened fire prior to the invasion of July 1944." He also asserted, "This land belongs to the natives[,] and a law authorizes the Government to buy the tracts some day. Meanwhile the military government has the problem of persuading the natives not to build sorely needed homes on their land because the Government may condemn it for military purposes. The natives have no place to go, however."[64] Trumbull's critique of the US military's land taking policy and the lack of homes for CHamorus drew attention to the military's authoritarian policy. Consequently, the building of modern homes for Americans evidenced another example of the colonial inequalities in Guåhan.[65]

Military Base Life

The US Air Force's Public Information Office also justified militarization through the newsletter it published for American servicemen stationed in Guåhan. In 1947 an unknown author stated, "Meanwhile, naval administration continues to provide homes, free education, schools, hospitalization, pay war claims, rebuild towns, villages, and public buildings, construct roads, and foster new business and industry."[66] Military officials believed it was important to inform servicemen and their families of the "positive" projects they had contributed to the island through periodicals such as the *Guam Daily News* and the *Pacific Profile*. In turn, the media legitimized the military's need to occupy the island since modernization was presented as only being possible under US governance. From 1944 to 1950, for example, the US Navy determined which off-island companies could establish businesses on the island since Guåhan remained under naval rule, with the navy controlling immigration via its security clearance program. Moreover, the military took credit for bringing other modern services to the civilian public, such as commercial banking, public libraries, a bus line, and a daily tabloid newspaper.[67] Even though the military did encourage commercial growth on the island, the majority of these businesses served military personnel and their families. In actuality, only servicemen and their dependents had access to many of the early postwar commercial industries because they were built within the confines of US military bases. Thus, the modernization of Guåhan's commercial industries and the suburbanization of military homes primarily provided modern amenities to American military personnel and their dependents.

The creation of suburban life in military bases was a key component to settler militarism in Guåhan. The US Air Force described the island as having "shops, restaurants, and cafes, and in and out of them pour a stream of civilians, soldiers, sailors and Marines."[68] These stores and restaurants provided Americans the opportunity to engage in consumer activities, an important facet of American suburban life. As prewar Guåhan generally lacked suburban amenities such as shopping plazas and Western recreational activities, the military believed the island needed to be remade into a place that would satisfy their soldiers, and their dependents' consumer desires.[69] This settler social reproduction attempted to erase single-structure storefronts and bakeries that were sometimes operated out of a person's home. Furthermore, these consumer opportunities not only represented American ideas of modernity and democracy but also made living in Guåhan more palatable for American military personnel.

The military's advertisement of American suburban life in Guåhan was reflective of the patriarchal social norms found in the continental United States. For example, white American women who came to the island as civilian dependents were reminded "to keep house and cook three meals a day just as you would anywhere[,] and you certainly need equipment with which to do it."[70] Military life on bases reinforced white patriarchal social norms that included Cold War consumerism. The military ensured that modern appliances and equipment were available for purchase in post exchanges, which upheld gendered norms of female household labor and domesticity, even for families living thousands of miles away from the United States.[71] While periodicals such as *Guam Destination* and *Life* magazine highlighted these consumer opportunities in terms of modernization, many recreational activities were only available to military personnel and their dependents.

Some of the earliest postwar movie theaters, libraries, service clubs, bowling alleys, and golf courses were built within the confines of bases or were designated as military-only facilities.[72] These recreational activities concealed militarization through the promotion of suburban living. However, suburbanization also distracted servicemen from the challenges of living a regimented lifestyle away from their homes. Some Americans believed being stationed on an island exacerbated a soldier's feeling of isolation and negatively impacted his health. In 1947, for example, Vernon T. Bull wrote a letter to the US Navy in Washington, DC, requesting that his son be relocated to a naval base in the continental United States. According to Bull, his son's "morale is steadily growing worse" and the "isolation affected by this island [Guåhan] is severely affecting his health, both mentally and physically."[73] For some Americans, the prospect of being stationed in Guåhan only magnified a soldier's dissatisfaction with living on an island that did not have the same recreational and social comforts of life in the continental United States. In a satirical article, writer Ronald Levitt described the reaction of a man who had received orders to be stationed on Guåhan. This fictional character stated, "Oh no, not Guam. . . . Poor kid. . . . There is nothing there but palm trees and gooney birds. . . . You'll go nuts within a week . . . there's nothing to do there."[74] Bull's letter and Levitt's article were two notable examples that underscored the discontent soldiers had with living in Guåhan. This was similar to the frustrations that American soldiers had with living in Hawai'i, which they came to quickly realize was not a paradise due to its large Asian American and Kanaka Maoli population and limited island resources.[75] Thus, it was important to transform Guåhan into a place that offered the recreational activities representative of American suburban life.

Civilian and military periodicals played an integral role in obscuring militarization through the optics of tourism, in what the late I-Kiribati and African American scholar Teresia Teaiwa coined "militourism."[76] For example, the *Industrial Miners Gazette* reported, "To the lovers of beautiful scenery and delightful drives, attention is called to this picturesque view of the palm-lined drive which runs along the water front at the southern end of the island."[77] This periodical's characterization of Guåhan underscores how militarism and tourism functioned together to attract civilian workers, soldiers, or their dependents to the island.[78] Other periodicals made similar depictions. The Pacific Area Travel Association described Guåhan as being traveler friendly, stating, "The new influx of visitors will have an easy time getting a thorough look at Guåhan via the scenic highway that circles the entire 30 mile island. The northern section offers a rolling savanna that leads to ocean cliffs and the southern half is verdant and mountainous."[79] Military newsletters disseminated similar information to their soldiers. The US Air Force noted, "The flora and fauna of Guam will prove attractive to those who are interested in nature study. Wild orchids and ginger thrive in the jungles and a number of strange birds may be seen and photographed."[80]

Other American writers focused on the pristine rural appeal Guåhan would have for American audiences and settlers. In the early 1960s, Stuart Udall wrote, "While the northern part of Guam is completely modern, the native villages of the southern half still carry on an ancient way of life. It is not uncommon to see people riding along country paths on carabaos. Driving around the island one will pass through the villages of Umatac, Merizo, and Inarajan, and see the ruins of several early Spanish forts. One may also inspect the mysterious latte stones."[81] The military personnel, contractors, and travel companies disguised the militarization of the island through words such as "paradise" and "exotic." While their motives might have differed, the discursive consequences of these postwar views maintained the notion that the militarization of Guåhan offered something for all Americans. For soldiers and their families stationed on the island, consumerism and suburban life provided the backdrop for recreational activities in an exotic place. In addition to these opportunities, beaches were also sites for American recreation.

The commodification of Guåhan's beaches as recreational sites also remade the island into a place that appealed to American settlers. For example, *Life* reported,

> Plane crews back from the exhausting 17-hour bomber run to Tokyo, submarine crews on land for the first time in months, both find Guam a pleasant base for rest and relaxation. The marines stationed on the island usually work from 5 a.m. until 1:30 p.m. and are then free for the afternoon and night to swim in the craters blasted out of the shallow coral on the ocean's edge, to play ball, to drink beer or just to sack out in their tents.[82]

Moreover, military newsletters disseminated a similar message regarding the carefree nature of being stationed in Guåhan. The US Air Force noted, "Military courtesy and the usual customs of the service are observed, but the accent is on a minimum of regimentation. There is a certain freedom in military life overseas which is not possible on installations near metropolitan or suburban areas."[83] Civilian and military periodicals shaped how Americans understood Guåhan as a site of informal work and laid-back recreational beach activity as consolation for being stationed on the island. The US Air Force's Office of Public Information stated, "Guam is a swimmers paradise; its beaches are numerous and some of them resemble a Hollywood movie setting, particularly Tumon Bay and Talofofo which are the most popular. And Camp Dealy, a former rest camp, holds the pennant for beach parties and steak fries. Collecting specimens of marine life, gathering colorful sea shells, and taking pictures are SOP [standard operating procedure] at all beaches."[84]

Tourism articles also played a major role in positioning Guåhan within the larger sphere of militourism in Oceania. In the early 1950s historian Paul Carano wrote a travelogue that was geared toward military personnel and their families. As Carano stated, "Guam's beaches offer all the famed attractions of Miami, the Riviera, Waikiki—balmy weather, crystal-clear water, powdery white sand, scenic beauty, charming girls—and yet entail none of those famed resorts' expenses."[85] His depiction of Guåhan underscored its beaches, resorts, weather, and women but also claimed that the island of-fered cheaper resorts than those provided in Florida or Hawaiʻi. While Amer-ican servicemen and their families took advantage of the economic privileges of middle-class suburban life, most CHamorus suffered from the loss of their land and a shift toward full-time wage labor.

A few American newspapers were willing to criticize the military's gov-ernance of Guåhan and its people. In December 1946 the *Christian Science Monitor* noted:

> Then our Navy built huge installations which took up much of the farm-ing land. Now Guam produces only five percent of its own food. Many of the 23,000 natives have changed from small farmers to poorly paid wage earners. Though the things which they must buy from abroad are, because of shipping costs, very expensive, our Navy enforces a low standard of wages for native workers. It is difficult for a common laborer and his wife to earn enough money for food alone. . . . In general, people of the island feel that the Navy is not moving rapidly enough to relieve their economic distress.[86]

This article was significant because it revealed to American audiences that the taking of CHamoru-owned land and the exploitation of workers were foundational in the militarization of the island. It also exposed that notions of American democracy and capitalism were not fulfilled for the CHamorus of Guåhan, who were dispossessed from their land and had few employment opportunities.

American periodicals and the US military were integral in obscuring the militarization of the island through the modernizing of Guåhan's infrastruc-ture. This resulted in remaking Guåhan into a place suitable for American military occupation through the creation of bases, buildings, homes, roads, ports, and other structures. In a 1956 article for the *Saturday Evening Post*, former governor of Guåhan Ford Q. Elvidge stated, "Americans now have presented the people of Guam with an entirely new pattern for living."[87] In particular, this new pattern of living was centered on notions of military be-nevolence, modernity, and suburbanization. This shift not only marked a new era for Guåhan but also transformed how Americans in the continental United States came to perceive the island and its people. Specifically, peri-odicals authored by military officials and civilians provided the primary me-dium through which Americans came to know Guåhan as a burgeoning US military site.

While the US military facilitated expansion and modernization projects, it did not do so with the benevolent or philanthropic intentions portrayed in American periodicals. Rather, these commercial and infrastructure projects were undertaken with the objective of developing the island into a place that would serve US military operations while appeasing military personnel with suburban amenities. This process was accompanied by the transmission of ideas and cultural principles that informed the infrastructural development of Guåhan. This was most evident in the construction of Andersen Air Force Base and tract homes, which were made to reflect US suburban life and promote American military settlement. Overall, American representations of Guåhan played a crucial role in reifying the physical manifestation of military sites as examples of modernization and philanthropy.

Chapter 3

The Civilian Military Workers of Guåhan

> Camp Roxas was no walk in the park when I arrived on New Year's
> Eve 1951. I was taken aback by the primitive conditions, living in
> crowded Quonset huts with no heat protection. And they could be
> very hot. There would be 20, 30 [Filipino] men to a Quonset with
> mosquito nets hanging for a stifling effect. We had community bath-
> rooms, clean but public.
>
> —Donald Marshall, *Under the American Sun*

Donald Marshall was a white American who worked as the general manager and personnel director for Luzon Stevedoring from 1951 to 1955. For a
time, he worked at Camp Roxas, the largest company camp for Filipino
workers in Guåhan. Marshall's reminiscence is significant because it helps
uncover the harsh conditions that these workers had to endure. The center-
ing of their experiences exposes the various ways that US settler militarism
functioned.

In this chapter, I argue that US settler militarism in Guåhan produced
and depended on an exploitive hierarchical labor system that was predicated
on race and nationality. As geographers Wesley Attewell and Adam Moore
separately argue, the US government relied on private contractors to serve
as the US military's "lifeline of empire"[1] as they provided "logistical support"[2] in the recruitment of Filipinos and white Americans to work as civilian laborers in the construction of bases throughout the island. These military

workers were integral to the infrastructure that connected Guåhan to private contractors in the Philippines and the continental United States. By the late 1940s, approximately 28,000 Filipinos (mostly men) and 7,000 white Americans had migrated to the island.[3] In contrast, the military and its contractors employed only 5,831 CHamorus even though they constituted nearly half of the island's population of 59,498 people in 1950.[4] Eventually, the recruitment of Filipino and white workers led to the massive influx of settlers who became synonymous with military employment. Thus, the racialization of these military laborers was integral to the creation, expansion, and maintenance of the US military's infrastructure that spanned the globe.[5]

The US military and its contractors justified their recruitment of Filipino and white American laborers through a narrative that they were instrumental to the postwar "reconstruction and rehabilitation" of Guåhan.[6] Additionally, the military and its contractors argued that CHamorus did not have the skills nor could they provide enough workers to complete the military's infrastructure projects. The military's rationale obscured the fact that Filipinos were paid the lowest wages and were the most exploitable laborers due to their status as "US colonials."[7] Besides recruiting workers, the US military and its contractors regulated the social and working lives of their employees. Military bases became the focal point for the systematic exploitation of Filipino workers that resulted in the segregation of company camps, unequal wages, and uneven working conditions.[8] Civilian labor and militarism in Guåhan was actually part of a larger Cold War legacy in the military's reliance on Asian labor that included the Philippines, South Korea, and South Vietnam.[9] In the case of Guåhan, this process was based on the triangulation of CHamorus, Filipinos, and white Americans.

I begin this chapter by focusing on the racialization of military labor and exposing the connections that linked Guåhan, the Philippines, and the United States. The story then shifts to examine the immigration, work, and social experiences of Filipino and white American laborers. Following that is an investigation of CHamoru and Filipino labor discontent as it relates to the proposed Guam Wage Bill of 1956. As this chapter demonstrates, the creation of Guåhan's military labor system was predicated on hierarchies of race, indigeneity, and nationality that produced issues such as access to employment, the creation of a stratified wage scale, an unequal immigration policy, and the formation of company camps that were reflective of Jim Crow practices from the US South. Ultimately, military base employment led to the largest influx of settlers into Guåhan, which shifted the island's demographics in a way that remains today.

Searching for Civilian Military Workers

As was noted in chapter 2, the US military relied on the US Construction Battalion—commonly known as Seabees—to provide the bulk of the labor needed to build infrastructure used in the retaking of Japanese-occupied islands in the Pacific. These white American men constructed airstrips and roads in places such as Guåhan, Midway, Okinawa, Palau, the Philippines, Sa'ipan, and Tini'an.[10] In Guåhan, Seabees built the island's main highway, Marine Drive, as well as developing the airstrips at Tiyan and Orote Point in 1944.[11] At the conclusion of the war, the mass deployment of Seabees to Guåhan ended, which resulted in the US military needing to secure a new source of workers.

Military officials quickly dismissed the mass hiring of CHamoru laborers, whom they considered to be unproductive and inefficient workers. Specifically, naval officials believed that CHamorus were slow and "not willing to take initiative"[12] in the completion of work-related tasks and that they did not have the "background and the education necessary for training in the skilled trades."[13] The racializing of CHamoru laborers as unproductive, inefficient, and unskilled masked a historical legacy of US colonial-style education in Guåhan. Beginning in the early 1900s, the US military implemented an education system that stressed elementary English language, public health and sanitation, citizenship training, and vocational training in unskilled work.[14] This education was largely in preparation to teach CHamorus jobs that could primarily serve the US military. In addition, the majority of CHamorus in the prewar period were farmers and ranchers, which was a more self-subsistent way to survive. A smaller number of CHamorus had civilian military jobs or were employed with companies such as Commercial Pacific Cable and the Pan American Hotel. Therefore, most CHamorus were never given the opportunity to obtain the training necessary to be carpenters, electricians, engineers, mechanics, and other skilled workers. As for CHamoru women, statistics for their employment are scant. It appears that they were only hired as midwives, nurses, secretaries, and other office support staff positions, which also made them subservient to military officials.[15] Finally, most CHamorus were still struggling to survive and reunite with family members who had been scattered throughout the island due to the US military's bombardment.

The military weighed the possibility of recruiting other Micronesians such as Carolinians, but they too were racialized in similar ways to CHamorus. Military officials argued that "[Micronesians] worked in groups rather than as individuals" and "looked lazy, unenterprising, improvident, and both unable and unwilling to work at regular, sustained labor."[16] The racialization of Carolinians was based on Western notions of work and time that were different from those of Native Pacific Islanders. Instead, military officials preferred to hire Carolinians and other Micronesians primarily as "houseboys, cooks, and laundresses" for individual units and officers.[17] The infantilizing of Micronesians through their hiring as house servants mirrored the experiences of CHamoru and Filipino men who worked as stewards in the US military and Mexican men who worked in service industries in the continental United States during the same time period.[18] Since military employers could not discipline Carolinians and CHamorus into a Western work pace, they turned to a group of workers they already had control over.

During the war, the US military utilized Japanese prisoners of war (POWs) to augment Seabee labor.[19] They repaired roads, worked as gardeners,[20] maintained camps, served as carpenters, and provided sanitation support.[21] Though there were only 1,250 Japanese POWs in Guåhan (in comparison to the several thousand Seabees), they constituted a source of cheap labor that the military sought to exploit.[22] They too were racialized as a workforce that was perceived to be in "excellent condition."[23] Moreover, military officials argued, "many of them prefer[red] to remain prisoners there [on Guam] and draw their $0.80 daily pay than be repatriated."[24] While it is highly questionable whether Japanese POWs preferred to remain in Guåhan, it is clear that this rationale concealed the capitalist cost-saving strategies through the racialization of Japanese soldiers as being reliable workers. Furthermore, Japanese POWs were already under the control of the US military, which meant they were forced into their roles as exploitable labor due to their incarceration. The war's end resulted in the repatriation of Japanese POWs, leaving the military to search for another group of workers to recruit.

By 1946 the US military contemplated supplanting Seabee and Japanese POW labor with Chinese workers. The island commander of Guam, L. D. Herrle, suggested that the military recruit Chinese workers, who were racialized as being "better workers than Filipinos, Polynesians," and other people from the Pacific region.[25] Herrle and others also believed that Chinese workers were more amenable to labor discipline and were less likely to mingle with CHamorus.[26] The power to control workers was the common thread that linked Seabees, Japanese POWs, and the potential hiring of Chinese workers. CHamorus and other Micronesians were not vulnerable to deportation because they lived in Guåhan or resided on nearby islands across Micronesia. Thus, the military considered Chinese workers because they could be easily deported if they did not adhere to US military labor policy. Herrle's views reflect the earlier perceptions that Leland Stanford and other industrial capitalists had in their preference for hiring Chinese men to construct the transcontinental railroad.[27] The racialization that they were "docile, industrious, trustworthy, and reliable" mirrored the nineteenth-century discourse on Chinese laborers in the continental United States.[28] Herrle also claimed that CHamorus supported the temporary recruitment of Chinese workers so long as they were eventually deported.[29] However, it is unclear which specific "Guamanians" were consulted. Lastly, Herrle believed that the cultural differences between the Chinese workers and the CHamorus would deter these two groups from mingling, which was a common employment strategy that happened in other parts of Oceania, such as plantation labor in Hawai'i.[30] Finding workers who they believed would not threaten US settler militarism proved to be a difficult endeavor for military officials. However, as with the CHamorus and Carolinians before them, the mass recruitment of Chinese workers did not occur. This was partly due to the fact that the growth of pro-Communist sentiment in late 1940s China fostered political tensions between both nations. Furthermore, though the Chinese Exclusion Act of 1882 was repealed in 1943, Chinese migration to the United States was limited under the Johnson–Reed Act of 1924.[31] Given the US military's preference for privately contracted construction companies in the Philippines and elsewhere, it eventually disregarded the recruitment of Chinese workers and instead hired Filipinos and white Americans as the primary sources of civilian military labor.

Infrastructure of US Empire

A close investigation of military records reveals that the recruitment of Filipino military workers to Guåhan was founded on a preexisting agreement between the Philippines and the United States made in 1947.[32] In this exchange of notes, the US government wanted to hire Filipino men to assist in the repatriation of the bodies of US soldiers who had died in World War II and to serve as mess hall stewards for the US military.[33] The Philippine government viewed this agreement as an economic opportunity for its citizens and the Philippine state. Though the Philippines was a newly independent nation, it was still recovering from the economic and physical ravages of World War II.

After 1947 the primary recruitment of Filipino laborers to Guåhan shifted to the private corporations who were contracted to construct the majority of the infrastructure on the island. This pact was also significant because it established the wages and privileges these workers were supposed to receive, which some military contractors used as their standards. As contract workers, their compensation was suppose to include 15 centavos per hour, plus a 25 percent overseas pay differential, free laundry services, free medical and dental care, guaranteed transportation to and from point of hire, pay while in travel, compensation for service connected to injury or death, overtime pay, and holiday pay.[34] Military private contractors benefited the most economically from this agreement. For example, some contractors saved money by paying their workers in Philippine pesos instead of US dollars.[35] Moreover, the length of their employment was one year, renewable up to three years maximum. This limit on employment was intended to ensure that Filipinos could not apply for permanent residency, as individuals who lived in the United States (and by extension Guåhan) for five years could legally petition for naturalization via the McCarran-Walter Act of 1952.[36] However, companies did not always adhere to this agreement, which resulted in numerous cases of workers who did not receive all of their contractual privileges. One of the largest military contractors in Guåhan, the aforementioned Luzon Stevedoring (LUSTEVECO), played a vital role in the infrastructure that connected these and other labor matters between the Philippines and the United States.[37]

A close examination of LUSTEVECO exposes a historical legacy that connected it to US interests that date to the Spanish–American War of 1898.[38] Founded by US veterans of the Spanish-American War, LUSTEVECO became one of the leading cargo transportation companies in Southeast Asia.[39] After World War II, the company came under the ownership of Americans Edward M. Grimm and Charles Parsons, himself a World War II veteran. By 1947 LUSTEVECO was one of the largest military contractors in Guåhan.[40] The navy relied on LUSTEVECO to provide cargo transportation and construction work for naval projects throughout the island. Because it was based in the Philippines, the company's reliance on Filipino workers was already established, though a small number of white Americans—such as Donald Marshall—held supervisory and managerial positions. Moreover, LUSTEVECO depended on labor unions in the Philippines, such as the Philippine Consolidated Labor Union (PCLU), to assist in recruiting Filipinos.[41] When the time came for LUSTEVECO to recruit workers for Guåhan, mobilizing a large labor pool was a relatively easy task given its preexisting infrastructure that connected the company to the PCLU and other unions. As historian Kevin Escudero argues, this "imperialist and militarist network" was instrumental in providing a source of laborers who could be easily and quickly recruited to Guåhan.[42]

Similar to LUSTEVECO, Brown-Pacific-Maxon (BPM) had a previous relationship with the US government. BPM was a joint venture that included Brown & Root, Pacific Ridge, and Maxon Construction. In Guåhan, BPM primarily received contracts from the US Air Force. Unlike LUSTEVECO, BPM's worker pool consisted of workers from both the Philippines and white Americans, with many of the latter coming from the southern United States. BPM's preference for white American southerners was most likely based on the fact that the lead company, Brown & Root, was located in Texas. Additionally, BPM's recruitment of workers was reflective of racial and class differences.

Hired primarily as skilled workers, white Americans labored before and during World War II for Brown & Root's federal projects, such as the constructing of Corpus Christi Naval Air Station in Texas (1940) and the development of 359 US naval ships (1941).[43] In contrast, BPM hired Filipinos to work mainly as unskilled labor. Thus, BPM's hiring preference differed from that of LUSTEVECO, which openly recruited skilled Filipino workers. These uneven hiring practices were significant in the establishment of a racialized labor system that was formed in the late 1940s and early 1950s, and lasted until the 1980s.[44]

BPM's hiring practices also contributed to the racialization of military workers in Guåhan.[45] In 1954 Guam senator James T. Sablan shared his observations during a Guam congressional hearing. He argued, "The BPM construction company is a company somewhat owned or controlled by Southerners and they do not want to hire people other than Caucasians and the reason why they have Filipinos is because they give them a slave or low salary. Now as proof of that I don't think there is a single Negro in that unit."[46] White American Eugene Morgan came to Guåhan in the early 1950s as a civilian military worker. He recalled that there was a "heavy quota" for white workers from Texas and Oklahoma since Brown & Root was located in Texas.[47] Sablan's testimony and Morgan's observations expose BPM's reliance on white American and Filipino workers, with the latter receiving lower pay. This discrepancy in hiring practices and pay contributed to and perpetuated a racialized labor system that would lead to tenuous relationships among workers. With their ties to the colonial Philippines, the US military, and the Jim Crow South, BPM and LUSTEVECO facilitated the largest in-migration of Filipino civilian workers to the island.

Coming to Guåhan

The first postwar wave of Filipinos arrived on Guåhan in 1947 as workers for LUSTEVECO. They came primarily from the province of Iloilo in the Visayas.[48] For many of these laborers (who were mostly men), immigrating to Guåhan provided them with sorely needed employment opportunities since the Philippines was in a state of economic and political instability due to the aftermath of World War II and rising tensions around the issues of labor organizing and communism.[49] By the late 1940s, BPM also had begun to recruit Filipino workers to Guåhan, primarily from the province of Pangasinan. Although it is unclear exactly as to why BPM recruited Filipinos, it can be hypothesized that LUSTEVECO had set the precedent of hiring Filipinos a few years before, an effort endorsed by the US government through its exchange of notes with the Republic of the Philippines. Moreover, Filipinos already had a history of working for the US military at US Naval Base Subic Bay and Clark Air Force Base.[50] These preexisting connections were especially important since the US Navy had implemented a security clearance policy that required all people traveling to and from Guåhan to receive permission from the naval commander.[51] BPM was able to expedite the process of hiring Filipino workers through its recruiting station at Clark Air Force Base, located in Angeles City, Philippines.[52] According to former BPM labor recruiter Gorgonio Cabot:

> It [the recruitment of Filipinos] was well established already when I joined them. They already had plenty of publications. It was advertised, and we continued to advertise about qualified people who were willing to work in Guam. They write, write, write. They could only write, but they [labor applicants] could not come in because we were in Clark Air Force Base. They had to write a letter, addressed to me with the positions they were applying for. We give them a test. Laborers very easy, there's a fifty-pound bag there, carry it. But carpenters need to know how to read the measurer,

and know how to cut wood and carry fifty-pound bag too. You had to have a clean bill of health because the Philippines was full of tuberculosis.[53]

Cabot's statement unveils that the US Air Force aided BPM's recruitment of Filipino workers by permitting the company to utilize Clark Air Force Base as its recruitment center. The air force's relationship with BPM is significant because it exposes how US settler militarism depended on private contractors on other islands throughout its empire, such as Guantánamo Bay. In Cuba, the military relied on its close ties to contractors to recruit local workers. This overlap blurred the relationship between government and private employers in which the US military engaged various island communities.[54] However, before any workers could come to Guåhan, they had to pass a number of strict medical requirements, which was similar to the practice the US government had Mexican workers endure under the Bracero Program.[55]

Before entering Guåhan, workers had to provide certification that they were free from "tuberculosis, chronic malaria, amoebic dysentery, venereal disease, and communicable or infectious diseases."[56] Each employee also had to provide documentation that they had been vaccinated against smallpox and received inoculations against typhoid fever and tetanus.[57] The few Chinese laborers who came to Guåhan via China were also subjected to a battery of health inspection requirements that included isolation for a period of fourteen days.[58] Other migrant workers from Hawai'i and the continental United States also had to pass medical requirements (such as being free of smallpox and venereal diseases), but they were not as rigorous as the health inspections endured by Filipinos.

American perceptions of Filipinos as weak and diseased were widespread in prewar Philippines.[59] In light of BPM's practices, the US military and its contractors still viewed Filipinos as a "diseased" people in the postwar era. Contrary to the belief that these medical tests were intended to protect all the inhabitants of the island, a separate military order required that all military personnel or their families that employed Native "servants" be advised to have them examined for diseases as well.[60] Thus, these hierarchical health requirements based on race and national origin were also implemented to protect the military and their dependents, while simultaneously racializing Filipinos as being the most "diseased" of all recruited civilian military workers.[61] Consequently, it was the labor of these Filipinos—US colonials of the United States—and white Americans that subsequently helped to expand the military's presence on the island.[62]

The Working Lives of Civilian Military Laborers

Filipino men participated in both skilled and manual labor. Examples of manual work included clearing overgrown brush, farming, and stevedoring at Naval Base Guam in the village of Sumai. Semi-skilled and skilled work included carpentry, construction, electrical work, painting, plumbing, road paving, and roofing.[63] LUSTEVECO also recruited Filipina workers for skilled labor in Guåhan.

Filipina workers served as nurses and medical assistants in the company camps and never totaled more than 1 percent of the labor force.[64] In some instances, contractors hired women to work as hospital workers rather than nurses.[65] This practice reveals that contractors were able to pay them lower wages as general hospital workers, while still benefiting from their formal training as certified nurses. In turn, these workers were exploited as "cheap labor," which was and still is a common occurrence for overseas Filipina laborers throughout the world.[66] Furthermore, companies such as LUSTE-VECO only hired seven to eight hospital workers for Camp Roxas, which housed several thousand men.[67] Depending on how many workers needed medical attention, this imbalance in the patient-to-medical-worker ratio created a pressured work environment. BPM took a similar approach that mirrored a racial and gendered hierarchy that privileged white American men over all other workers, including white American women, which was then commonplace throughout the United States.[68] They hired, for example, a small number of white American women who held subordinate positions as assistant clerks, clerk typists, and secretaries.[69] BPM also preferred hiring white American men who served in managerial and skilled positions such as electricians, engineers, foremen, mechanics, and site supervisors.[70] Some of these men even had experience doing foreign contract work before coming to Guåhan.[71] By 1950, BPM's labor force comprised approximately one thousand white Americans and five thousand Filipinos.[72] In Guåhan, white American workers were privileged over CHamorus and Filipinos, which was most evident in the wages they were paid.

Military contractors used a hierarchical wage scale that paid white American workers more than CHamorus and Filipinos. Specifically, white American workers (classified as a nonlocal hire) received a "territorial post differential" (TPD) that gave them an additional 25 percent bonus on top of their base pay.[73] CHamorus (classified as local hires) were paid the second-highest wages (which were usually half the rate of a nonlocal hire), while Filipinos were paid the lowest wages (three-quarters of a local hire).[74] Though some Filipinos were also supposed to receive a TPD, there were numerous cases in which they indicated that it was withheld or never issued at all.[75] While it is unclear how many people received TPD bonuses, Filipinos were usually still paid below the US minimum wage, which was $0.75 in 1950.[76] In response to these allegations, the US military simply claimed it was unaware of the low wage issue and that private contractors were responsible for paying workers accordingly.[77] Not surprisingly, the US military's complacency in the regulation and enforcement of workers' wages and other compensation underscored the notion that the militarization of Guåhan trumped the protection of workers' rights. This corrupt practice also allowed the US military and its contractors to reduce employment costs. In turn, they justified paying the lowest wages to Filipinos since they were categorized as "alien" workers who were "unskilled." Though CHamorus received lower wages than white Americans, they still received higher wages than Filipino nationals because they were US citizens. However, because CHamorus had to be paid more than Filipinos, fewer of them were hired, while Filipinos could be paid the least and were more susceptible to labor discipline since they could be deported. White Americans could also be deported, but their investment in working in Guåhan was dissimilar to that of Filipinos.[78] For Filipinos, working for the military and its contractors was more lucrative and represented economic mobility since the Philippines was still recovering from the ravages of World War II, whereas white Americans generally saw work in Guåhan as temporary and transitional.[79]

Working as a civilian military laborer sometimes resulted in injury or death. In January 1948, Filipino workers Felix Sarmago and Felicisimo Caperas were killed in an industrial accident while working for Marianas Stevedoring (MASDELCO), a subsidiary of LUSTEVECO.[80] Other Filipino laborers, such as Teodoro Gorospe, likewise encountered workplace accidents. In June 26, 1959, Gorospe and an unnamed CHamoru worker came into contact with a hot wire at a voltage substation on Andersen Air Force Base and died of electrocution.[81] While information on the number of deaths is not available, the number of injuries that workers sustained on the job was recorded periodically. During the summer of 1947, BPM averaged seventy-four worker injuries per month (for a three-month span), which amounts to 2.4 injuries per day.[82] The dangerous work environments in building construction, heavy machinery, and explosives made CHamorus, Filipinos, and white Americans all susceptible to workplace injuries and/or death. In addition to coping with these hazardous conditions, workplace injuries placed a financial burden upon Filipino laborers.

Filipino worker Antonio E. Lo was sent back to the Philippines for hospitalization due to his gastric ulcer. Lo claimed that his employing company, LUSTEVECO, had guaranteed to pay for his hospitalization yet never did.[83] In some instances, military contractors such as LUSTEVECO simply repatriated workers to the Philippines instead of granting them medical treatment in Guåhan. Thus, the risk of injury and/or death, coupled with their employers' unwillingness to provide medical care, caused many Filipinos to become outraged. Moreover, the US military was able to absolve itself from liability and obligation since these workers were hired directly by LUSTEVECO. However, working for the US military also resulted in medical issues that happened later in life.

Before coming to Guåhan, Filipino worker Larry Mabini was a carpenter for the Japanese Imperial Military during World War II. He was hired in 1959 to work for Vinnell Construction in Guåhan as a carpenter and worked at military sites throughout the island that included the Navy's Public Work Center and NAS Hagåtña. Larry's daughter, former Guam senator Dr. Sam Mabini, recalls, "I was always curious because when my father passed away he was very asthmatic at the end. During his later years after he retired he started having asthma. There were questions even after he passed away because he was a carpenter and he worked in asbestos environments. As a little girl, we would go to some of these naval station facilities and sometimes he would tell me not to go in there because there was asbestos."[84] Sam's memory of her father reveals that military laborers were subjected to working conditions that potentially impacted their long-term health. While it cannot be fully deduced what led to Larry Mabini developing asthma later in his life, there is scientific evidence that links asbestos exposure to respiratory issues that can occur years after exposure.[85]

Company Camp Life

While workplace conditions served as a source of tension, life in company camps was both a positive and negative focal point of workers' lives in Guåhan. The military's contractor system allowed construction corporations to set up company camps where they administered the social lives of their laborers. There were several company camps—including Camp Asan, Camp Edusa, Camp Marbo, and Camp Magsaysay—scattered throughout the island. However, the largest camps were LUSTEVECO's Camp Roxas (initially named Camp Carter) and BPM's Camp #1, Camp #2, and Camp Quezon.[86] Filipino workers employed by LUSTEVECO lived in Camp Roxas, which was located near the present-day southern villages of Hågat and Sånta Rita. BPM housed its Filipino and white laborers in segregated company camps in the village of Mangilao, near the present-day University of Guam. Filipinos lived in Camp Quezon, while white Americans lived in Camp #1 and Camp #2. White American women also resided in BPM's camps but lived in separate quarters that were located away from the men. These companies established autonomous camps that had baseball fields, basketball courts, bowling alleys, chapels, churches, clothing stores, medical facilities, mess halls, movie theaters, and security patrols.[87] However, the social experiences in these camps were at times just as regimented as in the workplace. Thus, these company camps were sites of social control that worked in conjunction with Jim Crow racism, immigration policy, and labor discipline in the workplace.

The logic of white supremacy operated through Jim Crow racism that operated via racial segregation. For example, white American workers from BPM's company camp performed minstrel shows, which was advertised in the *Constructionaire,* a newsletter that was circulated in BPM's camps:

Rastus, why fouh your be so happy? Well Rufus, Monday night we's all gwana have a lot ob fun wid dem folks out front. Yeah, dat's all true an' deys gwana enjoy it too, I think. Dat is if dey goes along wid our stuff an' takes it in de proper spirit. Yeah, Rufus, an' if dey don't, git ready to duck 'cause deys no reefer ship in an' dey'll be throwin' coconuts. Come on now, make wid de big smile fouh all de folks out dere, 'cause dis aint no good sample ob our show di'logue.[88]

Interestingly, this show was also performed in Camp Quezon, which suggests that some white Americans were willing to incorporate Filipinos into their anti-Black sentiment. For white Americans and Filipinos, recreational activities were one of the few social opportunities outside of work. However, for employers, these activities veiled their promotion of welfare capitalism that attempted to discipline all of the workers living in company camps.

BPM, LUSTEVECO, and other contractors utilized welfare capital activities to disguise their objective of reducing worker discontent and the possibility of labor protest.[89] Camp Roxas and BPM's camps had baseball, basketball, bowling, and volleyball teams.[90] For example, the MASDELCO Warriors was a basketball team that represented Camp Roxas.[91] These sports teams not only competed within camps but also played against other company camp teams, CHamoru village teams, and against US military teams, thereby encouraging workers to think of themselves as representatives of their companies. These sports teams also played an integral role in generating camaraderie, conflict, and rivalry that included the women and children who were allowed to attend these events. Moreover, sports teams commonly nominated Filipina nurses who worked in the same camp to symbolically serve as a "team muse" who attended the games to inspire their performance. This act was also a reflection of the gender imbalance among Filipino laborers and the relegation of women as passive participants. For Filipino and white American men, sports became one of the activities that allowed them to engage in homosocial relations and display their masculinity in front of large crowds of fans. These expressions of masculinity also represented racial and national pride, especially during interracial competitions. For the companies, they believed these activities kept workers in good physical condition and could prevent laborers from drinking, fighting, and gambling.[92] By doing so, companies wanted to ensure that their workforce was efficient, healthy, and disciplined.

Filipinos and white Americans participated in numerous racially segregated social activities such as beach parties, bingo game nights, church services, dances, and holiday parades.[93] While workers did initiate these social activities, the reality was that their employers allowed them to participate in these gatherings while providing them the facilities to hold these events.[94] For example, contractors required all of their workers to obtain company police clearances if they wanted to participate in recreational activities and social gatherings outside of their respective camps.[95] One of the most common activities was to have beach parties. As shown in figure 3.1, one beach became synonymous with Filipino workers, who nicknamed it Rizal Beach in honor of the Filipino nationalist Jose Rizal. Rizal Beach was reserved for Filipino workers from Camp Roxas as a way to segregate them from a nearby beach that was designated for US military personnel. While the naming of the beach after Jose Rizal was an attempt to claim place and nationality, it also perpetuated a settler colonial logic of remaking Indigenous lands since the beach is the ancestral property of the Pangelinan-Bordallo families. Places like Rizal Beach were supposed to be sources of comfort, even though the companies viewed these sites and activities as profit-driven measures.

Originally from Iloilo, Visayas, in the Philippines, former LUSTEVECO worker Jose Savares came to Guåhan in 1952 as a timekeeper. He arrived in Guåhan via a cargo ship from the Philippines that took eight days. Savares recollected, "I got sick and I was very young. I missed my mom and cried. Some of the guys at the camp [Roxas] already knew us and they took care

Figure 3.1. Rizal Beach, 1950s. Source: Photograph courtesy of Humanities Guåhan (formerly known as Guam Humanities Council), *A Journey Home: Camp Roxas and Filipino American History in Guam*, an exhibition funded by the National Endowment for the Humanities, We The People Initiative.

of us. . . . The older guys helped take care of me. One of the older guys was my neighbor back in the Philippines. He would wake me and have coffee with me."[96] For Jose and other Filipino workers, homosocial relationships were integral in the acclimation to living in Guåhan. For many Filipinos, finding people who were from their hometowns was easy since LUSTEVECO, BPM, and other military contractors recruited from the same province or regions in the Philippines. Filipino workers also served as unofficial recruiters who encouraged their family and friends to apply for jobs to work in Guåhan. However, even homosocial support and welfare capitalism was not enough to mitigate the hardships of living in company camps.

Growing Discontent with Company Camp Life

In the early 1950s, both Filipino and white American workers commonly complained about the dilapidated conditions of company camps. Naval medical officer R. W. Jones reported on the unsanitary plight of the Filipino quarters at Camp Asan: "The cleanliness and sanitary condition of sleeping quarters is very unsatisfactory. A general field day is badly needed. Bunks need clean linen and the loose gear that is adrift should be stowed. Clothes are being dried in sleeping quarter."[97] These conditions were not isolated occurrences. As seen in figure 3.2, Filipino laborers also complained about the conditions of the Quonset huts that they lived in at Camp Roxas.[98] Contractors housed their employees in Quonset huts because they were cheap to build and could accommodate eight to twelve people, depending on the length of the buildings. As shown in figure 3.3, these structures usually had an exterior made of sheet metal and wood, which were cheaper materials than concrete. Thus, the hot and humid weather in Guåhan heightened the temperature inside these structures. L. Eugene Wolfe, an officer with the US Industrial Relations, recorded his investigation of Quonset huts at Camp Piti. As he observed, "Frequent rains, combined with gusty winds, tend to make these relatively unprotected types of building virtually uninhabitable. These

Figure 3.2. Inside a Quonset hut at Camp Roxas, 1950s. Source: Photograph courtesy of Humanities Guåhan, *A Journey Home: Camp Roxas and Filipino American History in Guam*, an exhibition funded by the National Endowment for the Humanities, We The People Initiative.

Figure 3.3. Damaged Quonset hut at Camp Roxas, 1950s. Source: Photograph courtesy of Humanities Guåhan, *A Journey Home: Camp Roxas and Filipino American History in Guam,* an exhibition funded by the National Endowment for the Humanities, We The People Initiative.

structures are partially open at either end and except for a four foot strip on both sides under the eaves everything in them is subject to not only the high humidity of the island but the actual wetting from blown rain during the rainy season."[99]

Another point of contention was the poor quality of food available to workers. In August 1949 civilian worker Dorothea Minor Baker wrote a letter to C. A. Pownall, the governor of Guam, describing the inadequate mess hall conditions at Camp Asan. She claimed, "Many of us, after spending several minutes in line, turn dejectedly away from the heavy, colorless, unappetizing food and work eight hours without nourishment. There are those who have lost from ten to thirty pounds in weight; those who eat and those who don't because in either instance, the food has no value."[100]

Baker's comments illustrate that women also deplored some of the conditions they had to live in. Even the food served to white American workers was unappealing enough to dissuade them from eating breakfast in the company camps. These laborers most likely had to rely on restaurants and grocery stores outside of the camps for some of their meals. However, the most telling part of Baker's letter was her indirect critique of the regimented schedule, which was a common feature of camp life.

As LUSTEVECO worker Consul Umayan stated, "There is a tight curfew at all camps, with lights out at eleven P.M. and a bed check at one A.M." He continued, "There is too much discipline. . . . If the men are not there when a bed check is made they get one disciplinary check against them. Four such points are cause for dismissal. That's not good for morale."[101] This strictly enforced work schedule, combined with poor housing and unappetizing food options, forced Umayan to leave Guåhan. Other workers such as white American electrician Louie Levine also resigned their positions and returned to the United States due to "unsatisfactory living conditions."[102] Levine's and Umayan's actions show that some workers did not accept their living conditions and opted to find other jobs or return home rather than continuing to work for their contractors and living in company camps. These frustrations over work and life in camps sometimes resulted in conflict.

The potential for violence concerned all camp residents. On March 14, 1949, George Anderson, a resident at Camp Asan, was awakened at 1:00 a.m. He recalled:

> My wife awakened me with the statement that someone had been peering through the window. Upon investigating, I noticed an individual walking rapidly away from the building at an estimated 100 feet away. Two other couples had also been aroused by the prowler, but were unable to apprehend him. I had just begun to drowse when I was again awakened approximately one hour later by footsteps outside my window. Arising in bed, I noticed through the ventilating louvers the figure of a man creeping below the window level. I investigated and found him peering through the window of the adjoining room. . . . I went to the front door of the quarters and noticed a dark complexioned individual walking rapidly about 30 feet away.[103]

Though Anderson was unable to apprehend this individual, his statement reveals the potential danger in company camps. Along these lines, Filipino and white American men armed themselves with various weapons, which the military perceived differently depending on the racial group.

White American workers often owned firearms while living in Guåhan. As naval officer A. J. Carrillo claimed, "It is common knowledge that practically everyone, in most of the housing areas, and [in] particular Base 18[,]

have in their possession firearms[;] this is apparent as, when leaving the island for the states they are left behind, in drawers, and under beds. They are
all aware however of the existing orders prohibiting the possession of [guns],
but [they] will not come forward and use the proper channels to keep them."[104]
Carrillo's report indicated that military and company camp officials did not
police white American workers for their possession of firearms without
proper registration and did little to resolve this issue. Essentially, the military condoned the white American ownership of weapons. In contrast,
military officials knew that Filipino workers at Camp Roxas also owned firearms and had a punitive response. In February 1950, US military officials
sent a detachment of 484 marines and sailors to search Camp Roxas for
firearms and other weapons. According to the *Guam News*, "1,500 out of
the 3,000 Filipino residents of Roxas had a weapon of some sort taken
away."[105] The newspaper article continued, "Some of the weapons [included]
were nine pistols, seven rifles, blackjacks, brass knuckles, pneumatic drills
filed to a sharp point, thousands of knives of all descriptions, scissors, cut-
lasses, razors, hatchets, files, machetes, butcher cleavers, bayonets, dynamite,
air and pistol rifles, and many others."[106] The newspaper makes no observation that many of the items confiscated were tools that construction workers
commonly used—knives, razors, hatchets, files, and machetes. This racialization of Filipinos as potential criminals was pervasive in other parts of Oceania. For example, Filipinos in pre–World War II Hawai'i were perceived as
violent, emotionally volatile, and having a propensity for criminality.[107]

Labor Activism and the Philippine Consulate

The Cold War was an era of anti-Communist hysteria in the United States
that made labor activism synonymous with Communist Party activity. As a
result, very few attempts were made to organize labor unions in Guåhan during the 1940s and 1950s.

Deportation was the primary means by which the US military and its contractors dealt with Filipino and white American workers who challenged
labor discipline. In May 1955, 227 Filipino workers of LUSTEVECO were
deported to the Philippines because they refused to sign individual employment contracts. These workers had come to Guåhan on a collective contract
between LUSTEVECO and the PCLU, the union that represented them.[108]
Because the PCLU had been suspended (due to reasons unknown), the US
Navy required these workers to sign new individual contracts. The laborers

feared that these new contracts would eliminate the overseas bonus that LUSTEVECO had promised them. Additionally, the US military had a stringent policy that required all contractors to deport Filipino laborers before "the third anniversary of their arrival on Guam" and if they attempted to change their nationality through naturalization or intermarriage with CHamorus.[109] This policy was in response to the passing of the McCarran-Walter Act of 1952, which removed all racial restrictions to naturalization and made foreign-born Asians eligible for US citizenship.[110] In some instances, contractors overlooked the maximum time limit and continued to employ Filipino workers regardless of the military labor policy. Their investment in transgressing military policy benefited them since recruiting, processing, and training new workers was time consuming and costly. As a result, some Filipino laborers were able to permanently settle in Guåhan through intermarriage with CHamorus or through naturalization. Moreover, the military had disguised its repatriation policy by claiming it protected the employment rights of CHamorus, but in reality it racialized Filipino workers, some of whom challenged military and contractor policies as Communists and threats to US national security. Filipinos and white Americans could be removed from Guåhan at any time, which made labor activism and unionization difficult for fear of being transported off-island. In response, the Republic of the Philippines ordered investigations regarding the experiences and treatment of Filipino workers in Guåhan.

The Philippine government launched at least two inquiries amid growing concerns that Filipino workers were being mistreated. In July 1952 the US deputy chief of naval operations in Guam sent a memo to US military officials and their contractors informing them that Philippine government officials had visited the island in December 1951. The memo stated, "As a result of these charges, which basically were politically inspired[,] an investigation committee of high Philippine government officials was sent to Guam."[111] However, this probe did not find any information that the US military and its contractors had exploited Filipino workers. In 1954 the Philippine government initiated another investigation and sent congressional representatives Justino Benito, Angel Castano, Rodelpho Ganzon, Roseller Lim, and stenographer Anselma B. Domondon to Guåhan.[112] These officials sought to ascertain if Filipino workers were being paid lower wages than other laborers on the island.[113] Though the investigation was inconclusive, it led to a growing suspicion that the US military and its contractors were in fact exploiting Filipino workers and that the Philippine government was invested in the protection of its citizens' wages.

In 1952 the Republic of the Philippines established a consulate in Guåhan, which was done in cooperation with the US government. According to Bayani Mangibin, a former Philippine consulate general to Guåhan, "One of the reasons we established a consulate here [was that] it was requested because there was no territorial government so the US was running everything; they requested the Philippine government to establish this consulate office in the early 1940s."[114] For the Philippine government, the consulate functioned to support Filipino workers. For the US government, the establishment of a consulate helped them manage the Filipino community in Guåhan. However, one of the consulate's most important objectives was to promote Filipino worker productivity.[115] Similar to other Asian nations, the Philippine government wanted to ensure that Filipino workers represented their country positively by serving as dependable laborers. Consulate officials also helped families in the Philippines locate Filipino workers in Guåhan who had "gone missing."[116] The consulate's role in supporting workers had expanded to the point that Filipino laborers made requests such as asking consulate officials to pay for their court fines, loan them money, help them raise funds to pay personal debts, and advocate for them to receive better positions.[117] While it is unknown if consul officials actually interceded in all of these cases, the consulate was invested in the protection of Filipino workers' rights.

The Philippine consulate in Guåhan also addressed various concerns such as the nonpayment of wages, excessive working hours, overtime work without corresponding pay, inadequate living quarters and food, unsanitary conditions of toilet and bath facilities, the threat of deportation, and intraracial violence. However, it is important to note that the Republic of the Philippines might have had additional motives in supporting their workers, such as the safeguarding of their remittances to the Philippines. These remittances served as an important source of revenue that helped stimulate the Philippine economy, which was later institutionalized with the establishment of the Philippine Overseas Employment Administration (POEA) in 1982.[118] Labor strife and issues of camp life culminated with the proposal of the Guam Wage Bill in 1956.

Guam Wage Bill of 1956

Filipino frustrations over work place safety, wages, and worker privileges reached a boiling point that resulted in the Guam Wage Bill of 1956. Proposed in the US Congress, the bill attempted to make Guåhan exempt from the Fair Labor Standards Act (FLSA) of 1938. This act was an important piece of legislation that guaranteed a minimum wage, provided overtime pay, set a maximum hour workweek, and prohibited the employment of minors. BPM, LUSTEVECO, the US State Department, the US Department of Defense, and the US Department of Interior were the largest supporters of the proposed bill to circumvent workers' rights as guaranteed by the FLSA. As an unidentified US naval official stated, "The Defense Department is interested mainly in stretching the defense dollar as far as it can go."[119] For the US government and its military contractors, the passing of the Guam Wage Bill would have allowed them to reduce their payroll expenses while still benefiting from the labor of CHamoru and Filipino workers. The bill called for exemptions similar to those that private corporations and the US government supported in other US territories, such as American Sāmoa, Puerto Rico, and the US Virgin Islands. In the 1940s, for example, private companies were able to obtain FLSA exemptions in Puerto Rico and the US Virgin Islands, and in 1956 the Van Camp Seafood Company was allowed an exemption in American Sāmoa to maximize tuna cannery profits. As historian JoAnna Poblete writes, this capitalist strategy to suppress the wages of laborers connected Indigenous people and Asian immigrants living in US territories to "the same imperial legacy."[120] However, this attempt to reduce worker rights and wages in Guåhan met fierce resistance from various governments and labor organizations that spanned the world.

The proposed Guam Wage Bill spurred one of the largest transnational labor movements in the Oceania, connecting opponents from Asia, Europe, the Pacific, and the United States.[121] This coalition was not a coordinated effort among CHamorus, Filipinos, and others on the island to halt the militarization of Guåhan; instead, CHamorus and Filipinos had parallel movements, and each used their own set of strategies to oppose the bill. Their shared objective was to protect their wages and labor rights. For example, in March 1956 the Guam legislature sent CHamoru representative Antonio B. Won Pat to testify at a US Congressional subcommittee in opposition to the proposed bill.[122] Won Pat testified that the proposed bill would "have an extremely disruptive effect on the economy of Guam. More than that, we feel that it would affect the morale by removing from the people of Guam the privileges of a statute to which its benefits have already been extended and by threatening a pattern by which benefits of other statutes may be weakened or removed."[123] For CHamorus such as Won Pat, the Guam Wage Bill represented the loss of both labor and political rights, which they had just obtained through the passage of the Organic Act. For CHamorus, it was another stark example of how US citizenship did not guarantee inclusion or equality. Facing similar circumstances, Filipinos in Guåhan and back in the Philippines also challenged the US government.[124]

Republic of the Philippines ambassador Carlos P. Romulo opposed the proposal through diplomatic notes. He stated, "All Asia is watching the American attitude on Filipinos in these islands and if the wage scale would be discriminatory and contrary to the democratic principles enunciated by the United States."[125] Romulo's statement was strategic because it reminded the US government that Cold War politics and alliances were at stake since nations throughout the world were keeping track of how the United States handled political and economic issues in its territorial possessions. Furthermore, the Philippine government threatened the US government that it would have fifteen thousand Filipino laborers return home if the proposed bill was passed.[126] Though the Guåhan wage provision generated CHamoru and Filipino discontent with the US government, their efforts were—as noted above—not unified. Some CHamoru politicians believed that their people were being overlooked for jobs due to the significant number of Filipino workers in Guåhan.[127] Others contended that the US military and its contractors preferred to hire Filipinos because they accepted "coolie pay."[128] These CHamoru politicians recognized the capitalist strategies that were being used to marginalize the employment of their community. This is likely one of several factors that explain why a labor movement between CHamorus and Filipinos did not materialize. Nevertheless, CHamorus and Filipinos were united in their support to defeat the bill since it threatened the economic livelihood of their people; this, despite the fact that access to military civilian jobs served as a source of conflict between their communities and in the militarization of the island.

While CHamorus argued their US citizenship entitled them to political rights, Filipinos used their own tactics to oppose the bill. The Philippine Trade Unions Council (PTUC) was one of the most outspoken critics of the Guam Wage Bill.[129] PTUC's strategy was to generate support from other labor organizations such as the American Federation of Labor—Congress of Industrial Organizations (AFL-CIO). In February 1956, PTUC representative Jose Hernandez wrote a letter to AFL-CIO president George Meany urging him to oppose the Guam Wage Bill.[130] The AFL-CIO agreed to support Filipino workers in Guåhan and in other US territories that faced proposed FLSA exemptions.[131] Furthermore, the Philippine government and the PTUC ramped up their efforts by seeking support from other international labor organizations, such as the Asia and Pacific Regional Organization (APRO) of the International Confederation of Free Trade Unions (ICFTU).[132] Leaders from the ICFTU pledged to "present formal papers of protest and petition the [US] department to take the cudgels for these brother workers."[133] In addition to the ICFTU, the International Labor Organization (ILO) also agreed to oppose the Guam Wage Bill.[134] The ILO held an annual conference, granting representatives from the Philippines an opportunity to voice their concerns. Therefore, the ILO was instrumental in providing the space and audience to inform other labor organizations throughout the world of the US government's attempt to violate the rights of the workers in Guåhan and in other US territories.

Mounting concerns over the spread of communism and the perception of the United States' prominence as the world's democratic leader also led to the defeat of the Guam Wage Bill. AFL-CIO legislative representative Walter J. Mason testified before a US congressional subcommittee that "For the congress at this critical juncture in world affairs to enact legislation which would institute substandard wages in an underdeveloped American possession would simply feed grist to the mills of the communist propaganda machine." Mason continued, "Our relationship with the peoples in underdeveloped areas which are under U.S. administration must be exemplary and beyond criticism. It might thereby jeopardize the success of an important phase of our nation's foreign policy."[135] His comments reveal that the AFL-CIO supported the workers in Guåhan because its leadership believed the passing of the Guam Wage Bill would foster Communist thought on the island and in other US territories. The AFL-CIO also believed that the expansion of democracy and workers' rights was interlinked with US foreign policy.[136]

Politicians in the Philippines also went on record in defiance of the bill and the discrimination embedded in it. As Philippine congressman Serafin Salvador asserted, "There is an overwhelming sentiment for an overhaul of our attitude towards America. We should look more to our Southeast Asian neighbors. This atmosphere, that is termed by [the] American press as anti-American[,] is generated by the discriminatory attitudes of the United States to the Philippines."[137] Other Philippine officials also urged their government to reexamine its relationships with other Southeast Asian countries rather than focus on ties to the United States. This would deal an enormous blow to the US government's reputation, since promoting American democracy and containing communism was crucial to the federal government's foreign policy.

The advocacy of government officials and labor representatives from Guåhan, the Philippines, and the continental United States resulted in the defeat of the Guam Wage Bill in the summer of 1956. However, this victory for Filipino labor would serve to heighten the US government's suspicion of laborers from the Philippines being Communist labor organizers.

As discussed in this chapter, the justification for the recruitment of Filipino laborers and the hierarchical labor system it produced was an important component to US setter militarism in Guåhan. The narrative that these workers "rehabilitated and reconstructed" the island concealed how the recruitment and control of these workers was integral to the military's infrastructure. To achieve their results, the US military and its contractors produced and depended on a hierarchical labor system that was predicated on racial and national differences that resulted in the segregation of company camps, unequal wages, and uneven working conditions. The apex of these matters culminated with the Guam Wage Bill, which, if passed, would have allowed the US government and its military contractors to reduce their payroll expenses while still benefiting from employing CHamoru and Filipino workers. This victory for the military and its contractors would have permitted them to maintain their control over the material and social conditions of their workers, while simultaneously making military expansion more profitable. Moreover, the military's willingness to support corporate-sponsored FLSA exemptions in Guåhan and other US territories made the imperial relationships between business and government more apparent. In response to the potential worsening of social conditions on the island, CHamorus and Filipinos engaged in an uncoordinated, top-down movement against US military interests and their contractors during a time of intense anti-Communist sentiment. Although these movements did not result in the building of a large-scale multinational collation of CHamorus and Filipinos, they did symbolize that the people of Guåhan were willing to oppose the US military.

After the defeat of the Guam Wage Bill, Filipinos continued to serve as military civilian workers. White Americans began to return to the continental United States, though a small number of white American male workers stayed and married CHamoru women. Furthermore, the multinational labor movement that had formed to oppose the bill no longer existed after 1957. (While the factors for its disappearance are unknown, it is most likely due to the fact that the leaders of the movement no longer maintained the coalitions since they achieved their respective objectives.) However, the working-class victory for CHamorus and Filipinos produced some unintended consequences that perpetuated the racializing of these communities within the backdrop of American fears of communism. Camp Roxas was the last company camp to close, in 1972, which resulted in the final dispersal of Filipino laborers. These workers went back home, settled in Guåhan, or moved to the continental United States. For the men who settled in Guåhan, they either married into CHamoru families or became naturalized US citizens who sponsored the immigration of their family members from the Philippines to Guåhan.

Chapter 4

Militarized Intimacies

In December 1954, Filipino worker Eddie De La Cruz accompanied a friend who wanted to visit his girlfriend who lived in the village of CHålan Pågu (Chalan Pago). After their arrival at her house, Eddie waited patiently in the living room. It was during this moment that Eddie and CHamoru Barbara Castro first laid eyes on each other. Barbara was the sister of the woman that Eddie's friend came to visit. Barbara and Eddie's attraction to each other was instantaneous. Barbara disobeyed her parents, even though they warned her not to date Filipino men, believing they were "violent." A year later, Barbara and Eddie were married.

One evening, Eddie returned to the Brown-Pacific-Maxon (BPM) company camp after 10 p.m. curfew and was reprimanded. Upon learning that Eddie had married a CHamoru woman, BPM managers ordered him to be deported. Rather than accept his expulsion from Guåhan and be separated from Barbara, Eddie decided to escape from BPM's barracks. With the help of Barbara and her family, Eddie evaded BPM's patrol authorities until he received his green card a few weeks later.[1] Eddie had gained the legal ability to permanently reside in Guåhan because the Guam Organic Act of 1950 granted US citizenship to CHamorus—and, by extension, spouses of CHamorus—and the McCarran-Walter Act of 1952 had guaranteed him access to permanent residency.

While Barbara and Eddie's extraordinary love story might simply appear as one couple's triumph in staying together, it actually reveals how deeply involved the US military and its contractors were in the regulation of the militarized intimacies that were produced in the postwar era. As literary scholar Nicolyn Woodcock argues, militarized intimacies are personal relations that "cannot be disentangled from the physical spaces where they happen and the geopolitical contexts that frame them."[2] For people like Barbara and Eddie, the context of their love story is the post–World War II militarization of Guåhan. And by intimacy, I mean a broad set of interactions that include dating, gossip, homosociality, rumor, sex, and violence.[3] In the case of Guåhan, these militarized intimacies were not only interracial but came as a direct result of US military occupation.

As discussed in previous chapters, the recruitment of military labor had a profound impact that permanently altered the island's demography from a prewar society mostly comprised of CHamorus to a postwar settler society. Specifically, Guåhan's population skyrocketed, increasing 166 percent from 22,290 people in 1940 to 59,498 people in 1950. This astronomical growth in the island's non-CHamoru population produced various militarized intimacies that the US military attempted to regulate.

In this chapter, I argue that the US militarization of Guåhan functioned through the creation of laws that were fused in the policing of radical organizing and the interracial intimacies among CHamorus, Filipinos, and white Americans. In the case of Barbara and Eddie De La Cruz, the military viewed their marriage with suspicion because they believed Filipino men were potential labor radicals who posed a threat to the US military. However, these very same intimacies were also moments of resistance. As historian Nayan Shah has argued regarding the early twentieth-century American West, colonized people have always "undermined the containment efforts of nation-states and empires."[4] Thus, Barbara and Eddie's relationship represented one example of how CHamoru women and Filipino men transgressed military policy.

The military promoted or stymied interracial encounters depending on if these intimacies advanced or disrupted the military occupation of the island. This process included the racializing of CHamorus, Filipinos, and white Americans. Typically, the military viewed Filipinos as what historian Moon-Ho Jung refers to as "seditious threats"[5] or "subversives" due to their role in the thwarting of the Guam Wage Bill, which the US government viewed as an act that undermined the militarization of the island.[6] On the other hand, CHamorus and white Americans were largely perceived more flexibly depending on their actions. For example, military officials believed CHamorus were largely loyal to the US military except in cases when they engaged in interracial marriage with Filipinos. Similarly, white Americans were only viewed as subversives if their actions harmed the US government's "moral" reputation as the leader of the free world.[7]

A major concern for the military was the emergence of interracial violence among CHamorus, Filipinos, and white Americans. These incidents were problematic because of the possibility that they could generate anti–US military sentiment among island residents and worldwide.[8] Thus, the US military's policing of interracial intimacies in Guåhan was intertwined with the prevention of radical labor organizing and the US government's self-projection as the moral leader of democracy. However, as the De La Cruz family story demonstrates, CHamorus, Filipinos, and even white Americans directly or indirectly challenged US military power in ways that shifted or intensified Western and Indigenous notions of gender, race, and sex.

The first section of this chapter focuses on the US Navy's surveillance of Filipinos living in Guåhan. As mentioned earlier, their role and the Philippine government's advocacy in defeating the Guam Wage Bill generated suspicion among military and government officials. The second part of this chapter examines Guåhan's militarized intimacies through dating, gossip, marriage, rumor, and sex. The final section investigates interracial violence and the creation of US military laws that attempted to prevent these types of encounters.

The Office of Naval Intelligence (ONI)

As sociologist Rick Baldoz has argued, US authorities believed that Filipino workers were engaged in a Communist conspiracy that linked left-wing labor activists in a spy ring that stretched across the world.[9] As discussed in chapter 3, the defeat of the proposed Guam Wage Bill of 1956 was largely due to an international movement that connected various labor organizations. This movement, coupled with Filipino labor organizing in the continental United States, provoked the military's trepidation over their presence on the island. Consequently, the military believed that the global labor radicalism that Filipinos engaged in now reached Guåhan. Even though labor organizing in Guåhan was not centered on the overthrowing of US capitalism,[10] their actions in thwarting the bill heightened the military's fear of Filipino labor activism since they comprised 65 percent of the island's entire workforce by 1950.[11] However, the US government's concern with Filipino organizing was also historically rooted in their resistance to US colonialism.

During the Philippine-American War (1899–1902), US Army officials viewed Filipinos as rebellious and threatening due to their willingness to engage in armed combat against the United States for their political independence. Throughout the war, the army utilized informants and spies to report on the activities of Filipino political leaders.[12] At the conclusion of this conflict, the military exiled several dozen Filipino political leaders to Guåhan.[13] Thus, the US government's encounter with Filipino radicalism was rooted in colonialism and war, which perpetuated the military's distrust of Filipinos even after World War II. Filipino labor posed a complicated scenario for the military because they were viewed as ideal workers who were also racialized as potential subversives.

This anxiety was amplified because of their growing population and close proximity to military bases. The military believed Filipino radicals could engage in sabotage, surveillance, and other activities that could undermine their occupation due to their employment as civilian military laborers.[14] Even with this paradox, the military and its contractors preferred to recruit Filipinos because this allowed them to keep payroll costs down since they could pay them the lowest wages. This capitalist cost-saving decision resulted in the military's continued surveillance of the Filipino community. Additionally, Filipino Americans who were US permanent residents or US citizens also stoked the military's concern since they could obtain entry into Guåhan from places such as Hawai'i or the continental United States.[15] Ultimately, the military feared Filipino workers because it believed they were loyal to the Republic of the Philippines.

In a memo written in 1956, an unidentified naval administrator stated, "There has been an increasing number of indications that Filipinos who obtain permanent resident status and U.S. citizenship feel their original loyalty to Phil govt, in spite of the fact they owe complete allegiance to U.S."[16] The report reveals that American officials viewed Filipinos as "perpetual foreigners" due to their racial and cultural background.[17] The US government's insecurity over Filipino loyalty was rooted in its belief that Filipinos' racial or ethnic identity trumped their nationality as US citizens or permanent residents. It is unclear how Filipinos from Hawai'i were able to change their status, but their legal right to remain in the United States and its territories troubled the US military. A steady stream of Filipino immigrants continued with the passing of the 1960 Aquino Ruling, a law that granted alien workers US permanent residency if they originally arrived in Guåhan before December 1952 and were still working at the time of its approval.[18] Even though military officials were suspicious of individual Filipinos, they also believed that the Filipino Community of Guam (FCG) posed the greatest threat because of their social and political influence and their ability to galvanize Guåhan's Filipino population.

Founded in 1954 and composed primarily of Filipinos who came to Guåhan as civilian military and private workers, the FCG was and still is one of the largest community organizations on the island. Filipinos throughout Guåhan came together for gatherings such as banquets, dances, picnics, and philanthropic events.[19] These functions provided attendees with the opportunity to share gossip and cultivate friendships. The FCG also published a monthly newspaper called *Filipiniana*, which discussed political issues in Guåhan and the Philippines. Additionally, the FCG sought to reform policies, as with the elimination of a tariff tax that the Philippine state charged Filipinos in Guåhan who were sending gifts to their relatives back home.[20] In response to Filipino political organizing, the US military deployed the Office of Naval Intelligence (ONI) to identify subversive activity.[21]

The ONI investigated individuals and organizations for cases of "espionage, sabotage, or subversive activities."[22] The ONI not only probed civilians but also contract workers who it believed posed a threat to the US military. For example, the military periodically conducted "loyalty checks" through written statements and interviews that resulted in the vetting of its civilian employees.[23] These and other tactics such as surveillance, information omission, and interrogation were the primary methods the ONI utilized to conduct its investigations.[24]

Declassified military records unveil that ONI officials deployed these tactics in their surveillance of the FCG. For example, in 1956 the FCG hosted a dinner with Philippine government representatives Justino Benito, Luis Hora, and Serafin Salvador. Based on surveillance information, US naval intelligence officer G. M. Adams reported: "Press accounts of this meeting indicate that [the Filipino] congressmen attacked alleged U.S. discrimination against Filipinos [in Guam]. In addition, according to reliable informants, Filipino residents of Guam joined in the discussion and were equally outspoken in condemning the United States position vis a vis the Philippines."[25]

Naval intelligence officials were alarmed by such FCG activities because of their ability to connect the Filipinos in Guåhan with Philippine government officials. These gatherings allowed individual Filipinos to voice their criticism of the US military's policies, which resulted in official Philippine government inquiries regarding labor policy and wages. Moreover, Adams's report reveals that the US military had informants who provided information to ONI officials. Thus, the military surveilled the FCG since it believed the organization could potentially mobilize the Filipino population on the island. In the same ONI report, Adams also claimed:

> The intelligence officer . . . has noted with interest the increased influence and prestige of the Filipinos on Guam. This is especially reflected in the increasingly important position of the Filipino Community of Guam. . . . This group has strong ties with the Philippines and if in the future there should be differences between U.S. and Philippine policy, it could reasonably be expected that the community would act as a significant pressure group here. Although there has been no evidence to indicate that the Filipino Community of Guam has been conducting espionage or subversion, it is in a position to sponsor these activities.[26]

This report also unmasks that the military was anxious over the FCG's political ties to the Republic of the Philippines and its influence among Filipinos living in Guåhan. Furthermore, the military feared that the FCG might serve as a political lobbying group that had enough power to rally the Filipino community. For the military, this was plausible given the fact that Adams's report coincided with labor organizing in opposition to the Guam Wage Bill of 1956. This scenario generated panic within the military, as the FCG's labor organizing could have led to an island-wide slowdown of military operations and maintenance, especially since Filipinos comprised the largest group of civilian workers. However, Adams's report provides no evidence that the FCG was engaged in spying. For example, ONI officer C. J. Endres noted, "The FCG, at present, seems to be a confused, unorganized, factional and inefficient organization which currently does not present a serious subversive problem."[27] Thus, military concerns of the FCG were unfounded and based on a racialized Cold War view of the organization as composed of political subversives and perpetual foreigners. Besides the FCG, military officials also monitored the Philippine consulate of Guåhan, presuming that its staff were politically subversive.

According to the ONI, consulate administrative officer Resurrecion A. Azada had developed a "group of agents" to obtain US military information.[28] While it is unclear what specific information this group was seeking, the fact that the consulate was investigating the military was troubling to US officials. In response, the US military reported this information to the Philippine government, which resulted in Azada's repatriation. It is unclear if

Azada was truly acting in a subversive manner, but the result of this incident demonstrates the military's distrust of Filipino institutions. While this singular case did not materialize into a larger national security issue, it did expand the ONI's surveillance to include all Filipino individuals, the FCG, the Philippine consulate, and, by extension, CHamorus.

Following the US reoccupation of Guåhan in 1944, US officials began to monitor CHamorus to determine their loyalty to the US government. In order to do this, the US military read all outgoing and incoming mail on the island. Military Intelligence officer Peyton Harrison noted, "Letters from Guam continued to be extremely repetitive. Descriptions of conditions and treatment during the Japanese occupation and reactions to these conditions revealed nothing new."[29] Harrison's observations expose the military's willingness to violate the privacy of CHamorus and their trepidation in seeking out individuals who they believed were subversives. Ironically, this act contradicted the military's liberation of Guåhan narrative that had projected CHamorus to be loyal and patriotic Americans, as demonstrated in CHamoru songs such as "Uncle Sam Please Come Back to Guam."[30]

During the 1950s the military feared the possibility of CHamoru and Filipino political solidarity. According to US naval officer W. B. Ammun, "Aliens who remain on Guam for long periods become more and more accepted in the local community. Their prestige and power increase, enabling them to influence the thoughts of local U.S. citizens, especially the politically naïve but otherwise loyal Guamanians."[31] Ammun's colonial and paternalistic attitude demonstrates that CHamoru and Filipino relations troubled the military because they could foster political solidarity and coalitional organizing. In order to curtail this possibility, military officials attempted to police CHamoru and Filipino intimacies that they viewed as posing the greatest threat to US military bases in Guåhan.

Dating, Marriage, and Sex

CHamoru and Filipino marriages transgressed military policy. As mentioned at the beginning of this chapter, BPM attempted to deport Filipino laborer Eddie De La Cruz for marrying CHamoru civilian Barbara Castro. Barbara recalled her reaction when she learned Eddie was supposed to be deported: "So I cried, I didn't know I was pregnant already and then I miscarried. The immigration man [Joe Gumataotao], his wife who is related to me, found out that I miscarried, he told me to hide him and don't give him to any patrol police man from BPM, because they will take him away and deport him and then [later] the green card came."[32] This family's story highlights their courage and resistance to the military's attempt to override US immigration law. Ironically, the Organic Act of 1950, which legally codified the military's condemnation of CHamoru lands through the granting of US citizenship, and the McCarran-Walter Act of 1952, which allowed spouses of immigrants to apply for naturalization, indirectly gave Filipinos the possibility to obtain permanent residency through marriage. In this case, Barbara and Eddie's marriage and their family ties and networks were instrumental in circumventing military policy. Additionally, the advice that Barbara received from CHamoru immigration officer Joe Gumataotao and the support of Barbara's family in helping Eddie evade BPM police patrol were integral in their violation of military law. The De La Cruz story also underscores the intense pressure that CHamorus and Filipinos experienced, as evidenced by Barbara's miscarriage. As historian Tessa Ong Winkelmann has argued regarding the early twentieth-century Philippines, interracial intimacies presented colonial governments "with the complicated task of controlling the behavior and private lives of their own citizens, as well as that of the native population."[33]

Barbara and Eddie De La Cruz's love story is one example of the militarized intimacies that emerged in the postwar era. As historian Rudy P. Guevarra Jr. argues in his work on Filipino and Mexican interracial relations, "multiracial/multiethnic settings ultimately lead to the formation of interethnic mixing and mixed race children through personal relationships, shared experiences, and overlapping histories."[34] For CHamorus and Filipinos in Guåhan, their shared culture, history, and religious identity made such relations possible. Both groups are from predominantly Catholic backgrounds and have a shared historical legacy of colonialism that included the American, Japanese, and Spanish empires, which brought similarities in food, language, and other cultural practices.

Julita Santos Walin met her Filipino husband in 1954, while he was playing in a baseball game that she had attended at Camp Roxas. She recalled, "I was engaged to a CHamoru when I met him [her future Filipino husband,] but you know the feeling is not that strong."[35] She continued, "A lot of CHamorus got married to Filipinos because they said they were good. The Filipinos are very nice to their wives. There are plenty Filipino who marry CHamorus."[36] Walin's experience echoes that of Barbara De La Cruz, emphasizing that marriages between CHamoru women and Filipino men were based on love.

Some government and military officials were skeptical of marriages between CHamoru women and Filipino men. Former US immigration officer and CHamoru master blacksmith, the late Joaquin Flores Lujan, remembered:

> During my time there [US Immigration Office in Guåhan] I came across people who marry for the green card only. I came across an H2 worker [Filipino worker] who married a ninety-year-old woman [CHamoru]. I remember when he brought in that lady; he has to bring in his wife, you know. I asked this man, he was maybe forty years old, I said, "You know, sir, I didn't ask you to bring your grandmother, I asked you to bring your wife." Then he said, "Sir, this is my wife."[37]

While it is unclear if this couple was truly marrying for love or if the Filipino man was granted permanent residency, Lujan's encounter with this couple reveals the skepticism that government officials had over CHamoru-Filipino marriages. This resulted in the US military's continued policing of these militarized intimacies.

In response to questionable CHamoru-Filipino unions, the US Navy relied on the security clearance program to deny return entry to Filipino men who married CHamoru women while they were employed as military laborers.[38] For these men, leaving Guåhan posed a major risk of temporary or permanent exile. This was especially problematic since many of them still had relatives and family members living in the Philippines. This conundrum forced Filipino men to choose between visiting their family in the Philippines or being separated from their spouses in Guåhan. In some instances, Filipino men simply adhered to military law that required them to return to the Philippines after three years of employment. For example, in 1956, it was reported that eighty Filipino men could not rejoin their CHamoru wives in Guåhan because the navy had denied their requests to reenter the island.[39] Even though the security clearance policy was an effective method of separating CHamoru-Filipino couples, it did not prevent all of them from being with each other.

Some CHamoru women resisted the military's attempt to separate them from their Filipino husbands. Olivia Benavente Savares, a CHamoru and former US naval employee, recollected, "In the 1950s, when a Filipino alien worker gets married to a local girl they get deported. They get deported but then the wife would follow or sometimes just stay here. But [for] most of the CHamoru ladies the husband who was deported, they followed their husband and they started working on their papers and eventually they would come back here."[40] For CHamoru women, the deportation of their Filipino husbands was not enough to impede them from being with their spouses. Instead, they circumvented military policy by moving to the Philippines to be with their husbands and then returned to Guåhan when they were allowed to do so.

Some CHamoru men were critical of interracial unions between CHamoru women and Filipino men. Chief program officer for the Guam Preservation Trust Joe E. Quinata remembered, "In some cases yes, there was a lot of conflict. You had local young CHamoru men that were against it because they [Filipino men] were taking away their potential brides."[41] For these single CHamoru men, the presence of Filipinos were a threat to their masculinity because they not only represented labor competition but also were rivals when it came to courting CHamoru women. Former leader of Nasion Chamoru and US Vietnam veteran Joe Ulloa Garrido had similar memories to that of Quinata. He recalled:

> It's the clash of culture. You got local fiestas where they have dances in the church or in the gym. And a bunch of Filipinos from Camp Roxas would come and go into the dance and go in there and ask the young ladies to dance and the CHamoru men would be standing there feeling hot under the collar. It was basically, "Hey, that's my girl, man; don't mess with her, or that's my niece, what are you doing." It's the culture—the protective nature of the local people in protecting their young daughters that causes all of this. There are three main ethnic groups from the Philippines that actually came to Guåhan and became part of our society. The Visayans, the Tagalogs, and the Ilocanos.[42]

Garrido's perspective on the tensions between CHamoru and Filipino men exposes the entangled ways that ethnicity and culture served as markers of difference that were not always based on race. In this instance, Filipino men were viewed as threats to CHamoru female chastity since women were expected to refrain from premarital sex and were to be chaperoned in public spaces. Garrido's observations are also a reflection of kostumbren CHamoru, which is the syncretism of ancient CHamoru and Catholic cultural values and practices that developed in the eighteenth and nineteenth centuries and still continues today.[43]

CHamoru-Filipino sexual relationships also demonstrate the persistence of Indigenous values related to sex. Shortly after World War II, a CHamoru woman named Linda began working at a bar near Camp Roxas to provide for herself and her two children.[44] Linda's friend Sandra[45] recalled:

> Linda had little education and no job opportunities. She would take her children to gather breadfruit, mangos, and bananas to help feed them. She ended up having several children, but no one knew who their fathers are except they were Filipinos from Camp Roxas. Some CHamorus helped her, but she was looked down on for having worked at the bar and having several children with different Filipino men. She eventually got sick and was bedridden. Her children would walk around the village looking for food. Linda eventually died, and her children were split up among family members, friends, and other people who would be willing to take them.[46]

Linda's story is one example of the militarized intimacies that were complex and tragic. In many ways, Linda's occupation transgressed the domestic expectations of kostumbren CHamoru since she worked outside the home and in a space that was predominantly inhabited by men.[47] For some CHamorus, Linda also violated kostumbren CHamoru through her participation in premarital sex and having several out-of-wedlock children. However, as CHamoru scholar Laura Marie Torres Souder argues, Indigenous values within kostumbren CHamoru also viewed "sexuality as an integral, desirable, and natural part of human existence . . . and while virginity and modesty have been ideal virtues that young girls have been expected to uphold, in practice it has been understood that imperfect behavior is a fact of human nature."[48] CHamoru women such as Linda who engaged in premarital sex challenged and also demonstrated how kostumbren CHamoru included the persistence of Indigenous values. Thus, not all CHamoru women who engaged in sexual relations before marriage were ostracized from society; rather, their actions were reflective of older CHamoru practices that were accepting of people who engaged in premarital sex.[49] Furthermore, the family and friends who were willing to care for Linda's children after her death also participated in kostumbren CHamoru through the practice of *ináfa'maolek* (to make good) which is the CHamoru belief that individual actions should be based on "mutual assistance, cooperation, reciprocity, interdependence, obligation, respect, peace, and reconciliation."[50]

Taxi-Dance Clubs

Taxi-dance clubs were one of the spaces that created anxiety for military officials due to the possibility of marriage between Filipino men and US citizens. As was the case in the continental United States, these clubs included large groups of Filipino men who purchased tickets that allowed them to dance with the women who worked there.[51] Former Camp Roxas resident, the late John Luces recollected, "Taxi dancers were in Hagåtña. They [other Filipino workers] would tell me it was expensive. When the music is on they ring the bell when it's time to release the lady. When you want to hold the lady longer you have to pay more for that lady."[52] The gyrating bodies of these men and women were intimately brought together in hot, humid clubs through the music of local jazz artists such as Louie Gombar, who became well known for playing the vibraphone in venues throughout the island.[53] Many of these men and women relied on local stores for clothes, shoes, and cosmetics to be used in preparation for a night in the clubs. Some of the dancers were CHamoru women, but many others were women from the territory of Hawaiʻi or the continental United States.[54] What concerned military officials the most was that these women were US citizens or US nationals, which meant Filipino men could obtain permanent residency (and by extension US citizenship) if they were to marry them. Similarly to the military, some CHamorus viewed these clubs with disdain because they believed they were spaces that violated kostumbren CHamoru through illicit sexual activity.

Some island residents believed that taxi-dance clubs posed a moral threat to their families.[55] The president of the Parent-Teacher Association (PTA) of Mangilao, a Mr. Siguenza, stated, "The conduct of the taxi-dancers is such that residents do not want their children exposed to it. The children are becoming uncontrollable. Demonstrations of the taxi-dancers is not conducive to good citizenship. . . . A man who goes to such places becomes addicted to them, the same effect as dope."[56] CHamoru educator Agueda Johnston echoed a similar concern: "Taxi-dancing and prostitution are one, so we are against taxi-dancers for that very reason. It is similar to prostitution."[57] These concerns over prostitution were punctuated through newspapers articles and rumors. The *Manila Times* reported, "The former wife of a navy officer who went into the entertainment business [taxi-dancer] made $10,000 in two months. On investigation by the authorities, she revealed that not all of the money was made in dancing alone."[58] Military officials reported in a March 1954 meeting that teenage CHamoru girls were being recruited to work as prostitutes based on a surveillance report that claimed a white

American male civilian was allegedly running a brothel out of his home.[59] News such as this alarmed the George Washington High School Parent-Teacher Association, the Guam Women's Club, the Vicariate Union of Holy Name Societies, and other organizations that opposed taxi-dance clubs. Proponents of banning the clubs characterized the men who attended them as contributing to "bad moral" behavior because they spent their money in the clubs instead of in support of their families.[60] Former Camp Roxas resident John Luces remembered:

> A lot of people in the camp go poor. Some of the wives in Iloilo, they write the camp and ask, "How is my husband doing? He never send money for us." The camp investigates and ask the worker, "What are you doing?" The worker say, "I am working and sending money home." He [camp investigator] would give the worker the letter saying how many months they never send money. Then the guy say, "I need air conditioner or I go bowling." The investigator say, "I don't care what you do, but you have family there and need to send money. From there on I get a third of your salary and send it back home. If that's not enough, I will cut half your salary." The guy [worker] try to cry, but the investigator tell him "your job is to take care of your family back home."[61]

Luces's observations corroborate what some members of the Guam legislature believed, which was that Filipino men were not sending remittances to their families. His memories also expose that companies took an active role to ensure that Filipino men were sending money back home by garnishing their wages. Filipina wives living in the Philippines exercised their agency by relying on company officials to enforce that their husbands sent remittances. CHamorus who attended these dance clubs also were perceived negatively because their actions were viewed as a violation of kostumbren CHamoru.

Although local conservatives led a movement to ban the taxi-dance clubs, some local CHamoru and white Americans were supportive of their existence. In a letter sent to the Guam Congress, local businessman Fred Moylan wrote:[62]

> To say the taxi dancers are prostitutes, this is wrong and [a] libel statement[,] for in all walks of life you have women or men with the desire for companionship. Some choose their companions early in life and later find out that they are not evenly mated and because of their religions, honor, children, etc. do not wish to be separated. Do you say then these people should not find enjoyment elsewhere, but to break up their homes, etc. No gentlemen,

we cannot dictate any domestic laws to govern a family's thoughts. This would be communism.[63]

Moylan's statement reveals how the politics of the Cold War informed his and others' belief that prohibiting these clubs would be an act of communism. He was also concerned that the government should not have the power to restrict the decisions that individuals made based on the generalization that all taxi dancers were prostitutes. However, it is possible that Moylan was also financially invested in the survival of these clubs, since he likely benefited from the patronage of people who purchased goods or services from his general merchandise stores, concession stands, and camera film development shops.[64]

Other proponents of taxi-dance clubs cited the importance of upholding capitalism and republicanism as an important part of the US political system. In a letter addressed to the Guam Congress, Dr. T. A. Darling noted: "We cannot legislate the abolition of any honest, free enterprise. If we do, we are communistic to that extent, going against what the constitution of the United States of America stands for. . . . It is beside the point entirely in considering whether its abolition should be considered, as such abolition is entirely unconstitutional and un-American, and un-democratic."[65]

Similarly to Moylan, Darling invoked Cold War rhetoric to argue against the closing of taxi-dance clubs because they were examples of free enterprise. For Darling and Moylan, the clubs represented capitalism and economic freedom, which they believed were important to preserving US democracy. In addition, Darling, Moylan, and others believed that the banning of the dance clubs would be a violation of the political rights of US citizens and would harm the US government's position as a proponent of democracy and capitalism more so than the negative moral implications that these dance clubs represented.

This issue of taxi-dance clubs was critical enough that the governor of Guam, Ford Q. Elvidge, decided to abolish these clubs in 1954.[66] Governor Elvidge was one of the staunchest critics of taxi-dance clubs in Guåhan. In a memoir documenting their time on the island, Elvidge's wife, Anita, recalled her husband's concerns:

I am having a time about those girls. At the bottom of every tavern brawl, there's one of them. Women are coming to my office [governor's office] to complain that their daughters want to become taxi dancers and their husbands are straying. . . . Security regulations don't have any effect unless the girls have police records or are subversive. They are coming onto the island by the plane load. They get money from these unattached Filipinos and are spending so much that the merchants welcome them. Some of the leading legislators are involved. One of them came to see me yesterday. He said he did not see how he could be against taxi dance business because he'd be interfering with private enterprise. His wife has a dress shop. They are getting into the service clubs. The welfare of our men is being affected.[67]

Governor Elvidge's comments unveil the financial investment that CHamorus and non-CHamorus had in the continued existence of these clubs. Dancers contributed to the island economy through their purchasing power, while local business owners profited from their patronage. Elvidge was not only concerned with the conflict over the prohibiting of taxi-dance clubs but was also distressed that the dancers were gaining access to US military service clubs. Similar to military officials, he viewed these halls as sites of potential subversive activity.

As was noted earlier, many local organizations supported the banning of taxi-dance clubs. For example, a representative of the Guam Women's Club told the legislature, "The existence of such dance halls has a bad moral influence on the young people of Guam and, from their operation, tragic home situations are developing. . . . If allowed to continue and multiply [they] will, in time, render this community a less desirable place in which to live and bring up children."[68] The Vicariate Union of Holy Name Societies stated similarly, "The continued existence of such establishments constitutes a danger to the common good and morality of the territory."[69] With the support of these organizations, Governor Elvidge in 1954 passed Public Law 2–054, Bill No. 127, which outlawed taxi-dance clubs. Interestingly, military officials remained publicly silent on the issue of taxi-dance clubs since they had long endorsed the operation of brothels near American bases.[70] However, the ONI continued to monitor the political debates surrounding them.

Enlisted men's dances were military-sanctioned spaces that fostered interracial dating and sex among CHamoru women and white American soldiers.[71] Young, unmarried CHamoru women throughout the island were bused onto bases to attend these dances. Some of these gatherings took place during holidays and had themes such as the "Thanksgiving Eve supper dance" or "Tea-Dance." As shown in figures 4.1, 4.2, and 4.3, at these dances, CHamoru women (who were sometimes outnumbered one to five) and American servicemen had intimate encounters that included dancing to jazz music, drinking sodas, and conversing closely with one another in hot, humid halls.[72] As CHamoru historian Christine Taitano DeLisle contends, enlisted men's dances were also spaces that moved women further away from "domestic spheres of

Figure 4.1. US Marines gather around a small group of CHamoru women at the Third Marine Division Dance, 1945. Source: Photo by Sgt. Robert Wilton, USMC. Reprinted with permission from *Leatherneck* magazine.

CHamoru hearth and home and the interiority" of kostumbren CHamoru.[73] Specifically, dances provided them the opportunity to transgress kostumbren CHamoru through the possibility of participating in premarital sex and by being in unchaperoned spaces while mimicking the "modern girl" look through the use of clothing and cosmetics that reflected 1950s American youth culture.[74] Ultimately, these dances were coupled with a racialized discourse that presented CHamoru women as Americanized, modern, and sexually available.[75]

In 1945 *Life* magazine published an article that featured photographs (which originally appeared in the US Marine magazine *Leatherneck*) of several CHamoru women, who were praised for their "glamour" and "beauty." The unidentified author wrote: "The U.S. Marines have long felt that somewhere, somehow, romance could be found in the fabled South Seas. . . . A bouquet of pin-up girls from Guam makes its appearance. . . . The young people all go to school and learn English. The impeccable cleanliness of the young Chamorro women of Guam has already become celebrated in the Pacific."[76]

Figure 4.2. Barbara Bordallo (left) sitting next to a sweaty unidentified US Marine at the Third Marine Division Dance, 1945. Source: Photo by Sgt. Robert Wilton, USMC. Reprinted with permission from *Leatherneck* magazine.

Figure 4.3. CHamoru women dancing with US Marines at the Third Marine Division Dance, 1945. Source: Photo by Sgt. Robert Wilton, USMC. Reprinted with permission from *Leatherneck* magazine.

American periodicals such as *Leatherneck* and *Life* were invested in creating a perception that CHamoru women were sexually available for military personnel stationed in Guåhan. In turn, the military's investment in promoting interracial dating and sex was to keep American soldiers content. In some instances, these dances produced militarized intimacies that resulted in love, marriage, and obligation.

Some American soldiers found resistance in their attempts to marry CHamoru women. In 1946 William P. Hinson requested to be discharged in Guåhan so he could marry a CHamoru woman he had impregnated. Hinson's mother, M. T. Hinson, sent a letter from Charleston, South Carolina, to the island commander of Guåhan, imploring him to deny her son's request for discharge:

> It is definitely against my wishes that he be permitted to marry a native. He also tells me this girl is to become a mother in the near future and he is

responsible for her condition. He might be but can we be positive of this? Bill has been stationed on this island about 14 months and of course, you know more about the social conditions than I, but they must be limited and so very different from our good old American customs. . . . It grieves me deeply to hear of this young girls [sic] condition and if we can make any restitution we would be so glad, but I don't feel as if a young boy's entire future, the giving up of his country, customs and family, should be sacrificed for one mistake—do you? Have a talk with Billy, try to show him that these inter-racial marriages just don't work out.[77]

M. T. Hinson's letter represents the colonial and racist sentiment some Americans had toward CHamoru women. This was based on the ideas that CHamoru women did not make suitable spouses due to their racial and cultural background. Hinson's racist attitude is punctuated in her suggestion that her son might not be the father of the baby, thus implying that CHamoru women were devious and looked for opportunities to improve their financial situations. In the end, the island commander granted M. T. Hinson's request because her son was a minor, and he was eventually transferred to the continental United States.

As scholars Judith A. Bennett and Angela Wanhalla note, military officials were empowered to "control the private lives of servicemen" when it came to marriage, which also included parental consent if either party was under the age of twenty-one.[78] This example reveals that even though the military and American periodicals encouraged interracial romance and sexual relationships, the military did not fully endorse interracial marriages and by extension upheld anti-miscegenation sentiment that was commonplace in the continental United States during this time period. In this instance, the military used its power to intervene and stymie interracial unions among CHamorus and American soldiers, similar to what it had customarily done to CHamoru-Filipino partners. In another example, American servicemen Edward Leiss wrote a letter in February 1946 requesting that Emily Perez, a CHamoru woman, be allowed to join him in New York:

When Miss Perez arrives here I shall be completely responsible for her, as we have been planning to be married. I come from a fairly well to do family which I am now living with and I can assure you she shall be very pleased here in every form. . . . I am quite certain that Miss Perez too comes from a nice family as she is quite a cultured lady so therefore we should find excellent happiness throughout life.[79]

Leiss's letter demonstrates that a colonial perception of Perez being "cultured" played a major decision in his request and justification for their marriage. His letter also underscored the fact that his family was wealthy enough to take care of them both. However, his story had a tragic ending: On April 5, 1947, Leiss sent a telegram to Guåhan that stated, "Please cancel request of Miss Emily Perez[;] complications at home force me the cancellation."[80] It can be inferred that his request to cancel Perez's transfer to New York was due to his family's objections to the interracial relationship, especially since Leiss had conveyed that his family, and not he, had the financial means to provide for Perez.

Interracial Violence and Protecting the US Military's Cold War Reputation

Interracial violence among CHamorus, Filipinos, and white Americans jeopardized the military's Cold War reputation. Felix Stump, US commander in chief of the US Pacific Fleet in 1954, issued a military memo regarding personnel conduct that stated:

> This leadership, based on an example of fine virtue, the highest traits of character and impeccable conduct and appearance[,] has been an important factor in the development of our country's worldwide responsibilities. Never has it been more important that the world have confidence in the leadership of the United States. That confidence must be justified by fitting demeanor and integrity, particularly of our officials abroad. Foreign opinion of our character and integrity is influenced by the bearing and deportment of the individuals of our service who are observed in official, social, and day-by-day associations.[81]

American military and government officials were cognizant that the actions of their soldiers influenced how other countries and individuals perceived them. They were also keenly aware that the various spaces their servicemen frequented, whether in a formal or informal capacity, were significant in safeguarding the US military's Cold War reputation.[82] This was necessary to the US government's foreign policy in protecting its diplomatic position in Asia while simultaneously trying to limit the growth of communism.[83] To do so, various policies were implemented to reduce the chances for servicemen to engage in activities that would be deemed harmful to the US government—most notably violence when interacting with CHamorus and Filipinos.

Bars, cafes, and restaurants in Guåhan were commonly designated as "out of bounds" due to being hotspots for interracial violence. For example, on March 28, 1948, a fight broke out between a group of American servicemen and a group of Filipino workers from Luzon Stevedoring at the Ranche Café, a CHamoru-owned restaurant in the village of Barigåda. According to police interviews and reports, an argument occurred between an American and a Filipino, starting a large-scale fight that involved two dozen men.[84] While it is unclear why this fight took place, an investigation claimed that rocks and beer bottles were thrown between the two groups. This violent encounter resulted in injuries for two American servicemen, who needed medical treatment, and the arrest of two Filipino men, Monico Vellar and Gregorio Velasco. Because bars and restaurants were common public spaces frequented by CHamorus, Filipinos, and white Americans, violent encounters often occurred in them. In response, the US military believed that prohibiting soldiers from entering certain establishments would mitigate disorderly behavior. Places such as the Aloha Tavern, Cosmopolitan Café, and Seven Sisters Café were restricted for military personnel.[85] The US military also passed laws regarding the use of roads in an effort to police behavior even while in transit.[86]

In 1947 Governor C. A. Pownall issued a general order, regulating that "naval and marine personnel will not stop their cars, park cars, loiter on roads, leave the road right-of-way for any purpose, or enter houses or buildings adjacent to the roads."[87] The military was convinced that laws controlling the use of roads were needed, since these spaces also became sites for violence that could damage the US military's reputation. However, these orders were not always followed. On June 7, 1949, Filipino LUSTEVECO employee Elisa Pelengon offered two sailors fifty cents each to give him a ride to Camp Roxas. Two American servicemen named Floyd C. Hammers and Freddie J. Lapervse agreed to take Pelengon, but on the way to Camp Roxas, Hammers and Lapervse decided to rob Pelengon. In his police interview, Pelengon stated, "When we were near the junk at the intersection of road to base 18, the drivers said, 'no more gas.' The driver told me to get out of the car and when I got out, the driver pointed a knife of about one foot blade and asked me to give him my money while his companion held me past."[88] This potentially fatal encounter resulted in Pelengon being robbed of sixty dollars and also sustaining a cut to his right hand in a scuffle over the knife. The military police eventually apprehended Hammers and Lapervse, who did not initially admit to the robbery. Instead Lapervse claimed in his police statement that

> I woke up and some flip was wanting a ride home, Hammers didn't want to take him home but he kept pestering and I said did you hear he said no. Then he kept getting hold of me like he was drunk, and something I remember asking him if he was one of those blow boy[s] and then he laughed, and put a dollar in Hammers jumper pocket and tried to get it back and Hammers told him to keep his hands out of his pocket, and then this flip turned to someone and said we robbed him.[89]

By World War II, the US military had adopted an active policy of incarcerating and/or discharging soldiers who were believed to be homosexual.[90] As such, Lapervse's accusation that Pelengon was gay and tried to sexually assault them was his attempt to discredit him. However, after several interviews, both Hammers and Lapervse admitted to robbing Pelengon in hopes of receiving leniency for their violent actions. While there is no record of what punishment they received, it is clear that the military's regulation of roads (and other spaces) was partly in response to the interracial violence that occurred in these spaces.[91] However, interracial violence was not isolated to bars, restaurants, and roads.

In 1949 CHamoru men and US soldiers engaged in armed conflict over an alleged theft in the middle of a road near Naval Air Station Hagåtña. A military report noted "that an altercation had taken place . . . between five or six marine enlisted men and several Guamanian guards at the J&G Motor Company garage."[92] The confrontation began when the group of marines decided to approach several CHamoru guards across the road from where they stated that missing tools were last seen. This confrontation escalated, and according to the American servicemen, some of the CHamoru men fired their rifles at them. One marine was hit in the head with a rifle butt and was hospitalized for his injuries. In another case of violence, two CHamoru taxicab drivers were charged with murdering an American seaman.[93] While it is unknown how many cases of interracial violence occurred in Guåhan during the 1940s and 1950s, knowledge of these incidents were pervasive due to the close and overlapping proximity of military and civilian spaces.[94] In addition, some military records remain classified, which makes it difficult to determine the number of these occurrences. Due to the pervasiveness of violence, the policy to restrict specific areas as out of bounds was expanded to include CHamoru villages.

In 1947 the government of Guam passed Executive Order 21–46, which required all nonpermanent residents of Guåhan to follow a specific protocol if they wanted to enter villages and residences. Specifically, they had to possess an invitation from the "head of the Chamorro household" (the father of the home they intended on visiting) and a pass from the commanding officer or their company camp supervisor.[95] Upon entering the village, these visitors were also required to check in at the local village police office in order to have their liberty card or pass verified.[96] This law attempted to deter Filipino laborers and white American soldiers and civilians from engaging in illicit activities. These policies not only made it arduous for these men to gain access to villages but also made it challenging for CHamorus to freely travel in their own homeland.

The village pass system posed a dilemma for CHamorus because many of them viewed it as a policy that safeguarded their families and communities but it was also a reminder of their colonial status since this regulation was imposed upon them. During a 1949 Guam Assembly meeting, Assemblyman Carlos P. Taitano stated, "If you want to continue to keep the undesirables out of our villages, we have to continue that way. . . . It is true that sometimes we don't know just when our friends or business associates are coming in, but if we don't continue the way we are at present, the whole pass system will be no good."[97] Assemblyman Leon Flores Jr. echoed Taitano's argument: "Foreign elements which might constitute a menace to our society should not be permitted to enter without a proper pass."[98] For CHamorus such as Taitano and Flores Jr., the village pass system represented a safety protocol that at times did make receiving off-island guests troublesome. However, other CHamorus viewed the pass system as another example of the military's colonial control over the island. Assemblyman Frank D. Perez contended:

> By following the present system of issuing a pass, I can safely say that we miss some good friends who can do good for our people. . . . It might be that the person requesting permission to enter a village is a newspaper reporter or someone else who would write articles regarding Guam and its people, when he return to the states. I have seen a lot of these military people going in and out of villages. As to whether or not they have a pass, I don't think it is my duty to ask, but it is my belief that all of them do not have the necessary pass. I think we can take care of that ourselves.[99]

CHamorus like Perez wanted to reclaim the facilitation of village passes instead of relying on the military. His comments demonstrate that some

CHamorus believed that the village pass program was problematic because it restricted all non-island locals, including journalists and writers who played an instrumental role in reporting the social and political conditions impacting Guåhan. American journalists and writers posed a threat because they had the ability to circulate information throughout the continental United States that highlighted the military's colonial rule of the island and its people. This was concerning for military officials since the 1950s was the beginning of decolonization movements that occurred throughout parts of the world. Therefore, the village pass system also served as a tool to censor unfavorable media reports on the US military's activities. With the passing of the Organic Act in 1950 and the establishment of the government of Guam, military officials would eventually transfer authority to the local civilian government to conduct village-screening procedures.

Race, Rumors, and Violence

Even with the village pass system and the military's broader policy of trying to control public spaces, interracial violence against CHamoru civilians was still pervasive. CHamoru women and children were sometimes the victims of racial and gendered violence. On March 30, 1948, a CHamoru woman named Regina San Cruz filed charges against an American serviceman, Roy Farmer, who was also her former boyfriend. According to statements given by a witness named Joseph Cruz and San Cruz herself, Farmer slapped San Cruz twice during a confrontation. San Cruz stated, "I asked him to return the things he was going to sell for me. He said that he would take them to the club and try to sell them. He took these two months ago to sell. I asked him to give me these things [jewelry and picture frames] that are mine . . . but he wouldn't do it and he hit me with his hand."[100] Nine days later San Cruz withdrew her complaint and charge against Farmer. It is unknown why she withdrew her complaint.

In another example, US serviceman Harrel LaVerne Hicklin pleaded guilty to "conduct to the prejudice of good order and discipline (indecent exposure)," in which he laid under the bed of a CHamoru woman "with his privates indecently exposed."[101] Unlike other instances of militarized violence, Hicklin actually pleaded guilty and was given an undisclosed punishment. On September 11, 1947, serviceman Wilbur Gardner raped a six-year-old CHamoru girl, lied to Guam police officers regarding his identity, and stole a pair of shoes, all in one day. Additionally, he was reported to have frequently exposed his penis in public to three female CHamoru children.[102] During his court-martial hearing, he was only found guilty of one out of the five charges against him, which was the rape of the CHamoru child. Gardner's punishment was unspecified, but the public harm he caused during this string of events highlights that the military's restriction policies were not sufficient to deter physical and sexual violence. Moreover, incidents such as these played an important role in complicating how CHamorus perceived interracial relationships with white Americans and Filipinos through rumors and gossip that took place during birthday parties, fiestas, rosaries, and at other family gatherings, which created multiple and competing narratives that subverted the state.[103] While it is unknown if any protests materialized in response to this incident and others, these interracial encounters were concerning to CHamorus.

Sexual violence also played a role in shaping the discourse on CHamoru–white American relationships in Guåhan.[104] According to the *Guam Gazette*, a US Marine approached an unnamed CHamoru woman on her låncho in Barigåda on September 15, 1945.[105] The marine, whose name the article did not identify, asked her for water and then physically assaulted and raped her.[106] On October 24, 1945, an American serviceman broke into a home in the village of Barigåda and attempted to rape a CHamoru woman.[107] Fortunately, the woman's daughter walked into the room and scared the attacker away. The unnamed CHamoru woman suffered bruises on her face, forehead, and neck. In some instances, CHamorus defended themselves against the US servicemen. The *Guam Gazette* reported that on October 13, 1945, Jose Borja Castro shot and killed two American servicemen who had broken into his home in Barigåda.[108] As these three cases reveal, militarized violence was commonplace—two sexual assaults and one home invasion in the village of Barigåda within the span of a month. Experiences such as these made CHamorus skeptical of the benevolence that the military had proclaimed during World War II and the narrative of the liberation of Guåhan. To some degree, this gendered and racialized violence helps explain why CHamorus and Filipinos responded with similar force.

On August 18, 1957, a Filipino man named Francisco Bernardo David, who worked as an accountant, stabbed Pacific Wholesalers president Gayle Shelton. When asked why he stabbed Shelton, David stated, "I was tired of being pushed around by Shelton."[109] David's action was just one of several violent incidents that occurred in the workplace. On September 17, 1960, George Fitzgerald, acting manager of the Federal Aviation Agency (FAA) in Guåhan, was shot and killed. According to the *Manila Times*, "Fitzgerald,

38, was shot to death . . . while trying to subdue a berserk Filipino employee of the FAA."[110] In another incident, two CHamoru men had "allegedly murdered a U.S. citizen on Guam," without giving a specific reason.[111] These examples of violence might seem unrelated, but when viewed through a "critical juxtaposing," they provide a documented pattern of CHamoru and Filipino violence against US soldiers and civilians.[112]

As discussed at the beginning of this chapter, Barbara and Eddie De La Cruz's story was symbolic of how the US military was invested in the monitoring of politically subversive activity. In order to do so, military officials attempted to control the militarized intimacies that occurred among CHamorus, Filipinos, and white Americans. While it is difficult to track how many interracial marriages occurred in Guåhan from 1946 to 1962, it can be argued that the US military was most concerned with interracial marriages that involved Filipino men and US citizens.[113] Some of the tactics they utilized included deportation, the regulation of security clearances, and the management of village passes. In contrast, the US military took a more ambivalent stance when it came to policing the interracial dating and sex involving CHamoru women and white American men. In fact, the military promoted these interactions through events such as enlisted men's dances. The military's primary concern with CHamoru–white American relations was the potential of violence, which potentially harmed the US government's Cold War reputation. Thus, the creation of laws that controlled social interactions was predicated on the racialization of each group of people. A by-product of this racial stratification was interracial and gendered violence. Not all interracial violence can be attributed to the military's social policies, but it was a major contributor to various antagonisms and conflicts.

By the late 1950s, CHamoru politicians called for the end of the security clearance program because large-scale subversive activity never materialized and the program prevented the development of the island's economy. In contrast, the military and the federally appointed officials of Guåhan supported the program throughout the 1960s. For example, Richard Barrett Lowe, governor of Guam from 1956 to 1960, was a staunch supporter of the security clearance program even though local CHamoru politicians wanted to end the policy. On April 24, 1957, Lowe issued a statement that said, in part, "I have no objections to agitation of the problem on the part of loyal private citizens, but these loyal citizens should realize that they may be aligning themselves with subversive groups who seek the same result but with a far different motive."[114] Lowe's comments mirror those of other military officials who believed that subversive groups would overrun Guåhan. A year later, Lowe maintained his support for the program. In a letter addressed to the Guam legislature, he argued, "The relaxation of the entry regulations to encourage tourism would also open the doors again to hordes of undesirables . . . which would have a serious effect upon the morals of our people. . . . How can we distinguish between a bona fide tourist, a prostitute, or a spy, without some sort of screening or clearance regulations."[115] Lowe's concern with lifting the security clearance policy now included the potential entry of undesirable and immoral people who might harm the US government's reputation. While Lowe and other government officials were troubled by the growth of "undesirables," the deplorable security screening policy separated families and stunted the local economy in hopes of protecting the island from a threat that never materialized. This immigration policy was a part of a larger colonial apparatus that attempted to control social relations throughout the island.

Chapter 5

From Breadbasket to Naval Air Station

Today almost half the island's 225 square miles are occupied by airfields, supply depots, housing areas, baseball diamonds, and other
adjuncts of America's great strategic base in the Pacific. The roar of
heavy trucks, the chug of tractors, and the bang of hammers are
heard everywhere as new warehouses go up, roads are driven thru
jungled hills, and war's last remaining scars are removed.
—Walter Simmons, *Chicago Daily Tribune*, September 5, 1948

Tiyan was a place away from the life they had in reality. That to them
was their saving grace for the core of the family. That was a part of
her [Benavente's mother's] Tiyan story, and what was really a tragedy
was after the war, they thought it was going to go back to them. . . .
Their love for Tiyan had been spoiled by the perpetual taking by the
US and the condemnations.
—Ed Benavente, May 4, 2013

When the US military retook Guåhan from Japanese forces during World
War II, Tiyan was selected for construction of Naval Air Station Hagåtña
(NAS Hagåtña), which became the primary settler gateway in postwar
Guåhan (it is now the home of the A. B. Won Pat International Airport).
The complex history of Tiyan and NAS Hagåtña as a settler colonial site is
interwoven with stories of CHamoru survival. This chapter brings together

the major themes of the book and reveals what it was like to live near the base.

In this chapter, I argue that NAS Hagåtña (which closed down in 1995 due to the Base Realignment and Closure Commission of 1993) was the physical culmination of settler militarism because it was the postwar gateway for military and civilian settlers to arrive on the island. Before World War II, the region of Tiyan consisted primarily of lånchos for CHamorus and other island residents who lived in or near Hagåtña. However, World War II transformed Tiyan into an airfield under Japanese occupation, and the airfield was subsequently expanded into a sprawling military base under US control. Like other military bases on the island, NAS Hagåtña became a settler focal point that attempted to transform the cultural, environmental, and physical landscapes of the region. But as discussed throughout this book, CHamorus transgressed the US military's attempt to erase the history and meaning of Tiyan through their memories that still exist today.

Tiyan before World War II

As discussed in chapter 1, the naming of villages and places in Guåhan is part of a larger Indigenous practice of perceiving the human body as being an extension of the land, sky, and ocean. Located in the central part of the island, Tiyan derives from the CHamoru term *tuyan*, which means "stomach" or "belly."[1] The place name of Tiyan is also connected to the neighboring village of Barigåda. CHamorus of the pre–World War II era sometimes referred to parts of Tiyan and Barigåda as Jalaguac or Alaguag, which is related to the CHamoru word *kalaguak*, meaning the "sides of the body."[2]

CHamorus recall Tiyan as a place of community and agricultural value. It was home to one of the largest numbers of lånchos on the island, totaling at least seventy-eight family estates.[3] Many of the families who lived in Hagåtña and, later, Barigåda had lånchos in Tiyan. As Justo Torre Leon Guerrero remembered, "Back then, it was common for households to have ranches separate from their Agaña homes."[4] CHamoru activist, the late Ed Benavente, corroborated Leon Guerrero's memory, recalling how his mother would tell him, "In the old days, every week they would go up to the ranch [in Tiyan] and would stay there for six days and then go to the church back in their town of Hagåtña. . . . That's where they would intermingle with their neighbors, share food, have meetings, lunch and dinner with family and neighbors."[5] On any given weekend, Tiyan was a place where laughing, singing, dancing, talking, and children playing were common sights and sounds. In some instances, these gatherings were due to birthday parties, fiestas, or rosaries, but they often were simply an opportunity for family to spend time with each other while completing chores such as clearing brush, planting crops, harvesting fruits and vegetables, or tending to livestock. Thus, the maintenance and perpetuation of ancestral, cultural, and family ties were intertwined with the land.

For the families who had lånchos in Tiyan, the phrase "breadbasket of Guam" described the agricultural bounty that the land produced. Ed Benavente remembered his mother frequently reminiscing that "the soil was so fertile, even if you throw a seed, any kind of seed, it will grow anywhere."[6] CHamorus from other villages also knew of Tiyan for its rich agriculture. CHamoru rights activist Antonio Artero Sablan recalled, "Tiyan use to be the breadbasket of Guam; that's where all the fertile soil and big farming occurred."[7] Some of the most common foods grown and harvested at Tiyan were bananas, breadfruit, coconuts, corn, and taro. These fruits and vegetables, combined with the meat that came from the ranching of animals such as chickens and pigs, were used to create delicious food such as *champulado*, fina'denne', kelaguen, and *tinaktak*.[8] The mouth-watering aromas of these foods being prepared traveled from låncho to låncho throughout the region. For some, Tiyan continues to represent the island's breadbasket in the postwar era because it is the site of Guåhan's international airport, which brought US. military dependents to the island and, later, tourists who spend money in support of the island's economy.[9] Tiyan was not the first site that served as a gateway for militourists[10] in Guåhan, but it is the place that transformed the island into a postwar settler society.[11]

In the 1980s, CHamorus began imaging a new meaning of Tiyan as the breadbasket of Guåhan through the transformation of the island's economy. Specifically, unprecedented amounts of off-island investment flowed into Guåhan, resulting in an accelerated decade of tourism that brought hotels, restaurants, and retail shops.[12] At the center of this process was the airport, which experienced a dramatic expansion of flights, visitors, and the physical growth of its facility that continued into the early and mid-1990s. As a result, tourism is now Guåhan's number-one industry.

Tiyan, World War II, and the Making of Guamu Dai Ni

As was noted in chapter 1, the transformation of Tiyan into an airfield began with the Japanese military invasion of Guåhan during World War II. In late

1942 the Imperial Japanese Navy (IJN) commissioned the construction of an airfield, which was named Guamu Dai Ni (Guam No. 2) in reference to it being the second runway on the island.[13] This airfield was a strategic site for the IJN because it was used to facilitate and transport supplies throughout Micronesia and because Guåhan (which was renamed Omiya Jima, meaning Great Shrine Island) provided a large amount of agriculture for the Japanese military.[14] To complete the construction of Guamu Dai Ni, the IJN forced CHamorus to provide the labor.

The CHamorus who were forced to labor at Tiyan varied in age and gender. Typically, the Japanese military forced CHamorus aged ten to sixty years old to work for them.[15] The late US Marine general and CHamoru Ben Blaz was fourteen years old when he began working at Tiyan. He stated in his memoir, "We used picks, shovels, axes, machetes, and whatever we could improvise to clear the trees and undergrowth of the jungle, pull out huge rocks, and finally level the ground. . . . We hated it."[16] CHamoru Alberto Babauta Acfalle remembered a similar experience. He was fourteen years old when the Japanese military invaded Guåhan. He recalled, "At that time it was all jungle[,] and big rocks had to be moved from the area, so that airplanes could land and take off."[17] For these young CHamorus, age or gender did not exempt them from the intense manual labor of constructing the airfield. Instead, they were exposed to the trauma of military occupation and violence that scarred them physically and mentally for the rest of their lives. In addition, the physical toil and burden was heightened due to the lack of modern heavy equipment.

The working conditions at Tiyan were excessive and extreme. Alberto Babauta Acfalle stated,

> As we worked in Alaguag [Tiyan], some people got sick because we were working in the rain and on sunny days we worked in the heat of the sun. They would build a fire out of dead coconut leaves, which gave us light and warmth, but some men were already sick because of the constant heat and wetness. Some were so weak that they could not even carry their own bodies.[18]

Ben Blaz also remembered

> joining four or five other men in lashing ropes to large rocks and then around our waists dragging them off like we were cattle. . . . At the end of the day, I would hobble back to our farm so tired that my mother would have to

force me to eat to keep up my strength, and in the morning I would awake still exhausted from the day before and begin all over again.[19]

For both Acfalle and Blaz, backbreaking labor, sickness, and dangerous working conditions were a daily reality. Moreover, adverse weather conditions such as 85-degree weather with 85 percent humidity and monsoon-like rain did not excuse them from their daily labor. Figure 5.1 shows the vastness and density of the jungle in which CHamorus were forced to work. It was both the fear of death through execution and the hope of survival that motivated CHamorus to endure this traumatic experience.

For the CHamorus who lived through World War II, Tiyan was imbued with new meaning predicated on the militarization of the island. Ben Blaz recalled his emotions at the completion of Guamu Dai Ni:

So when the airstrip was finished, it was not possible to simply dismiss it as something we were forced to do. All of us looked at it with a kind of pride

Figure 5.1. Hagåtña airfield, October 1944. Source: US National Archives and Records Administration.

and proprietorship. It was ours. We had made it. And then we'd be struck by what the Japanese intended to use it for, and the emotional conflicts would tear us once again. . . . But to this day, I cannot arrive at the international airport or depart from it and not remember the agony that went into its original creation.[20]

Tiyan was no longer just a place known for its lånchos. During and after the war, it came to represent a site of pain and pride that was connected to the blood, sweat, and tears of the people who worked and died there. For many CHamorus, the sounds of working at Tiyan were "haunting."[21] CHamoru US military veteran John C. Benavente recollected, "My uncle was forced to work at Tiyan. He had no military experience, and when I came back to Guam he told me about how he reacts to artillery being fired at the air base [Tiyan] and he told me by listening to the rotation in the air it makes a certain sound when it's going to come real close. He was able to tell from that experience if the round is going to come close or go overhead."[22] Benavente's uncle's experience underscores how some CHamorus were frequently exposed to the possibility of death due to their close proximity to the US military's bombing of Tiyan. As Benavente astutely pointed out, even though his uncle had not served in the military, he had been exposed to enough bombing and live fire that he knew when to be concerned.

Constructing NAS Hagåtña

During and after World War II, US settler militarism functioned through the military's frequent practice of using the same airfields, roads, and harbor facilities that the Japanese had earlier occupied.[23] In Guåhan, the US military did exactly this by occupying sites such as Tiyan, where the Japanese base Guamu Dai Ni was located. Instead of returning the land to its prewar owners, the US Navy began converting Guamu Dai Ni into NAS Hagåtña on September 1, 1944. By 1954, NAS Hagåtña totaled approximately 1,820 acres, 1,593 of which were privately owned prior to June 1950 and had to be condemned using declarations of taking at the total amount of $260,371.00.[24] It also housed nineteen units that included 1,522 officers and 9,506 enlisted personnel.[25] Other facilities that were constructed included a mess hall galley that accommodated two thousand men, eighty-seven married officers' quarters, housing for the Coast Guard, a steam plant, and recreation facilities such gyms, basketball courts, and baseball fields.[26] Construction

of these facilities produced sights, smells, and sounds that were unprecedented on the island. The reflection of buildings and sheet metal, the rum-
bling of heaving equipment, and the smell of vehicle exhaust permeated the
entire area and consequently remade the environment. Ultimately, this
process resulted in the transformation of Tiyan from lånchos to a modern
military base.

In as early as 1947, the US military had begun hiring contractors to con-
struct base facilities and provide the majority of the workers to complete
these various projects. As mentioned in chapter 4, former BPM employee
Eddie De La Cruz worked as a carpenter at NAS Hagåtña from 1947 to
1948.[27] BPM was one of the largest contractors on the island that served the
US military. According to former BPM Filipino recruiter Gorgonio Cabot,
"BPM got the biggest navy contracts to build the island of Guam, including
Andersen [Air Force Base]."[28] One of BPM's primary responsibilities at NAS
Hagåtña was erosion control of all taxiways, hardstands, aprons, and working areas.[29] In some instances, NAS Hagåtña employed its own contract
workers directly, and that sometimes included Filipinos and white Americans. In 1951 there were twenty-six CHamorus employed as non–civil ser-
vice/contract personnel.[30] In 1957 it was reported that NAS Hagåtña had
two hundred Filipino contract workers under its payroll.[31] These Filipino
contract workers were manual laborers who assisted in the loading and un-
loading of military air transport airplanes and other civilian aircraft. Thus,
the labor of civilian workers was instrumental in establishing NAS Hagåtña
as a settler colonial site.

Making Suburbia at NAS Hagåtña

One of the most important roles of NAS Hagåtña was its transportation of
military personnel and civilians traveling to and from the island. The US
Navy allowed Pan American World Airways to provide commercial air flight
service beginning on October 21, 1946, and it allowed the airline to use
Quonset huts on the base for a hotel and galley.[32] The navy's contracts with
commercial airlines quickly expanded to include other companies such as
Philippine Air Lines and Transocean Air Lines.[33] The need for more commercial flight access increased with the US government's expansion of its
military presence in Guåhan. This increased the island's temporary and
permanent population of military dependents and contract workers. By
1957 NAS Hagåtña had an average of 4,200 airline passengers per month.[34]

American soldiers stationed in Guåhan used these commercial airlines to take rest-and-relaxation (R&R) breaks in Asia and on other neighboring Pacific islands.[35] Additionally, these contracts were significant because they gave NAS Hagåtña a revenue stream to help pay for the maintenance and expansion of the base. In many ways, the first "glimpse of Guam" a person would experience was arriving at NAS Hagåtña.[36] This view was coupled with sights of clear blue water, coral reef, lush jungle, and a burgeoning military presence. Ultimately, NAS Hagåtña served as the postwar settler colonial gateway that eliminated, remade, and sustained the arrival of settlers to the island.

NAS Hagåtña resembled an American suburb with all of the accouterments of mass consumerism that attempted to keep soldiers and their wives happy. The *New York Times* reported, "Life on Guam is comfortable even though it is somewhat limited. Good housing is provided for the military personnel and their families, along with such facilities as commissaries and post exchanges, movies, restaurants and privately operated stores. And, with the mountains, the beaches and the lush vegetation, there is all the natural beauty one's heart and eyes may desire."[37] These natural and consumer activities were just some of those created and marketed to American families living in Guåhan. This strategy to appease and attract military settlers to Guåhan was similar to other US military bases throughout the world.[38] As historian Lauren Hirshberg has argued regarding the militarization of Kwajalein (an atoll in the Marshall Islands), the US military created "a mythical landscape of small-town Americana onto Kwajalein," with the goal "to support a comfortable suburban family lifestyle."[39] At the center of this process were the wives of US soldiers, who participated in a variety of social activities and other forms of domestic consumerism. For example, the Aloha Committee of the Armed Forces Officers' Wives Club at NAS Hagåtña published a booklet that served as a resource for newly arriving officers' wives by providing information on schools, child-care centers, post exchanges, commissaries, laundry services, post offices, beauty shops, banks, church services, military clubs, movie theaters, and clothing stores on base and throughout the island.[40] The name of the Aloha Committee itself exposed that Americans were unfamiliar with CHamoru culture and language, as "aloha" is a Kanaka Maoli (Native Hawaiian) concept.[41] The Aloha Committee's booklet reveals that white American women were central to the settling and suburbanization of NAS Hagåtña through their social and consumerist activities. This included shopping for the household, discussing women's magazine articles, watching movies and television shows, and hosting lunch gatherings that included card games and tea. These moments were all reflective of suburban spaces that emerged in the Cold War era. While these activities allowed women to participate in consumerism and gendered norms of Western domesticity, they also functioned to spread consumerism throughout the island as businesses were created to cater to American women. Ironically, NAS Hagåtña came to represent a place for the gathering of American women and their children, similar to how Tiyan had been a gathering place for CHamoru families in the prewar period.

CHamorus were cognizant of how white Americans living in Guåhan perpetuated consumerism, conformity, and racial segregation. As a child and teenager, former Guam senator Hope Cristobal remembered:

> Of course the people who lived there [NAS Hagåtña] lived in concrete homes. It was very different from outside. We didn't have those nice-looking concrete homes, two-story with the nice yards, well kept, maintained. They drove nice cars, they dressed well, and they looked different; they're all beautiful blond looking. Sometimes you see them tanning themselves in their yard. I would say, "Wow, is there a beach in there?" So NAS Agaña was a land just for special people. I thought they were the elite. Those are the rich people who live up there. They're different; we are down here. That's kind of the attitude I developed about there.[42]

For some CHamorus like Cristobal, NAS Hagåtña symbolized US Cold War suburbanization through consumerism, conformity, and segregation that worked together in creating privileged spaces and experiences for settlers. Her comments also demonstrate that CHamorus were acutely aware of how military bases not only transformed the physical landscape but also the island's demography. This was not only reflected in class and consumer differences but also in the racial background of the people living inside NAS Hagåtña.

Domestic violence was one of the ways that the suburban dream could also become a nightmare. On July 17, 1954, NAS Hagåtña's Medical Department responded to a domestic disturbance call from one of the family housing neighborhoods. Upon arriving, they found a Mrs. Parson bleeding from a head wound. She claimed that "she and her husband had been playing games and she got hurt."[43] Upon further investigation, Mr. and Mrs. Parsons admitted that they had gotten into a fight that resulted in the throwing of rocks, kitchen dishes, and coffee mugs. As a result, Mrs. Parsons sustained two lacerations on her head, two bruises on her neck, and a fractured left mandible.[44] It was also reported that both Mr. and Mrs. Parsons were found to be intoxicated. The reason for their violent encounter was never recorded. Although records of domestic violence incidents at NAS Hagåtña are scant, examples such as this one show the discontent that military suburban base life could not mask.

The Dangers of NAS Hagåtña

NAS Hagåtña brought the possibility of "premature death"[45] to the people living in nearby villages through terrorizing jet blasts of frequent low altitude and night-landing exercises, helicopters and warplanes crashing into nearby mountains, and the poisoning of environments and communities with military toxins.[46] For the residents living near NAS Hagåtña, the fear of aircraft accidents was their daily reality. One of the first documented postwar airplane crashes occurred in March 1947 when a military plane's engine caught on fire and crashed into Mt. Barigåda.[47] Miraculously, the two-man crew escaped without injury. On September 19, 1960, a World Airways plane (under charter to the Military Air Transport Service) carrying seventy-one military personnel and fifteen military dependents departed NAS Hagåtña after a routine refueling stop. It exploded moments after takeoff and slammed against the side of Mt. Barigåda, killing seventy-seven people.[48] Another crash occurred at NAS Hagåtña in 1962 that resulted in the death of three crewmembers operating a navy cargo plane for the military transport service.[49] The frequency of these crashes near NAS Hagåtña produced flames and debris that littered the bases and the surrounding areas. These crashes also produced sights, sounds, and smells that terrorized the nearby residents. While the military might have viewed these occurrences as inevitable incidents that occur on or near bases, NAS Hagåtña's existence threatened the lives and safety of the people of Guåhan.

CHamorus did not simply accept the dangers that NAS Hagåtña's aircraft posed to the surrounding villages. In 1954 the Guam legislature (led mostly by CHamorus) submitted Resolution no. 160 requesting that the navy and the governor of Guam address this issue:

> George Washington High School is located in the path of aircraft taking off
> and landing at the Naval Air Station; and whereas, such aircraft constitute a

danger to the more than 1900 students attending the high school; and whereas, appropriate markings on the buildings of the high school would serve to warn aircraft that they are passing over a highly congested area . . . the legislature does hereby respectfully request the Governor of Guam to take such steps as he may deem necessary and proper to provide for the painting of the word "school" or some other appropriate designation on the buildings at George Washington High School in such manner as to be clearly visible to pilots of aircraft approaching or leaving the Naval Air Station. . . . The legislature does hereby respectfully request the Governor of Guam to take such action as he may deem necessary and proper to bring such designation to the attention of the proper officials of the military air force and the civilian airlines in order that their pilots may both be aware over which they are traversing and may detour around the school area to whatever extent is possible.[50]

For island residents, sending their children to school every day was a fearful experience. The roaring sounds of low-flying military and civilian airplanes were a constant reminder that their children might not come home from school. The actual crashes of planes near the base reified their anguish. Their request was not only an attempt for aircraft to reroute their approach to NAS Hagåtña but also a formal acknowledgement that held the governor of Guam (appointed by the president of the United States) and the military responsible for the possible death of their children.

While low-flying military aircraft posed the most visible danger to residents living near NAS Hagåtña, there were other more insidious threats to nearby villagers. Naval officials realized that the rainfall NAS Hagåtña received threatened to flood neighboring villages such as Tamuneng due to runoffs that were a result of the base's elevated location and its western cliff line. Naval officials reported, "During periods of very heavy rainfall which sometimes occur, the run-off from the NAS Agaña is so rapid as to exceed the capacity, resulting in flooding of the Tamuning area which contains commercial and residential developments."[51] One of the proposals to resolve this issue was to drill dry wells in the sink areas around the base.[52] Flooding of communities due to typhoon rainfall was a significant issue, but there were other less publicly known issues with runoff from NAS Hagåtña. CHamoru rights advocate Catherine Punzalan Flores McCollum recalled that "some Chamorros believe the atomic bomb tests in the atolls is connected. This [Tiyan] is a runoff area. There are a lot of contaminants. That is one of the issues. People were housed in naval areas coming up with cancer caused by contamination."[53] Though it is difficult to determine how many planes used for nuclear testing in Micronesia were washed at NAS Agaña, the military acknowledged that there was an issue in which any kind of runoff from the base could reach and impact neighboring villages. While chemical runoff from NAS Hagåtña posed a possible environmental threat to nearby communities, it was the discovery of mustard gas that posed a credible risk to those living near Tiyan.

During World War II the US military transported chemical weapons such as mustard gas and napalm to Guåhan. These and other related items that included chemical weapon kits and unknown liquids were found in the village of Mongmong, which was once part of NAS Agaña.[54] In the postwar era, chemical weapons and other related items were typically dumped in large underground pits. Anthony J. Ramirez, former Guam museum curator (since deceased), recalled, "Sometimes the military would dig these large pits and just dump it all instead of selling it for surplus; sometimes they would dump vehicles. It was part of their inventory process. There are still a lot of toxic dumpsites."[55] The burying of these toxic chemicals was harmful to the residents living in neighboring villages, especially with the possibility of canisters leaking into the soil, the underground water table, and natural runoffs. These weapons of mass destruction also represented the slow killing of all island residents due to the increased chances of cancer and reproductive abnormalities. Similarly to Runit Dome in the Marshall Islands, the navy's practice of burying chemical weapons and waste in pits was part of a larger legacy of military dumping that reflected settler colonial polices that accelerated the death of all people living in Guåhan.

Perceptions of NAS Hagåtña

American newspapers and periodicals described Guåhan as being a place useful for war. During World War II, the island became synonymous with US military power in the Asia-Pacific region. In 1945 the *Chicago Daily Tribune* published an article that reported, "From Guam's airfields planes can roar on either offensive or defensive missions, as necessity may dictate."[56] The article continues, "Long range bombers shuttling from the United States via Honolulu and Kwajalein may be refueled and serviced at Guam prior to departure from final hopoff bases on Okinawa or northern Japan."[57] This view of Guåhan as a site of military might persisted throughout the Cold War era. The *New York Times* reported,

Most of the United States nuclear retaliation power in the Pacific is con-
centrated on this peaceful South Seas island. . . . Equally important to the
overall defense of the Pacific is this island's role as a supply center between
Hawaii and the Philippines, Formosa, Okinawa and Japan. Pot-bellied
C-124 troop carriers and the sleek C-54's and Super Constellations of the
Military Air Transport Service stop here on their flights east and west. The
Agaña Naval Air Station, on the west coast of this hourglassed-shaped island,
is an important part of the Fleet Air Wing, and it is the headquarters of Rear
Admiral M.E. Murphy, Air Naval Commander of the Marians [sic]."[58]

For American readers, visions of military bases, aircraft, bombs, and nuclear
power are what they most likely imagined when thinking about Guåhan.
This reified the island as a place that would eventually become the tip of
America's spear. Moreover, NAS Hagåtña became recognizable as the por-
tal for the US military throughout Oceania and the continental United States.
Ultimately, NAS Hagåtña represented American military strength for its war
capabilities and its utility as being "as large as the municipal air stations in
the United States."[59]

For military personnel, NAS Hagåtña reflected the modern busyness of
air terminals in the United States. US military sergeant Jack Sher recalled:

Agaña used to be the hub of the Pacific war, the GI Grand Central Station
for the war-bound headed toward Okinawa, the Philippines, Saipan and
China. Now it's the take-off spot for men reporting back to their units after
time out on Guam. Then, some of them will turn up here at Agaña terminal again. Because this is also the place where soldiers say good-by to GI
life and monotony in the Pacific and sweat out planes that will take them
through Oahu toward California, Ohio, Kentucky, Illinois and Maine. The
passenger waiting room is a long, low, modern building about three times
the size of the dance floor at the Copacabana in New York—and twice as
crowded. There are never enough seats for the uniform-clad crowd which
swirls in and out from predawn morning until late at night. You have to be
careful making your way across the terminal, to avoid tripping over tired
infantrymen sacked out on their duffel bags and sailors curled up on the
white canvas of side. Everyone is bushed or nervous or asleep, everyone but
the men behind the priorities desk working to clear passengers and freight
to keep the works running smoothly. . . . Looking around the Agaña terminal, at the restless, churning activity of men and cargo pushing in all di-
rections, toward the land of the lotuses and louses, toward the embarkation

points, toward home, you knew that it had been too long. Looking around Agaña terminal, you got a mixed-up feeling about it. You were glad it was all over. You were glad for yourself, because it meant going home soon for you, too, and then you were glad for everybody else."[60]

For soldiers such as Jack Sher, leaving Guåhan was an emotional experience because it meant that he and the other people at NAS Hagåtña had survived World War II.

As the Cold War continued throughout the 1950s and 1960s, Guåhan's importance to the United States was inextricably tied to its capabilities as a nuclear military site. In 1962 the *New York Times* reported:

> But everybody knows that Guam's prosperity is based on nuclearage weaponry. That's why hundreds of millions of dollars have been poured into the island. There are about 45,000 Guamanians on the island and there is hardly one whose economic existence is not tied in one way or another to the Strategic Air Command or to the Naval bases here. . . . There is a strange reversal of attitudes between the military and civilians toward the nuclear-age realities. Civilians talk and think of the nuclear age in terms of contracts and construction and buying power and jobs. They want the base to be bigger and bigger and its commander to build more houses and buy more eggs. To the military the nuclear age is not an abstract thing or a matter of contracts but a physical presence with which they live day and night and whose potential hideousness they are quite aware. The airmen have an almost missionary belief in the importance of nuclear deterrence, as vivid as an evangelist's conviction that the knowledge of hell can save men from sin.[61]

By the 1960s, a new view of Guåhan was emerging. This perception was that the island was no longer just a military site but a nuclear one. In many ways Guåhan became part of the larger legacy of US nuclear testing in Micronesia that connected it to the Pacific Proving Grounds program, which resulted in approximately 105 atmospheric and underwater nuclear tests.[62] The *New York Times* article's Christian overtones that were used to justify US military motives was similar to how the US military rationalized the taking of the Marshall Islands to use it for nuclear testing. This article also perpetuated the narrative (which still exists today) that CHamorus and other island residents were grateful and supportive of the military for bringing suburbanization and economic opportunities to Guåhan even though the military did not gainfully employ CHamorus.

The Gates and Roads of NAS Hagåtña

NAS Hagåtña's existence as a military base was "normalized" due to its location in the center of the island, which put it in nearby proximity to surrounding villages.[63] In addition, island residents could gain entrance onto the base when they had permission to leave the island via the civilian terminal located in NAS Hagåtña. Another normalizing factor was that civilians could drive around the majority of the perimeter of the base using public roads. In contrast, other bases in Guåhan—such as Andersen Air Force Base in the north and Naval Base on the western coast—were isolated from civilian communities. The navy, however, viewed NAS Hagåtña's proximity to surrounding villages as a security issue that required the tightening of the roads and gates that allowed access to the base.

A naval report from 1947 stated, "There is altogether too much unauthorized vehicular traffic on the taxiways—this should be curtailed as it causes considerable dust and is a source of concern to sentries in airplane parking area. It is suggested that a jeep patrol, with authority to stop, investigate, and report where indicated, all unauthorized traffic be instituted.[64] Administrators believed an increased military patrol presence would deter any possibility of security breaches. By the late 1940s, officials at NAS Hagåtña called for greater restrictions and surveillance of its nearby roads.

> The security problem at the Naval Air Station, Agaña, with the widely dispersed buildings thereon, lack of fencing around Supply and Public Works Compounds, through highways, and lack of means of inspection of cars leaving the area, is extremely difficult at the best. . . . The subject road [Route 8], which is only occasionally patrolled and allows through public traffic, is considered as particularly detrimental to the welfare of the Station.[65]

NAS Hagåtña officials also surveyed Route 8 and found that 51 percent of all vehicles on the station used this road to enter or exit the area.[66] The navy's proposal to resolve this supposed security issue was to close the road off to all non–NAS Hagåtña personnel, which was problematic because Route 8 was the most direct route between the central and western parts of the island.[67] This proposal never came to fruition, but it did represent another example of how the military attempted to control and alter this region of the island.

The navy requested that Route 10, located on the eastern part of NAS Hagåtña, also be closed to nonmilitary personnel due to the cost of maintenance. Specifically, naval administrators claimed,

The section of Route 10 on this station has never been surfaced with black top or cement, and consequently requires an abnormal expenditure of labor and funds to keep it in a useable condition. . . . Since it is a part of the Island Highway system and is subject to heavy traffic by vehicles in transit across the station having no business to conduct on the station, it is considered that this is a misapplication of funds granted under the appropriation Aviation Navy.[68]

In this instance, the navy's strategy to have a portion of Route 10 closed was based on having the road classified for military use only. The US Navy supported the reclassification of the road through security patrols that occurred approximately once an hour.[69] Naval administrators also claimed that other roads existed that could serve as satisfactory substitution. They argued that the alternative highway was similar in quality, cheaper to maintain, and half a mile longer than Route 10.[70] The navy's attempt to close Route 10 produced resistance from civilian administrators. Civil administrator P. S. Tambling responded, "To close the road without providing an alternative route in the same general area would enforce hardships on the residents of the Barrigada and Price Road areas. Many of the residents in these areas are employed by military activities at the north end of the island and still others have farms at the north end of the island to which they commute daily."[71] Tambling also believed that closing Route 10 would cause a rerouting of all traffic in the area, which would increase the amount of travel by 3.8 miles and represented an "arbitrary closing of an established traffic route" that was unwarranted and did "not appear to affect the security" of the base.[72] Based on the information provided, Governor C. A. Pownall ruled that Route 10 through NAS Hagåtña would not be closed and opted to relocate Highway 10 around the northeast end of the base.[73] Pownall's decision was one of the few moments in which the government of Guam, which was led by officials appointed by US Congress, did not acquiesce to the navy's request and did not act as a monolithic agent for the US government. Pownall's ruling demonstrates that as governor, he did have some agency when it came to dealing with the US military.

While roads of NAS Hagåtña served as one flashpoint of anxiety for the military, another place of contention was its gates. For CHamoru legislators, the gates of NAS Hagåtña were spaces that sometimes resulted in humiliating interactions with naval security. On March 5, 1960, the chair of Guam's Committee on Labor and Education, James T. Sablan, attempted to enter NAS Hagåtña to escort CHamoru politicians M. U. Lujan and A. C.

Cruz, using a guest pass that had been issued to him by a naval administrator. Sablan was denied entry when he arrived at the security gate and was then told to "get a visitor's pass, just like everyone else." Sablan recalled this encounter as a "humiliating experience" and believed the guest pass was "meaningless and pointless" if the military security refused to recognize as a valid document.[74] CHamoru politicians F. T. Ramirez, Joaquin A. Perez, and A. L. Cristobal were also denied entrance to NAS Hagåtña while attempting to use guest passes authorized by the US Navy. On October 19, 1961, all three men attempted to access the Pan American Terminal to greet US Congressman Michael J. Kirwan from the state of Ohio. However, navy security told the men that their guest passes allowed them to enter the base but they "would need another pass for the car."[75] Ramirez, Perez, and Cristobal argued with security and showed the guards that their passes gave them authorization to access navy and air force facilities in Guåhan. After the event, Ramirez wrote a letter that expressed his frustration and anger by stating, "Since a car pass is all anybody needs to get into NAS, in any event, the possession of these guest passes thus become meaningless."[76] He went on to remind naval officials, "As you might know, we frequently need to go to the airport to meet and greet various governmental personages" and that all three men returned their guest passes to the US Navy chief of staff Captain G. M. Winne as an act of protest.[77] In closing, Ramirez reminded Captain Winne, "We did not ask for the guest passes and are perfectly willing to continue, as everyone else does, to obtain the necessary car pass from the Security Office at the gate. What we do not wish to continue doing is ending up in bootless arguments with the Naval personnel over whether our guest passes mean what they quite clearly say."[78] Ramirez's letter to Captain Winne underscores the anger that some CHamoru politicians had with the military's policies regarding access to NAS Hagåtña. In many ways, the security gates represented the contradiction and inconsistency of military policy that generated discontent among some CHamorus. NAS Hagåtña was a reminder to CHamoru politicians that they were still living as colonial subjects whose Indigenous homelands were occupied. While the navy attempted to control the paths and gates leading to NAS Hagåtña, it also wanted to regulate the boundaries between the base and surrounding villages.

By the early 1950s, some CHamorus, such as Ed Calvo, attempted to reestablish their lånchos at Tiyan. In response, the navy acted quickly to determine boundary lines and ruled that Calvo's pig enclosure, which was made out of chicken wire and metal posts, was two feet within the unmarked perimeter of NAS Hagåtña.[79] Calvo was therefore ordered to remove his pigpen.

Other non-CHamoru landowners, such as Charlie Corn, a wealthy businessman in Guåhan and the Philippines, also constructed buildings near
NAS Hagåtña. Similar to Calvo's case, the navy ruled that the roof over-
hang of Corn's buildings extended into the boundary of NAS Hagåtña.[80]
The navy wanted these buildings removed, as well, but took a more amenable and patient tone by stating, "Efforts will be made to eliminate these
encroachments, if possible, upon the return to Guam of Mr. Corn who is
presently in the Philippines."[81]

Interracial Intimacies at NAS Hagåtña

NAS Hagåtña also became a site that dictated and controlled the legality of
interracial intimacies. Specifically, the commanding officer at NAS Hagåtña
had the power to approve of marriages that occurred among CHamorus and
American servicemen stationed at the base. In 1953, American serviceman
Douglas Anthony Anderlini and CHamoru Benita Pereda Sablan had to petition naval officer S. Gazze to get married. The petition required documentation that included a financial statement, health certificates, a chaplain's
statement, an affidavit from Sablan certifying freedom to marry, and a copy
of Sablan's birth certificate.[82] As discussed in chapter 4, the US military took
an active role in promoting romantic and sexual relationships among CHamoru women and American servicemen. The navy's power to control marriages was another example that reminded CHamorus that they lacked
autonomy on their home island.

NAS Hagåtña also became a site for interracial violence. On Sunday, October 9, 1949, American servicemen Donald E. Shoemaker, Ramson T. Tew Jr.,
Robert D. Talley, and William B. Prince were involved in a confrontation
with CHamoru security guards at the J&G Motor Company, which was
located 200 meters outside the main gate of NAS Hagåtña. Shoemaker claimed
that he just returned from liberty and noticed that his toolbox was open and
missing tools.[83] Shoemaker then enlisted the help of Tew, Talley, and Prince
to search for the tools, believing that he had lost them on the road near the
main gate. While they were on the road outside of the main gate, they
claimed that without warning or reason, the "Guamanian" security guards
at the J&G Motor Company garage "starting using abusive language" and
"cursed" at them.[84] According to the four men, the CHamoru guards then
began throwing rocks and firing their guns at them.[85] This confrontation
culminated with Tew sustaining injuries to his head from being hit with a

rifle and the rest of the marines running back to NAS Hagåtña. Several days later, NAS Hagåtña security officials completed their investigation and could only confirm that Tew suffered an injury to his head.[86] They could not locate the CHamoru guards who worked at J&G Motor Company. While many of the details surrounding this incident could not be corroborated, the fact that these marines identified their assailants as "Guamanians" most likely caused concern with NAS Hagåtña officials. Furthermore, the close proximity of this violent interaction to NAS Hagåtña most likely solidified the military's rationale in wanting to control the boundaries between the gates of NAS Hagåtña and its surrounding communities.

In 1995 NAS Hagåtña was closed as a result of the Base Realignment and Closure Commission of 1993. This resulted in NAS Hagåtña being returned to the government of Guam to be fully utilized as an international airport, now known as the Antonio B. Won Pat International Airport. For the tourists and military dependents who travel to Guåhan every year, the international airport hides the wounds that date back to World War II. However, for Tiyan families and other CHamorus, these scars are still present. As discussed earlier, NAS Hagåtña was constructed over the place that was the center of their social and familial life. Tiyan also represents the backbreaking labor that many of their ancestors were forced to endure under Japanese occupation. The US military continued to reopen these wounds as it condemned the entire region, using a legal mechanism that made resistance daunting and implementing settler colonial policies that sought to transform the nearby environment and villages. However, the memories of what Tiyan use to be and how it has been transformed is a symbol of CHamoru survival, which continues today.

Conclusion

As discussed throughout this book, US settler militarism in Guåhan drastically transformed the island. This was predicated on a co-constitutive process that included CHamoru land dispossession, discursive justifications for the remaking of Guåhan, the racialization of civilian military labor, and the military's policing of interracial intimacies. In order to acquire large tracts of land, the US military relied on the GLCC and declarations of taking to conceal the coercive strategies it used to force CHamorus to accept settlements after World War II. While some CHamorus were forever separated from their ancestral properties, others continued to rely on their lånchos for physical sustenance and cultural perpetuation. By charting these counternarratives of land stewardship and survival, my goal has been to highlight that their postwar relationship to the land has endured.

Part of this settler colonial project was filtered through the optics of American visitors and military officials who perpetuated a discourse that justified military occupation through modernization and development. Specifically, the construction of Apapa Harbor, houses, and roads became examples of the military's benevolence and contribution to improving the island and the lives of CHamorus. In reality, however, these infrastructure projects were built with the intention of improving and streamlining military operations. This process also promoted American military settlement through the transmission of cultural principles that supported the idea of US Cold War suburban life on the island. Ultimately, the discursive justifications for the US military occupation of Guåhan reified the cultures of settler colonialism.

The US militarization of Guåhan also depended on the creation of a hierarchical labor system that was predicated on race and nationality. In order to construct bases throughout the island, the military and its contractors primarily recruited Filipinos, along with some white American southerners, to Guåhan. The military's contractors preferred to hire Filipinos because of a capitalist cost-saving strategy that made it financially advantageous to recruit them based on race and nationality. In turn, CHamorus increasingly relied on the government of Guam for employment in the civil sector.[1] The apex of these uneven hiring practices and the exploitation of workers culminated with the proposed Guam Wage Bill of 1956. CHamorus and Filipinos opposed this proposal in order to protect their labor rights during a time of intense anti-Communist sentiment. Thus, the immediate postwar military expansion of the island led to an influx of Filipino settlers—who now comprise the second-largest ethnic group in Guåhan—and the creation of a Filipino labor class that still persists in the military and tourist industries.

The US military was also highly invested in policing interracial intimacies among CHamorus, Filipinos, and white Americans. These interracial encounters functioned to support or transgress military occupation in a variety of ways. For example, a by-product of military occupation was the accelerated influx of laborers who at times came into conflict with CHamorus, which resulted in interracial and gendered violence. In order to regulate these intimacies, military officials created laws that dictated the use of public spaces such as bars, clubs, restaurants, and roads. The military also utilized other tactics that included deportation, the denial of security clearances, and the requirement of passes to enter CHamoru villages. While interracial conflict in Guåhan changed over time, its roots partly derived from US military occupation and the creation of laws that fueled interracial antagonism.

The construction of NAS Hagåtña represented the physical manifestation of settler militarism. Before World War II, this area primarily contained lånchos for CHamorus who lived in the surrounding villages. However, Japan transformed the region into an airfield during the war, and then the United States developed it into a military base. As a US naval air station, it became a focal point for the influx of settlers and ultimately became the site for Guåhan's international airport.

The early 1960s marked an important shift in the US militarization of Guåhan. In August 1962, President John F. Kennedy passed Executive Order 11045, which ended the US Navy's security clearance program that gave it the authority to regulate the travel of all civilians to and from the island. This change in military policy accelerated Guåhan's transformation into a postwar settler society. Specifically, it was the foundation for the development of the island's tourism industry that flourished in the 1980s and 1990s. Migrants from all over Asia, the continental United States, and other parts of Micronesia began settling in Guåhan for these employment opportunities. The emergence of tourism also blossomed simultaneously with the suburbanization of the island. Up until the 1960s, suburbanization was concentrated in military bases. However, Executive Order 11045 and the continued US militarization of the island brought suburbanization outside the gates of bases through prefabricated and tract-style homes, shopping plazas, and recreational activities in central Guåhan.

Then, in November 1962, Typhoon Karen (category 5) struck Guåhan and other parts of Micronesia, resulting in one of the most destructive events in the island's history. Over 90 percent of all civilian buildings were damaged.[2] This catastrophic event was the powder-keg moment that led to the largest exodus of CHamorus for the continental United States. The diasporic CHamorus who left the island were seeking improved economic and educational opportunities since the US military's governance and occupation of the island that spanned approximately sixty-one years had produced bleak possibilities.[3] My paternal grandparents, mentioned at the beginning of this book, were part of this group of CHamorus to leave their home island in the 1960s.

Finally, the US government's entrance into the Vietnam War was another important shift in US settler militarism that perpetuated the CHamoru diaspora. In 1965 the US government began deploying soldiers to Vietnam, which led to a significant enlistment or drafting of CHamorus. Those who enlisted often did so because of the "liberation of Guåhan" narrative that was promulgated after World War II or due to the fact that economic opportunities on the island were marginal.[4] Regardless of their reasons for joining, CHamorus from Guåhan and the Commonwealth of the Northern Marianas experienced the largest casualty rate per capita of any ethnic group in the Vietnam War.[5] Some CHamorus remained in the military after the war ended, which led to their permanent settlement outside of Guåhan as they were stationed in other parts of the United States or the world.

With the fall of Saigon in 1975, Guåhan once again became a temporary or permanent home for diasporic Southeast Asians. From April to November 1975, the US government processed over 112,000 Vietnamese refugees in Guåhan in what became known as Operation New Life. As scholar Evyn Lê Espiritu Gandhi argues, the "humanitarian rhetoric that newspapers and politicians used to describe Operation New Life" served to justify US settler militarism.[6] To carry out Operation New Life, the US military set up several refugee camps, or "tent cities," throughout the island; the three largest were located at Andersen Air Force Base, Asan Beach, and Orote Point. For non-CHamorus and American audiences in the continental United States, these camps and the military's discourse of humanitarianism were instrumental in concealing the legacy of CHamoru land dispossession that dated back to the Spanish era. For CHamorus, these tent cities were another reminder of their status as colonial subjects. However, one event threatened the military's projection as a benevolent nation.

During Operation New Life, several hundred Vietnamese refugees engaged in various acts of protest throughout Guåhan's tent cities that challenged the US government's "humanitarian" project and "benevolence."[7] For these repatriates, their objective was to return to Vietnam since some sought to reunify with family members who remained there; others reported that they had been coerced or forced to leave their homeland.[8] This politically contentious issue culminated with the US government agreeing to their demands and with 1,500 Vietnamese refugees given a ship to return to Vietnam. Upon their return, these repatriates were met with suspicion and were imprisoned in labor camps that are sometimes referred to as "re-education camps."[9] Ultimately, their actions served to unmask the military's humanitarian discourse and transgressed US settler militarism since they wished to return home instead of moving to the United States.

By drawing attention to the postwar history of the militarization of Guåhan, I urge everyone to consider how settler militarism functions not only through the actions of people but also via sites such as military bases. In many ways, Guåhan demonstrates how the US military transformed the island into the tip of America's spear and that settler colonialism can occur even with a small settler population. However, my second goal has been to highlight how CHamorus have survived. In some instances, CHamorus and their allies have been successful in halting US military expansion. This legacy of resistance continues today through the actions of organizations such as Filipinos for Guåhan, Independent Guåhan, Prutehi Litekyan, and We Are Guåhan, just to name a few. In closing, I hope this book can serve to inspire a critical engagement of how military bases in Guåhan affect the lives of those living back home and in the diaspora. Finally, I encourage those of you reading this book to document your elders' stories of survival. Preserving their words will help perpetuate their memories and experiences, which can nourish the minds and souls of future generations.

Notes

Introduction

1. Lâncho comes from the Spanish word *rancho*, which means "ranch" in English. For more on the CHamoru lâncho, refer to Laura M. Thompson, *Guam and Its People: With a Village Journal by Jesus C. Barcinas* (Princeton, NJ: Princeton University Press, 1947).

2. *Champulado* is a chocolate rice pudding that is served warm or cold. *Fina'denne'* is a spicy sauce used as a condiment that is composed mainly of soy sauce, vinegar, lemon, and chili peppers. Red rice is short-grain rice that is combined with *achote* seeds. *Kelaguen* is shredded coconut with chopped chicken, meat, or seafood that is combined with lemon juice and hot pepper.

3. CHamorus are the Indigenous people of the Mariana Islands, whereas Guamanians can be anyone regardless of race or ethnicity that resides in Guåhan.

4. Alex Lockie, "Trump Promised 'Fire and Fury' for North Korea If It Continued Threats—Hours Later, It Threatened Strikes on Guam," Business Insider, August 8, 2017, https://www.businessinsider.com/north-korea-trump-missile-threat-guam-fire-fury-2017-8.

5. Camila Domonoske, "Why Is North Korea Threatening Guam?," NPR.org, August 9, 2017, https://www.npr.org/sections/thetwo-way/2017/08/09/542384201/why-is-north-korea-threatening-guam.

6. Will Ripley, "North Korea Revives Guam Threat ahead of US-South Korea Drills," CNN.com, October 15, 2017, https://www.cnn.com/2017/10/13/asia/north-korea-guam-threat/index.html.

7. Daniel Immerwahr, *How to Hide an Empire: A History of the Greater United States* (New York: Farrar, Straus and Giroux, 2019), 9.

8. Matt K. Matsuda, *Pacific Worlds: A History of Seas, Peoples, and Cultures* (New York: Cambridge University Press, 2012), 2.

9. For more on the militarization of Hawai'i, refer to Kyle Kajihiro, "The Militarizing of Hawai'i: Occupation: Accommodation, and Resistance," in *Asian Settler Colonialism: From Local Governance to the Habits of Everyday Life*," eds. Candace Fujikane and Jonathan Y. Okamura (Honolulu: University of Hawai'i Press, 2008), 170–194.

10. Judy Tzu-Chun Wu, "The Dead, the Living, and the Sacred: Patsy Mink, Antimilitarism, and Reimagining the Pacific World," *Meridians: Feminism, Race, Transnationalism* 18, no. 2 (October 2019): 314.

11. Alfred Thayer Mahan, *The Influence of Sea Power upon History, 1660–1783* (London: Sampson Low, Marston & Co., 1890), 28.

12. White House Office of the Press Secretary, "Fact Sheet: Advancing the Rebalance to Asia and the Pacific," November 16, 2015, https://obamawhitehouse.archives.gov/the-press -office/2015/11/16/fact-sheet-advancing-rebalance-asia-and-pacific.

13. Ron Crocombe, *Asia in the Pacific Islands: Replacing the West* (Suva, Fiji: IPS Publications, 2007), 353; and Michael Lujan Bevacqua, "American-Style Colonialism," Guampedia.com, accessed June 6, 2020, https://www.guampedia.com/american-style-colonialism/.

14. David Vine, *Base Nation: How the U.S. Military Bases abroad Harm America and the World* (New York: Skyhorse Publishing, 2015), 86; and Frank Quimby, "Fortress Guåhån," *Journal of Pacific History* 46, no. 3 (2011), 370.

15. Danica M. Sirmans, "Indo-Pacom Wraps Up Valiant Shield 2018," *Navy Public Affairs Support Element West*, September 25, 2018, https://www.af.mil/News/Article-Display/Article /1644211/indo-pacom-wraps-up-valiant-shield-2018/.

16. The Mariana Islands is an archipelago that includes fifteen islands. Out of the fifteen islands, only Guåhan, Luta (Rota), Sa'ipan, and Tini'an are inhabited. Guåhan is the only island that is a US territory; Rota, Sa'ipan, and Tini'an are politically connected as the Northern Mariana Islands, which is a commonwealth of the United States.

17. David Vine, *The United States of War: A Global History of America's Endless Conflicts, From Columbus to the Islamic States* (Oakland: University of California Press, 2020), 2–3.

18. Juliet Nebolon, "'Life Given Straight from the Heart': Settler Militarism, Biopolitics, and the Public Health in Hawai'i during World War II," *American Quarterly* 69, no. 1 (2017), 25.

19. For more on empire and infrastructure, refer to Vernadette Vicuña Gonzalez, *Securing Paradise: Tourism and Militarism in Hawai'i and the Philippines* (Durham, NC: Duke University Press, 2013); Manu Karuka, *Empire's Tracks: Indigenous Nations, Chinese Workers, and the Transcontinental Railroad* (Oakland: University of California Press, 2019); Nadine Attewell and Wesley Attewell, "Between Asia and Empire: Infrastructures of Encounter in the Archive of War," *Inter-Asia Cultural Studies* 20, no. 2 (2019): 162–179; Deborah Cowen, "Following the Infrastructures of Empire: Notes on Cities, Settler Colonialism, and Method," *Urban Geography* 41, no. 4 (2019): 469–486; Andrew Friedman, "US Empire, World War 2, and the Racialising of Labour," *Race and Class* 58, no. 4 (2017), 23–38; and Laleh Khalili, "The Infrastructural Power of the Military: The Geoeconomic Role of the US Army Corps of Engineers in the Arabian Peninsula," *European Journal of International Relations* 24, no. 4 (2017), 911–933.

20. Vine, *Base Nation*, 4.

21. Sasha Davis, *The Empires' Edge: Militarization, Resistance, and Transcending Hegemony in the Pacific* (Athens: University of Georgia Press, 2015), 2.

22. For more on CHamoru resilience, refer to Tiara R. Na'puti, "Disaster Militarism and Indigenous Responses to Super Typhoon Yutu in the Mariana Islands," *Environmental Communication* 16, no. 5 (2022), 612–629.

23. Gerald Vizenor, "Aesthetics of Survivance: Literary Theory and Practice," in *Survivance: Narrative of Native Presence*, ed. Gerald Vizenor (Lincoln: University of Nebraska Press, 2008), 1. I thank Kēhaulani Vaughn for our conversations on Native survival.

24. Michael P. Perez, "Chamorro Resistance and Prospects for Sovereignty in Guam," in *Sovereignty Matters: Locations of Contestation and Possibility in Indigenous Struggles for Self-Determination*, ed. Joanne Barker (Lincoln: University of Nebraska Press, 2005), 172.

25. My gratitude goes to Keith L. Camacho for our discussions on US empire and CHamoru complacency and complicity.

26. Audra Simpson and Andrea Smith, "Introduction," in *Theorizing Native Studies*, eds. Audra Simpson and Andrea Smith (Durham, NC: Duke University Press, 2014), 13.

27. Nicolyn Woodcock, "Narratives of Intimacy in Asian American Literature," in *Oxford Research Encyclopedia* (August 30, 2019), 1, DOI: 10.1093/acrefore/9780190201098.013.1173. For more on militarized intimacies, refer to Nicolyn V. Woodcock, "Militarized Intimacies: War, Family, and Transpacific Asian American Literature (PhD diss., Miami University, 2019).

28. Patrick Wolfe, "Settler Colonialism and the Elimination of the Native," *Journal of Genocide Research* 8, no. 4 (2006), 388. My appreciation goes to Charlie Sepulveda for our conversations on settler colonialism.

29. Haunani-Kay Trask, *From a Native Daughter: Colonialism and Sovereignty in Hawai'i* (Honolulu: University of Hawai'i Press, 1999), 25.

30. J. Kēhaulani Kauanui and Patrick Wolfe, "Settler Colonialism Then and Now: A Conversation between J. Kēhaulani Kauanui and Patrick Wolfe," *Politica & Societa* 2 (2012): 235–258.

31. Roxanne Dunbar-Ortiz, *An Indigenous Peoples' History of the United States* (Boston: Beacon Press, 2014), 8.

32. Cynthia Enloe, *Maneuvers: The International Politics of Militarizing Women's Lives* (Berkeley: University of California Press, 2000), 3.

33. Candace Fujikane and Jonathan Y. Okamura, "Introduction," in *Asian Settler Colonialism: From Local Governance to the Habits of Everyday Life in Hawai'i*, eds. Candace Fujikane and Jonathan Y. Okamura (Honolulu: University of Hawai'i Press, 2008), 6.

34. Setsu Shigematsu and Keith L. Camacho, "Introduction: Militarized Currents, Decolonizing Futures," in *Militarized Currents: Toward a Decolonized Future in Asia and the Pacific*, eds. Setsu Shigematsu and Keith L. Camacho (Minneapolis: University of Minnesota Press, 2010), xxvi.

35. JoAnna Poblete, *Islanders in the Empire: Filipino and Puerto Rican Laborers in Hawai'i* (Urbana: University of Illinois Press), 3.

36. Dean Itsuji Saranillio, *Unsustainable Empire: Alternative Histories of Hawai'i Statehood* (Durham, NC: Duke University Press, 2018), 20.

37. Iyko Day, *Alien Capital: Asian Racialization and the Logic of Settler Colonial Capitalism* (Durham, NC: Duke University Press, 2016), 19.

38. Jodi A. Byrd, *The Transit of Empire: Indigenous Critiques of Colonialism* (Minneapolis: University of Minnesota Press, 2011), xxx.

39. For more on the defining of settlers, refer to Lorenzo Veracini, "Natives Settlers Migrants," *Politica & Societa* 1, no. 2 (2012): 187–240; and Rebekah Garrison, "Settler Responsibility: Respatialising Dissent in 'America' beyond Continental Borders," *Shima* 13, no. 2 (2019): 56–75.

40. Fujikane and Okamura, "Introduction," 5.

41. For more on settler militarism and prisoner of war camps, refer to Juliet Nebolon, "Settler-Military Camps: Internment and Prisoner of War Camps across the Pacific Islands during World War II," *Journal of Asian American Studies* 24, no. 2 (June 2021): 299–335.

42. Vicente M. Diaz, *Repositioning the Missionary: Rewriting the Histories of Colonialism, Native Catholicism, and Indigeneity in Guam* (Honolulu: University of Hawai'i Press, 2010), 11.

43. The policy of *reducción* would later be expanded to the neighboring islands of Sa'ipan and Tini'an. The CHamorus living on these islands were relocated to Guåhan, where they were forced to live.

44. Other Spanish forts included Fort San Luis (1737), Fort Santiago (circa 1700s), Fort San Fernando (1750), Fort Santo Angel (1756), and Fort Soledad (1810). For more information on

Spanish-era forts, refer to Daryl A. Haun, "Spanish Forts of Guam Overview," Guampedia.com, https://www.guampedia.com/spanish-forts-of-guam-overview/.

45. For more on the Spanish moral justification of colonialism, refer to Robert C. Perez, "Guantánamo and the Logic of Colonialism: The Deportation of Enemy Indians and Enemy Combatants to Cuba," *Radical Philosophy Review* 14, no. 1 (2011): 25–47.

46. For more on inter-imperial rivalries, refer to Christen T. Sasaki, "Emerging Nations, Emerging Empires: Inter-Imperial Intimacies and Competing Settler Colonialisms in Hawai'i," *Pacific Historical Review* 90, no. 1 (2021): 28–56; and Augusto Espiritu, "Inter-Imperial Relations, the Pacific, and Asian American History," *Pacific Historical Review* 83, no. 2 (2014): 238–254.

47. Walter Lafeber, *The New Empire: An Interpretation of American Expansion, 1860–1898* (Ithaca, NY: Cornell University Press, 1998), 197; and Saranillio, *Unsustainable Empire*, 9.

48. Robert F. Rogers, *Destiny's Landfall: A History of Guam* (Honolulu: University of Hawai'i Press, 2011), 117–119.

49. Sasaki, "Emerging Nations, Emerging Empires," 31; and Espiritu, "Inter-Imperial Relations," 239.

50. For more on Tini'an and the atomic bombs dropped on Japan, refer to Dan A. Farrell, *Tinian and the Bomb: Project Alberta and Operation Centerboard* (Tinian: Micronesian Productions, 2018).

51. Quimby, "Fortress Guåhån," 361.

52. Rogers, *Destiny's Landfall*, 212; Quimby, 361, and Andersen Air Force Base, "Andersen Air Force Base History," January 31, 2007, https://www.andersen.af.mil/About-Us/Fact-Sheets /Display/Article/414630/andersen-air-force-base-history/.

53. Rogers, 232.

54. Mong Palatino, "1975: The Start and End of Conflict in Southeast Asia," *The Diplomat*, December 1, 2015. https://thediplomat.com/2015/12/1975-the-start-and-end-of-conflict-in -southeast-asia/.

55. For more on settler militarism, Vietnamese refugees, and Operation New Life in Guåhan, refer to Evyn Lê Espiritu Gandhi, *Archipelago of Resettlement: Vietnamese Refugee Settlers and Decolonization across Guam and Israel-Palestine* (Oakland: University of California Press, 2022).

56. Gandhi, *Archipelago of Resettlement*, 79. For more on military humanitarianism, refer to Jana K. Lipman, "'A Precedent Worth Setting . . .': Military Humanitarianism—The U.S. Military and the 1975 Vietnamese Evacuation," *Journal of Military History* 79 (January 2015): 151–179; and Heather Marie Stur, "'Hiding behind the Humanitarian Label': Refugees, Repatriates, and the Rebuilding of America's Benevolent Image after the Vietnam War," *Diplomatic History* 39, no. 2 (April 2015), 223–244.

57. For more on Operation New Life and Vietnamese refugees in Guåhan, refer to Jana K. Lipman, *In Camps: Vietnamese Refugees, Asylum Seekers, and Repatriates* (Oakland: University of California Press, 2020); Yến Lê Espiritu, *Body Counts: The Vietnam War and Militarized Refuge(es)* (Oakland: University of California Press, 2014); and Trụ Trần Đình, *Ship of Fate: Memoir of a Vietnamese Repatriate*, trans. Bac Hoai Tran and Jana K. Lipman (Honolulu: University of Hawai'i Press, 2017).

58. Tiara R. Na'puti and Michael Lujan Bevacqua, "Militarization and Resistance from Guåhan: Protecting and Defending Pågat," *American Quarterly* 67, no. 3 (September 2015), 837.

59. For more on the US military's attempt to transform Pågat into a firing range, refer to Na'puti and Bevacqua, "Militarization and Resistance," 837–858.

60. For more on the history of Litekyan, refer to Mike T. Carson, Anthony Tamayo Jr., Victoria-Lola M. Leon Guerrero, Brett Storie, Monique Storie, and Mary E. Camacho, *Lina'la':*

Portraits of Life at Litekyan (Mangilao: University of Guam Richard Flores Taitano Micronesian Area Research Center, 2018).

61. In 1899 the United States acquired 36,030 acres of Spanish Crown lands in Guåhan as part of the Treaty of Paris. The United States owned 48,014 acres in 1937, occupied 56,985 acres in 1948, and owned 39,287 acres in 2010. This statistical information was obtained from Paul Carano and Pedro C. Sanchez, *A Complete History of Guam* (Rutland, VT: Charles E. Tuttle, 1964), 335–336; Catherine Lutz, "US Military Bases on Guam in Global Perspective," *Asia-Pacific Journal: Japan Focus*, http://www.japanfocus.org/-catherine-lutz/3389; and Michael F. Phillips, "Land," in *Kinalamten Pulitikåt: Siñenten I Chamorro/Issues in Guam's Political Development: The Chamorro Perspective* (Hagåtña: Political Status Education Coordinating Commission, 2002), 2–8.

62. Kelly Lytle Hernández, *City of Inmates: Conquest, Rebellion, and the Rise of Human Caging in Los Angeles, 1771–1965* (Chapel Hill: University of North Carolina Press, 2017), 4.

63. Valerie J. Matsumoto, *Farming the Home Place: A Japanese American Community in California, 1919–1982* (Ithaca, NY: Cornell University Press, 1993), 219–220.

64. For more on Native/Indigenous oral history and oral traditions, refer to Jennifer S. H. Brown and Elizabeth Vibert, eds., *Reading beyond Words: Contexts for Native History* (Toronto: University of Toronto Press, 2003); and Peter Nabokov, *A Forest of Time: American Indian Ways of History* (New York: Cambridge University Press, 2002).

65. Each interview lasted approximately one hour and took place where the interviewee felt the most comfortable. During these interviews, I encouraged my interviewees to narrate their experiences. I only asked them specific questions when the content from the interview prompted me or if they had exhausted their comments on a particular topic. I met the majority of my interviewees through my networks with community organizers, educators, family members, friends, political activists, and scholars. I also utilized a snowball sampling approach in which one of my interviewees would introduce me to additional people I could potentially interview.

66. Rogers, *Destiny's Landfall*, 217–218.

67. Carano and Sanchez, *A Complete History*, 329; Vicente M. Diaz, "'Fight Boys, til the Last . . .': Islandstyle Football and the Remasculinization of Indigeneity in the Militarized American Pacific Islands," in *Pacific Diaspora: Island Peoples in the United States and across the Pacific*, eds. Paul Spickard, Joanne L. Rondilla, and Debbie Hippolite Wright (Honolulu: University of Hawai'i Press, 2002), 175; and Rogers, 217.

68. For more on the entanglement of natural disasters and militarism, refer to Na'puti, "Disaster Militarism."

1. CHamoru Land Stewardship and Military Land Taking

1. Ben Blaz was thirteen years old when Japan occupied Guåhan during World War II. After high school, he completed his bachelor's degree at the University of Notre Dame in 1951 and earned a master's degree from George Washington University in 1963. He joined the US Marine Corps at the beginning of the Korean War and rose to the rank of brigadier general, becoming the first CHamoru to achieve this position. He also served as Guam's delegate to the US Congress for four terms, beginning in 1985 and lasting until 1993. Ben Blaz, *Bisita Guam: Let Us Remember Nihi Ta Hasso* (Mangilao: University of Guam Micronesian Area Research Center, 2008).

2. In the CHamoru language, Tiyan means "belly" or "stomach," which references its location in the central area of Guåhan. The place name of Tiyan follows the CHamoru Indigenous practice of naming specific areas of the island after a human body part. Another example

is the village of Barigåda, which means "flank" or central Guåhan. However, CHamoru adults from the prewar era also referred to Tiyan as Jalaguac or Alaguag. The word *tuyan* or "stomach" has also been referred to this same area of Guåhan. The use of all four names has been documented in the historical record, but this book will refer to this area as Tiyan, the most commonly used term by CHamorus in the postwar period and today. From 1944 to 1995, Tiyan was under control of the US Navy and was primarily used as a naval air base (the US Navy permitted the government of Guam to operate an international airport terminal on Tiyan). The Base Realignment and Closure Commission closed the air base in 1995 and returned ownership of the entire property to the government of Guam. Today, Tiyan is the location of the A. B. Won Pat International Airport.

3. Anne Perez Hattori, "Guardians of Our Soil: Indigenous Responses to Post–World War II Military Land Appropriation on Guam," in *Farms, Firms, and Runways: Perspectives on U.S. Military Bases in the Western Pacific*, ed. L. Eve Armentrout Ma (Chicago: Imprint Publications, 2001), 186. For more on liberal empire and the notion of the gift of freedom, refer to Mimi Thi Nguyen, *The Gift of Freedom: War, Debt, and Other Refugee Passages* (Durham, NC: Duke University Press, 2012).

4. For more on notions of liberation and loyalty in Guåhan, refer to Keith L. Camacho, *Cultures of Commemoration: The Politics of War, Memory, and History in the Mariana Islands* (Honolulu: University of Hawai'i Press, 2011).

5. Michael F. Phillips, "Land," in *Kinalamten Pulitikåt: Siñenten I Chamorro/Issues in Guam's Political Development: The Chamorro Perspective*, ed. Political Status Education Coordinating Commission (Hagåtña: Political Status Education Coordinating Commission, 2002), 14.

6. In the United States, most places are referred to as cities, whereas in Guåhan they are all known as villages regardless of their size and population.

7. Paul Carano and Pedro C. Sanchez, *A Complete History of Guam* (Rutland, VT: Charles E. Tuttle, 1966), 20; and Carmen Artero Kasperbauer, "The Chamorro Culture," in *Kinalamten Pulitikåt: Siñenten I Chamorro/Issues in Guam's Political Development: The Chamorro Perspective* (Hagåtña: The Political Status Education Coordinating Commission, 2002), 36.

8. Lawrence J. Cunningham, *Ancient Chamorro Society* (Honolulu: Bess Press, 1992), 170.

9. Vicente M. Diaz, *Repositioning the Missionary: Rewriting the Histories of Colonialism, Native Catholicism, and Indigeneity in Guam* (Honolulu: University of Hawai'i Press, 2010), 11; and Anne Perez Hattori, *Colonial Dis-Ease: US Navy Health Policies and the Chamorros of Guam, 1898–1941* (Honolulu: University of Hawai'i Press, 2004).

10. Christine Taitano DeLisle, "A History of Chamorro Nurse-Midwives in Guam and a 'Placental Politics' for Indigenous Feminisms," *Intersections: Gender and Sexuality in Asia and the Pacific* 37 (2015), http://intersections.anu.edu.au/issue37/delisle.htm; and Hattori, *Colonial Dis-Ease*, 122.

11. Jillette Leon-Guerrero, "Hagåtña," Guampedia.com, accessed July 1, 2020, https://www.guampedia.com/hagatna/#Origin_of_village_name_in_Chamoru.

12. Robert F. Rogers, *Destiny's Landfall: A History of Guam* (Honolulu: University of Hawai'i Press, 1995), 74–75.

13. Connie Blaz Snipes, interview with author, May 24, 2013, Dédidu, Guåhan. Hereafter cited as C. Snipes interview, May 24, 2013.

14. Hattori, *Colonial Dis-Ease*, 16.

15. Joe E. Quinata, interview with author, June 20, 2012, Los Angeles, CA. Hereafter cited as J. Quinata interview, June 20, 2012.

16. Michael Lujan Bevacqua, "Låncho: Rancho," Guampedia.com, accessed July 1, 2020, http://Guampedia.com/lancho-ranch/.

17. John S. Unpingco, interview with author, May 29, 2013, Assan, Guåhan. Hereafter cited as J. Unpingco interview, May 29, 2013.

18. In 1898 the United States defeated Spain in the Spanish-American War, which established that United States as an overseas colonial power. The Treaty of Paris resulted in the United States gaining protectorate rights over Cuba and ownership of Guåhan, the Philippines, and Puerto Rico. For more on the ascendancy of US empire in the Pacific, refer to Julian Go, "The New Sociology of Empire and Colonialism," *Sociology Compass* 3, no. 5 (2009): 775–788; and Julian Go, "Modes of Rule in America's Overseas Empire: The Philippines, Puerto Rico, Guam and Samoa," in *The Louisiana Purchase and American Expansion*, eds. Sanford Levinson and Bartholomew Sparrow (Lanham, MD: Rowen & Littlefield, 2005).

19. To Authorize the Secretary of the Navy to Transfer Land for Resettlement in Guam, and for Other Purposes, S. 1362, 79th Cong., 1st sess., Miscellaneous Bills, no. 119, September 25, 1945.

20. Typically, naval captains were stationed in Guåhan for two to three years. Once their term was over, another naval captain was appointed and served as commanding officer and naval governor of the island.

21. Rogers, *Destiny's Landfall*, 115.

22. Political Status Education Coordinating Commission, "Public Proclamation of United States Sovereignty over Guam, August 10, 1899," in *Hale'-ta Hinasso': Tinige' Put Chamorro* (Hagåtña: Political Status Education Coordinating Commission), 22.

23. Hattori, *Colonial Dis-Ease*, 102.

24. Robert K. Coote, *A Report on the Land-Use Condition and Land Problems on Guam* (Washington, DC: US Department of the Interior, 1950), 19.

25. Coote, *A Report on the Land-Use Condition*, 19.

26. L. M. Cox, E. J. Dorn, K. C. McIntosh, M. G. Cook, and Allen H. White, *The Island of Guam* (Washington, DC: Government Printing Office, 1926), 45.

27. Guam Preservation Trust, "Exploring Guam's Cultural Heritage," accessed on July 1, 2020, http://cardandcardbeta.com/cultural_orientation/.

28. For more on CHamoru agriculture in the pre–World War II era, refer to Elyssa Juline Santos, "'Practicing Economy': Chamorro Agency and US Colonial Agricultural Projects, 1898–1941" (master's thesis, University of Hawai'i at Mānoa, 2018).

29. Similar to Hawai'i, the US government knew that a Japanese attack in Guåhan was imminent. By October 1941 all naval dependents had been evacuated from the island.

30. Two of the hardest-hit villages were Hagåtña and Sumai. These two places represented the civic and commercial centers of Guåhan and were the two most populated villages as well. The naval governor resided in the village of Hagåtña, which is the capital of Guåhan, and the Pan American Company operated clippers (flying boats) and the US Marine Corps barracks were located in Sumai. For more on the history of Hagåtña, refer to Jillette Leon-Guerrero, "Hagåtña," Guampedia.com, accessed July 1, 2020, http://guampedia.com/hagatna/. For more on the history of Sumai, refer to James Oelke Farley, "Broken Spear: The Roller Coaster Existence of Sumay, Guam (1900–1941)," in Mariana History Conference (Mangilao: Guampedia.com, 2012), 9–41, https://issuu.com/guampedia/docs/marianas_late_colonial_history/17; and James Perez Viernes, "Fanhasso I Tao Tao Sumay: Displacement, Dispossession, and Survival in Guam" (master's thesis, University of Hawai'i at Mānoa, 2008).

31. Dirk Anthony Ballendorf, "Guam Military Action in World War II," in *Guam History: Perspectives*, vol. 1, eds. Lee D. Carter, William L. Wuerch, and Rosa Roberto Carter (Mangilao: University of Guam Micronesian Area Research Center, 1998), 229. Even though the Japanese

had taken control of CHamoru residences in coastal villages, for the most part they did not confiscate CHamoru lånchos except for near Tiyan.

32. For more on the Japanese military governance of Guåhan, refer to Wakako Higuchi, *The Japanese Administration of Guam, 1941–1944* (Jefferson, NC: MacFarland & Company, 2013).

33. Rosa Roberto Carter, "Education in Guam to 1950: Island and Personal History," in *Guam History: Perspectives*, vol. 1, eds. Lee D. Carter, William L. Wuerch, and Rosa Roberto Carter (Mangilao: University of Guam Micronesian Area Research Center, 1998), 202.

34. Not all CHamorus initially perceived Japanese soldiers negatively. However, this changed with the impending American invasion in 1943 and the subsequent surrender of Japanese forces in Guåhan. Refer to Carter, "Education in Guam to 1950"; and Mark-Alexander Peiper, "Guam Survivor Recalls WWII Forced March," *Pacific Daily News*, June 22, 2004, http://166.122.164 .43/archive/2004/june/06-22-17.htm.

35. In August 1944 US forces defeated Japan and reoccupied Guåhan. Subsequently, the US Navy created an area called Naval Operating Base Guam, the predecessor of Naval Base Guam. The people of Sumai were never allowed to move back to their prewar homes and are given one day a year known as "back to Sumai" to visit the graves of their relatives, now located inside Naval Base Guam.

36. The Japanese military also forced some CHamoru women into sexual servitude. Along with women from Korea and Japan, they served as "comfort women" for Japanese soldiers and were subjected to physical and sexual abuse. For more on comfort women, refer to Maria Rosa Henson, *Comfort Woman: A Filipina's Story of Prostitution and Slavery under the Japanese Military* (Lanham, MD: Rowman & Littlefield, 1999); and Tony Palomo, *An Island in Agony* (Washington, DC: Library of Congress, 1984).

37. Palomo, *An Island in Agony*, 142. For more on the forced labor of CHamorus at Tiyan, refer to Jose M. Torres, *The Massacre at Atåte* (Mangilao: University of Guam Press, 2021).

38. These averages are based on contemporary figures because historical averages were not recorded. For more on Guåhan's average temperatures, humidity, and rainfall, refer to Weather US, https://www.weather-us.com/en/guam-usa-climate.

39. Palomo, *An Island in Agony*, 142.

40. For more on the role of CHamoru interpreters from Sa'ipan during World War II, refer to Keith L. Camacho, "The Politics of Indigenous Collaboration: The Role of Chamorro Interpreters in Japan's Pacific Empire, 1914–45," *Journal of Pacific History* 43, no. 2 (2008): 207–222.

41. Palomo, *An Island in Agony*, 148.

42. In response to the Japanese military's murdering of CHamorus in Malesso', CHamorus organized and killed several Japanese soldiers in the Malesso' area. For more, refer to Torres, *The Massacre at Atåte*.

43. For more on intimate relationships and colonial memories, refer to Ann Laura Stoler, ed., *Haunted by Empire: Geographies of Intimacy in North American History* (Durham, NC: Duke University Press, 2006).

44. Kathleen R. W. Owings, ed., "The War Years on Guam: Narratives of the Chamorro Experience," vol. 1 (Mangilao: University of Guam Micronesian Area Research Center, 1981), 263.

45. D. Colt Denfeld, "'To Be Specific, It's Our Pacific': Base Selection in the Pacific from World War II to the Late 1990s," in *Farms, Firms, and Runways: Perspectives on U.S. Military Bases in the Western Pacific*, ed. L. Eve Armentrout Ma (Chicago: Imprint Publications, 2001), 54.

46. For more on communism, containment, and the Cold War, refer to John Lewis Gaddis, *The Cold War: A New History* (New York: Penguin Books, 2005); Robert J. McMahon, *The Cold War: A Very Short Introduction* (Oxford: Oxford University Press, 2003); and Leslie Holmes, *Communism: A Very Short Introduction* (Oxford: Oxford University Press, 2009).

47. Prabhakaran Paleri, *National Security: Imperatives and Challenges* (New Delhi: Tata McGraw-Hill, 2008), 45.

48. Rogers, *Destiny's Landfall*, 207. For more on the US military and the Cold War, refer to Chalmers Johnson, *Blowback: The Costs and Consequences of American Empire* (New York: Metropolitan Books, 2000); and Chalmers Johnson, *The Sorrows of Empire: Militarism, Secrecy, and the End of the Republic* (New York: Henry Holt, 2004).

49. L. J. Watson, "Status of Investigations of Land and Claims Commission. Proposed Issuance of T.A.D. Orders to OinC to Confer with Office of CNO," August 20, 1945. RG 38, US National Archives and Records Administration, College Park, MD.

50. The majority of the families from Sumai were moved east into the newly created village of Sånta Rita. A portion of Tamuneng was used as an air force base called Harmon Field (which was returned to the government of Guam in 1949). The portion of land used for the naval radio towers is now referred to as Radio Barrigada, and the land at Tiyan was primarily ranch and farmland of the families who lived in the surrounding villages of Barigåda, Hagåtña, and MongMong-To'to-Maite'. Furthermore, portions of Yigu became Northwest Field, which is now known as Andersen Air Force Base.

51. The military's strategy in using Western law to acquire land in Oceania also occurred in places such as the Marshall Islands.

52. Land and Claims Commission, Guam to the Chief of Naval Operations, "Scope of Program and Request for Personnel—Report on," December 18, 1945. RG 38, US National Archives and Records Administration, College Park, MD.

53. John C. Fischer, "Statement of Chief Justice of Guam for Secretary John T. Koehler Concerning the Status and Situation of the Land Acquisition Program on Guam Insofar as the Courts Are Involved," January 8, 1950. RG 38, US National Archives and Records Administration, College Park, MD.

54. From 1900 to 1941 and from 1945 to 1950, the US Navy administered all of the public schools on Guåhan. These schools taught CHamorus a minimal understanding of English and math. For example, the core curriculum for public schools in Guåhan was predicated on the teaching of the English language (students were punished if they spoke CHamoru in school), math, health/sanitation, and citizenship. Moreover, the highest level of schooling students could obtain was middle school. If they wanted to earn a high school degree or a college degree, they had to attend school off-island. Thus, this prewar education system placed landowners at a disadvantage when interacting with commission officials. For more on Guåhan's prewar education system, refer to Pilar C. Lujan, "The Role of Education in the Preservation of the Indigenous Language of Guam," in *Kinalamten Pulitikåt: Siñenten I Chamorro/Issues in Guam's Political Development: The Chamorro Perspective* (Hagåtña: Political Status Education Coordinating Commission, 2002), 17–25; and Robert A. Underwood, "American Education and the Acculturation of the Chamorros of Guam" (PhD diss., University of Southern California, 1987).

55. The governor of Guam and the navy had the authority to appoint the judge of the superior court until 1950.

56. Many CHamorus in the past and present have expressed concern over the appraisal of land in postwar Guåhan. Specifically, they have argued that the military frequently compensated landowners for their property based on the value of when they first occupied private lands instead of the time of when the settlements were filed. This resulted in lower settlements since the military did not take into account inflation. For more on military land taking, refer to Phillips, "Land," 2–16.

57. Louis J. Rauber, "Guam Land and Claims Commission and Guam Land Transfer Board," September 24, 1948. RG 313, US National Archives and Records Administration, San Bruno, CA.

58. The request for a civilian committee to evaluate the navy's administration in American Sāmoa and Guåhan suggests that naval governance on both islands was problematic. It also highlights that American Sāmoa and Guåhan were both integral sites in the creation of the US military's Pacific base network.

59. "Military necessity" refers to the idea that certain actions prohibited in times of peace are allowed during times of war. For more, refer to Luis Paulo Bogliolo, "Rethinking Military Necessity in the Law of Armed Conflict" (Brasilia: University of Brazil, 2012); and Nobuo Hayashi, "Military Necessity as Normative Indifference," in *Georgetown Journal of International Law*, vol. 44, 2013, 675–782, https://www.law.georgetown.edu/academics/law-journals/gjil/recent/upload/zsx00213000675.PDF.

60. Ernest M. Hopkins, Maurice J. Tobin, and Knowles A. Ryerson, "Hopkins Committee Report on the Civil Governments of Guam and American Samoa," March 25, 1947. Hopkins Report Vertical File, Nieves M. Flores Memorial Library, Hagåtña, Guåhan.

61. Hopkins, Tobin, and Ryerson, "Hopkins Committee Report."

62. Rogers, *Destiny's Landfall*, 216.

63. For more on gift culture, refer to Nicholas Thomas, *Islanders: The Pacific in the Age of Empire* (New Haven, CT: Yale University Press, 2012); and Nicholas Thomas, *Entangled Objects: Exchange, Material Culture, and Colonialism in the Pacific* (Cambridge, MA: Harvard University Press, 1991).

64. Hattori, "Guardians of Our Soil," 190.

65. Cesar J. Ayala and Jose L. Bolivar, *Battleship Vieques: Puerto Rico from World War II to the Korean War* (Princeton, NJ: Markus Wiener Publishers, 2011), 58.

66. Carlos P. Taitano, personal communication to author, October 10, 2008, Los Angeles, CA. In 2007 and 2008 I had the opportunity to have several conversations with Carlos P. Taitano (since deceased), who frequently told me that CHamorus were afraid of the US military. This was especially the sentiment among CHamorus who were adults during World War II. Taitano had many interactions with American officials because he was a businessman, Guam congressional member, lawyer, and a US military officer. He was also an instrumental member of the Guam Congress walkout and was the only CHamoru present at the signing of the Organic Act of 1950.

67. US House Sub-Committee on Public Lands, November 22, 1949, RG 38, US National Archives and Records Administration, College Park, MD, 56. Hereafter cited as US House Sub-Committee, November 22, 1949.

68. Guam Congress, Senate, Subcommittee on Territories of the Senate, Committee on Interior and Insular Affairs, S. 1215, 11th Legislature, August 4, 1971, Federal Land Taking, Vertical File, Nieves M. Flores Memorial Library, Hagåtña, Guåhan. The quotation for this record is a 1971 reference to the 1940s and 1950s.

69. Federal Land Taking Questionnaire of Felicita Santos San Nicolas, April 10, 1974, Federal Land Taking, Vertical File, Nieves M. Flores Memorial Library, Hagåtña, Guåhan.

70. Federal Land Taking Questionnaire of Delfina Cruz, April 10, 1974, Federal Land Taking, Vertical File, Nieves M. Flores Memorial Library, Hagåtña, Guåhan.

71. Joe T. San Agustin, interview with author, May 5, 2013, Dédidu, Guåhan. Hereafter cited as J. San Agustin interview, May 5, 2013.

72. Antonio Artero Sablan, interview with author, April 17, 2013, Hagåtña, Guåhan. Hereafter cited as A. Sablan interview, April 17, 2013.

73. Federal Land Taking Questionnaire of Ciriaco C. Sanchez, April 10, 1974, Federal Land Taking, Vertical File, Nieves M. Flores Memorial Library, Hagåtña, Guåhan.

74. Federal Land Taking Questionnaire of Fancisco S. Santos, April 11, 1974, Federal Land Taking, Vertical File, Nieves M. Flores Memorial Library, Hagåtña, Guåhan.

75. Federal Land Taking Questionnaire of Urelia Anderson Francisco, April 10/11, 1974, Federal Land Taking, Vertical File, Nieves M. Flores Memorial Library, Hagåtña, Guåhan.

76. C. A. Pownall, "Availability of Guamanians for Consultation and Evidence," December 28, 1946, RG 313, US National Archives and Records Administration, San Bruno, CA.

77. Camacho, *Cultures of Commemoration*, 137. For more on strategies of resistance, refer to James C. Scott, *Domination and the Arts of Resistance: Hidden Transcripts* (New Haven, CT: Yale University Press, 1990).

78. Ed Benavente, interview with author, May 4, 2013, Mangilao, Guåhan. Hereafter cited as E. Benavente interview, May 4, 2013.

79. J. Quinata interview, June 20, 2012.

80. C. Snipes interview, May 24, 2013.

81. Jose P. De Leon, "Reoccupation of Privately-owned Home, Request for," July 29, 1946, RG 313, US National Archives and Records Administration, San Bruno, CA.

82. K. B. Salisbury, "Reoccupation of Privately-owned Home—Request for," August 15, 1946, RG 313, US National Archives and Records Administration, San Bruno, CA.

83. Phillips, "Land," 10.

84. Harold Schwartz, "Policy Regarding Disposition of Government-owned Property Remaining on Lands Released for Guamanian Uses," January 23, 1948, RG 313, US National Archives and Records Administration, San Bruno, CA.

85. Federal Land Taking Questionnaire of Galo Lujan Salas, April 10, 1974, Federal Land Taking Vertical File, Nieves M. Flores Memorial Library, Hagåtña, Guåhan.

86. US House Sub-Committee on Public Lands, November 22, 1949, 54.

87. US House Sub-Committee on Public Lands, November 22, 1949, 54.

88. Joaquin Pangelinan Perez, interview with author, May 6, 2013, Hagåtña, Guåhan. Hereafter cited as J. Perez interview, May 6, 2013.

89. There are several dozen military recreational areas throughout the island. Most of these sites are located inside military bases and installations. However, Tomhom Beach and Admiral Nimitz Golf Course were two of the earliest areas designated as recreational facilities for the military. Tomhom Beach is located on the western coast of Guåhan. Today, it is the center of Guåhan's tourist industry, where the majority of the island's department stores, hotels, and restaurants are located. The development of Guåhan's tourist industry began in the late 1970s. As a result, Guåhan's economy primarily relies on tourism from Japan and US military spending and employment. For more on tourism in the Pacific, refer to Vernadette Vicuña Gonzalez, *Securing Paradise: Tourism and Militarism in Hawai'i and the Philippines* (Durham, NC: Duke University Press, 2013); and Teresia Teaiwa, "Reading Paul Gauguin's *Noa Noa* with Epeli Hau'ofa's *Kiss in the Nederends*: Militourism, Feminism, and the 'Polynesian' Body," in *Inside Out: Literature, Cultural Politics, and Identity in the New Pacific*, eds. Vilsoni Hereniko and Rob Wilson (Lanham, MD: Rowman & Littlefield, 1999), 249–264.

90. Simon A. Sanchez, "Resolution Adopted by the Guam Congress on 1 May 1948," May 10, 1948, Land Taking (Federal) Vertical File, Nieves M. Flores Memorial Library, Hagåtña, Guåhan.

91. Sanchez, "Resolution Adopted by the Guam Congress."

92. Doloris Coulter, "Editor's Note," *Guam Echo*, June 30, 1948, 5.

93. In 1946 the US Navy constructed a golf course in the village of Barigåda called Admiral Nimitz Golf Course. A large portion of this golf course was constructed on privately owned land for military personnel.

94. John T. Koehler, "Guam Land Acquisition Program," April 18, 1950, RG 38, US National Archives and Records Administration, College Park, MD, 11.

95. Koehler, "Guam Land Acquisition Program," 11. Most major American companies were prohibited from setting up businesses on Guåhan. However, this would change with the lifting the security clearance in 1962.

96. Robert A. Underwood, interview with author, April 22, 2013, Mangilao, Guåhan. Hereafter cited as R. Underwood interview, April 22, 2013. Robert Underwood is the former president of the University of Guam. From 1993 to 2003, he served as delegate to the US Congress and sat on several congressional committees. The village of Piti is located on the western coast of Guåhan, near US Naval Base Guam.

97. Catherine Punzalan Flores McCollum, interview with the author, May 7, 2013, Hagåtña, Guåhan. Hereafter cited as C. McCollum interview, May 7, 2013.

98. Evidence regarding how much land the military has paid for or simply acquired for free is unclear due to the scant documents that exist. This is especially the case for land that the military acquired for free since it simply occupied it during World War II and never returned it.

99. Shannon J. Murphy, "Institute of Ethnic Affairs," Guampedia.com, accessed on May 1, 2020, http://www.guampedia.com/institute-of-ethnic-affairs/. Thompson was the first American anthropologist to study pre–World War II Guåhan and was author of *Guam and Its People* (1941). Not only were Collier and Thompson members of the Institute of Ethnic Affairs, they were also contributors to the *Guam Echo* and spent much of their time in the postwar years lobbying for CHamorus to be given US citizenship. Collier and Thompson would eventually divorce. Collier then married Grace E. Volk in 1957. For more on Laura M. Thompson, refer to Rebecca A. Stephenson, "Laura Thompson," Guampedia.com, accused on May 1, 2020, http://www.guampedia.com/laura-thompson/.

100. John Collier, "Guam Citizens," *Washington Post*, December 4, 1946, 6.

101. For more on Doloris Coulter and the Institute of Ethnic Affairs, refer to Doloris Coulter Cogan, *We Fought the Navy and Won: Guam's Quest for Democracy* (Honolulu: University of Hawai'i Press, 2008).

102. Cogan, *We Fought the Navy and Won,* 61.

103. Murphy, "Institute of Ethnic Affairs."

104. The Indian Reorganization Act (IRA) is also known as the Indian New Deal or the Wheeler-Howard Act. In theory, this policy gave authority back to American Indian tribes to govern their remaining lands. However, the act did not return or compensate them for the land that had been taken and settled. The ultimate goal of the IRA was to reverse the Dawes Act of 1884, which was an assimilative policy that divided tribal lands into individual parcels. It also gave corporations access to plots of land that the US government deemed as excess.

105. For more on John Collier's life and experiences as a US government official, refer to Jodi A. Byrd, *The Transit of Empire: Indigenous Critiques of Colonialism* (Minneapolis: University of Minnesota Press, 2011); and John Collier, *From Every Zenith: A Memoir; and Some Essays on Life and Thought* (Thousand Oaks, CA: Sage Books, 1963).

106. *New York Times*, "Forgotten Guam," February 20, 1946, 23.

107. For more on the Guam Congress walkout, refer to Cogan, *We Fought the Navy and Won*; and Anne Perez Hattori, "Righting Civil Wrongs: Guam Congress Walkout of 1949," in *Kinalamten Pulitikåt: Siñenten I Chamorro/Issues in Guam's Political Development: The Chamorro Perspective* (Hagåtña: Political Status Education Coordinating Commission, 2002), 57–69.

108. Hattori, "Righting Civil Wrongs," 58.

109. Vanessa Warheit, dir., *The Insular Empire: America in the Mariana Islands* (Palo Alto, CA: Horse Opera Productions, 2009), DVD.

110. Kristin Oberiano, "Territorial Discontent: Chamorros, Filipinos, and the Making of the United States Empire on Guam" (PhD diss., Harvard University, 2021), 232–233.

2. The Remaking of Guåhan

1. For more on the social roles of local media in the Pacific, refer to Francis Dalisay, "Social Control in an American Pacific Island: Guam's Local Newspaper Reports on Liberation," *Journal of Communication and Inquiry* 33, no. 3 (July 2009): 239–257.

2. Christine Taitano DeLisle and Vicente M. Diaz, "Itinerant Indigeneities: Navigating Guåhan's Treacherous Roads through CHamoru Feminist Pathways," in *Allotment Stories: Indigenous Land Relations under Settler Siege*, eds. Daniel Heath Justice and Jean M. O'Brien (Minneapolis: University of Minnesota Press, 2021), 147.

3. Christina Klein, *Cold War Orientalism: Asia in the Middlebrow Imagination, 1945–1961* (Berkeley: University of California Press, 2003), 7.

4. Vernadette Vicuña Gonzalez, *Securing Paradise: Tourism and Militarism in Hawai'i and the Philippines* (Durham, NC: Duke University Press, 2013), 12.

5. Mark L. Gillem, *America Town: Building the Outposts of Empire* (Minneapolis: University of Minnesota Press, 2007), xv. For more on militarized suburbanization, refer to Lauren Hirshberg, *Suburban Empire: Cold War Militarization in the US Pacific* (Oakland: University of California Press, 2022); Matthew Farish, *The Contours of America's Cold War* (Minneapolis: University of Minnesota Press, 2010); and Catherine Lutz, *Homefront: An American City and the American Twentieth Century* (Boston: Beacon Press, 2002).

6. Raymond Williams, *Keywords: A Vocabulary of Culture and Society* (New York: Oxford University Press, 1983), 208. For more on US modernization, refer to David Ekbladh, *The Great American Mission: Modernization and the Construction of an American World Order* (Princeton, NJ: Princeton University Press, 2010).

7. In the prewar era, the military suggested minor infrastructure improvements with the dredging of Apapa Harbor and the paving of the road that would later become known as Marine Corps Drive. The US government did not fully fund these projects because Guåhan was used as a coaling station and had little strategic value. Guåhan then became vital to American military operations due to World War II, nuclearism, and the Cold War.

8. David Hanlon, *Remaking Micronesia: Discourses over Development in a Pacific Territory, 1944–1982* (Honolulu: University of Hawai'i Press, 1998), 10.

9. For more on US military public health policies in Hawai'i, refer to Juliet Nebolon, "'Life Given Straight from the Heart': Settler Militarism, Biopolitics, and Public Health in Hawai'i during World War II," *American Quarterly* 69, no. 1 (2017): 23–45.

10. Anne Perez Hattori, *Colonial Dis-Ease: US Navy Health Policies and the Chamorros of Guam, 1898–1941* (Honolulu: University of Hawai'i, 2004), 40–41.

11. For more on US colonial health and education policies, refer to Hattori, *Colonial Dis-Ease*; Christine Taitano DeLisle, "A History of Chamorro Nurse-Midwives in Guam and a 'Placental Politics' for Indigenous Feminism," in *Intersections: Gender and Sexuality in Asia and the Pacific* 37 (March 2015), http://intersections.anu.edu.au/issue37/delisle.htm; and Robert A. Underwood, "American Education and the Acculturation of the Chamorros of Guam" (PhD diss., University of Southern California, 1987).

12. For more on the importance of US naval power, refer to Alfred Thayer Mahan, *The Influence of Sea Power upon History, 1660–1873* (Boston: Little, Brown, 1890); George C. Herring, *From Colony to Superpower: U.S. Foreign Relations since 1776* (New York: Oxford University Press, 2008); and Steven High, *Base Colonies in the Western Hemisphere, 1940–1967* (New York: Palgrave Macmillan, 2009).

13. During the Spanish period, ports in the villages of Hagåtña and Humåtak (Umatac) were utilized more frequently. While Spain was the first foreign nation to use Apapa Harbor as

a port, in the mid to late nineteenth century, it was the US Navy in the early twentieth century that primarily relied on it for commercial and military use. For more on the history of Apapa Harbor, refer to Robert Rogers, *Destiny's Landfall: A History of Guam* (Honolulu: University of Hawai'i Press, 1995); and Michael R. Clement Jr. and Marie Ada Ayong, "Apra Harbor," Guampedia.com, accessed August 1, 2020, http://www.guampedia.com/apra -harbor/.

14. Henry P. Beers, *American Naval Occupation and Government of Guam, 1898–1902* (Washington, DC: Navy Department, 1944), 5; RG 313, US National Archives and Records Administration, College Park, MD.

15. Beers, *American Naval Operations*, n.p.

16. For more on US corporate interests to find and create consumers, refer to Walter LaFeber, *The New Empire: An Interpretation of American Expansionism 1860–1898* (Ithaca, NY: Cornell University Press, 1998); and Matthew Frye Jacobson, *Barbarian Virtues: The United States Encounters Foreign Peoples at Home and Abroad 1876–1917* (New York: Hill & Wang, 2000).

17. For more on the US military's interest in Pearl Harbor, refer to John R. Eperjesi, "Basing the Pacific: Exceptional Spaces of the Wilkes Exploring Expedition, 1838–1842," *Amerasia Journal* 37, no. 3 (2011): 1–17; and Jon Kamakawiwo'ole Osorio, "Memorializing Pu'uloa and Remembering Pearl Harbor," in *Militarized Currents: Toward a Decolonized Future in Asia and the Pacific*, eds. Setsu Shigematsu and Keith L. Camacho (Minneapolis: University of Minnesota Press, 2010), 3–14.

18. J. F. Beane, *From Forecastle to Cabin* (New York: Editor Publishing Co., 1905), 272, Vertical File, Nieves M. Flores Memorial Library, Hagåtña, Guåhan.

19. Mary Augusta Channell, "A Bit of Guam Life," *The Independent*, 1902, 607–608, Guam History Vertical File, Nieves M. Flores Memorial Library, Hagåtña, Guåhan.

20. DeLisle and Diaz, *Itinerant Indigeneities*, 148. This road would later become the southern end of Marine Corps Drive.

21. George L. Dyer, "The Present Condition of Guam," *The Independent*, April 20, 1905, 886, Guam History Vertical File, Nieves M. Flores Memorial Library, Hagåtña, Guåhan.

22. Dyer, "The Present Condition," 932. For more on the construction of modern roads and highways, refer to Tom Lewis, *Divided Highways: Building the Interstate Highways, Transforming American Life* (Ithaca, NY: Cornell University Press, 2013); and Earl Swift, *The Big Roads: The Untold Stories of the Engineers, Visionaries, and Trailblazers who Created the American Superhighways* (New York: Mariner Books, 2012).

23. L. M. Cox, E. J. Dorn, K. C. McIntosh, M. G. Cook, and Allen H. White, *The Island of Guam* (Washington, DC: Government Printing Office, 1926), 50.

24. DeLisle and Diaz, *Itinerant Indigeneities*, 148–149.

25. Jay Earle Thomson, *Our Pacific Possessions* (New York: Charles Scribner's Sons, 1931), 247, University of the Philippines Diliman, University Archives and Records Depository.

26. "The Way Houses Were Made in the 1900s," Hunker.com, accessed August 1, 2020, https://www.hunker.com/12567970/the-way-houses-were-made-in-the-1900s.

27. Beane, *From Forecastle to Cabin*, 253.

28. Beane, 253.

29. For more on pre–World War II pole and thatched homes, refer to Lawrence J. Cunningham, "Pole and Thatched Homes," Guampedia.com, accessed August 5, 2020, http://www .guampedia.com/pole-and-thatched-homes/.

30. For more on CHamoru material culture, refer to Judy Selk Flores, *Estorian Inalahan: History of a Spanish Era Village in Guam* (Hagåtña: Irensia Publications, 2011); and Michael Lujan

Bevacqua, "Lâncho: Ranch," Guampedia.com, accessed July 1, 2020, https://www.guampedia .com/lancho-ranch/.

31. Dyer, "The Present Condition," 886; US Air Force, *Guam: Key to the Pacific* (Guam: Andersen Air Force Base, 1947), 13, University of Guam, Richard F. Taitano Micronesian Area Research Center; and Nicholas Yamashita Quinata, "Wood and Tin Houses," Guampedia.com, accessed August 1, 2020, http://www.guampedia.com/wood-and-tin-houses/.

32. For more on race and nationality during World War II, refer to T. Fujitani, *Race for Empire: Koreans as Japanese and Japanese as Americans during World War II* (Berkeley: University of CA Press, 2013); and John W. Dower, *War without Mercy: Race and Power in the Pacific War* (New York: Pantheon, 1987).

33. *Life*, "Guam: U.S. Makes," 71. The generalization of Pacific Islanders as being impressed by military might and goods is a major issue in Melanesian studies of World War II. Refer to Lamont Lindstrom, *Cargo Cult: Strange Stories of Desire from Melanesia and Beyond* (Honolulu: University of Hawai'i Press, 1993).

34. For more on the racialization of labor during World War II, refer to Andrew Friedman, "U.S. Empire, World War 2 and the Racialising of Labor," *Race and Class* 58, no. 4 (2017): 24.

35. DeLisle and Diaz, "Itinerant Indigeneities," 147.

36. Julie Greene, *The Canal Builders: Making America's Empire at the Panama Canal* (New York: Penguin, 2009), 1–3.

37. *Life*, "Guam: U.S. Makes," 65.

38. Henry L. Larson, "The Story of Guam," *Navy News*, January 5, 1946, Guam History Vertical File, Nieves M. Flores Memorial Library, Hagåtña, Guåhan.

39. For more on US military and benevolent paternalism, refer to Mary A. Renda, *Taking Haiti: Military Occupation and the Culture of U.S. Imperialism, 1915–1940* (Chapel Hill: University of North Carolina Press, 2001).

40. *Public Relations Newsletter*, "Community Relations Stressed by UnderSecNav," November 18, 1949, vol. 1, no. 37, RG 313 Naval Government Unit, US National Archives and Records Administration, San Bruno, CA.

41. *New York Times*, "Guam Is Declared New Pearl Harbor," April 22, 1945.

42. *New York Times*, "Guam Is Declared," n.p.

43. In the postwar era, the US government invested in military infrastructure expansion throughout the Asia-Pacific region that included places such as Hawai'i, Japan, the Marshall Islands, Okinawa, the Philippines, and South Korea, to name a few. For more on the militarization of the Marshall Islands, refer to Hirshberg, *Suburban Empire*.

44. Harold H. Martin, "Heart Trouble in Paradise," *Saturday Evening Post*, November 1, 1947.

45. US Air Force, *Guam: Key to the Pacific*, 13.

46. *New York Times*, "Guam Converted into Big Fortress," December 6, 1944.

47. *New York Times*, "Guam Is Declared."

48. For more on manifest destiny, refer to Anders Stephanson, *Manifest Destiny: American Expansionism and the Empire of Right* (New York: Hill & Wang, 1996); Robert J. Miller, *Native America, Discovered and Conquered: Thomas Jefferson, Lewis and Clark, and Manifest Destiny* (Lincoln, NE: Bison Books, 2008); Frederick Jackson Turner, *The Significance of the Frontier in American History* (Eastford, CT: Martino Fine Books, 2014); and Amy S. Greenberg, *Manifest Destiny and American Territorial Expansion: A Brief History with Documents* (New York: Bedford/St. Martin's, 2011).

49. For more on ecological theory, refer to Elizabeth M. DeLoughrey, "The Myth of Isolates: Ecosystem Ecologies in the Nuclear Pacific," *Cultural Geographies* 20, no. 2 (2012): 167–184; and

Elizabeth M. DeLoughrey, "Heliotropes: Solar Ecologies and Pacific Radiations," in *Postcolonial Ecologies: Literatures of the Environment*, eds. Elizabeth M. DeLoughrey and George B. Handley (New York: Oxford University Press, 2011), 235–253.

50. Hanlon, *Remaking Micronesia*, 10.

51. Anthony Leon Guerrero, "The Economic Development of Guam," in *Kinalamten Pulitikåt: Siñenten I Chamorro/Issues in Guam's Political Development: The Chamorro Perspective* (Hagåtña: Political Status Education Coordinating Commission, 2002), 91. For more on US military bases and Cold War operations in Guåhan, refer to Mark Forbes, "Military," in *Kinalamten Pulitikåt: Siñenten I Chamorro/Issues in Guam's Political Development: The Chamorro Perspective* (Hagåtña: Political Status Education Coordinating Commission, 2002), 39–44; and Rogers, *Destiny's Landfall*.

52. Anthony Ramirez, personal communication, Barigåda, Guåhan. August 3, 2009.

53. Keith L. Camacho, *Cultures of Commemoration: The Politics of War, Memory, and History in the Mariana Islands* (Honolulu: University of Hawai'i Press, 2011), 2.

54. *Navy News*, "Island Rebuilding to Include Modern Homes for Guamanians," February 10, 1946, Vertical File, Nieves M. Flores Memorial Library, Hagåtña, Guåhan.

55. Former residents and descendants of the village of Sumai are permitted to visit Naval Base Guam once a year, on what is known as "Back to Sumai Day." This includes various ceremonies and speeches that take place on the former village site. The village cemetery still exists; CHamorus are allowed to visit their ancestors only with navy permission.

56. Janice J. Beaty, *Discovering Guam: A Guide to Its Towns, Trails and Tenants* (Tokyo: Faith Book Store, 1968), 18.

57. Laura Thompson, "Crisis on Guam," *Far Eastern Quarterly*, November 1946, 165; *Guam Echo*, Vertical File, Nieves M. Flores Memorial Library, Hagåtña, Guåhan.

58. The suburbanization outside of military bases did not become widespread until after 1962. In August 1962 the security clearance program was lifted, and in November 1962 Typhoon Karen destroyed 90 percent of the island's structures, which also made the construction of new homes necessary. Private contractors adopted the Kaiser prefabricated homes model that was made with reinforced rebar and concrete. However, these homes were problematic because they absorbed heat easily. For more information on Kaiser prefabricated homes on Guam, refer to Nicholas Yamashita Quinata, "Kaiser Pre-Fab Homes," Guampedia.com, accessed August 20, 2020, http://www.guampedia.com/kaiser-pre-fab-homes/

59. Walter Sullivan, "Guam Mushrooms into a Metropolis," *New York Times*, November 30, 1948.

60. Lauren Hirshberg, "Home Land (In)security: The Labor of U.S. Cold War Military Empire in the Marshall Islands," in *Making the Empire Work: Labor and United States Imperialism,* eds. Daniel E. Bender and Jana K. Lipman (New York: New York University Press, 2015), 341; and Lauren Hirshberg, "Nuclear Families: (Re)producing 1950s Suburban America in the Marshall Islands," *OAH Magazine of History* 26, no. 4 (2012): 2–3.

61. *Territorial Sun*, "$20 Million Capehart Project Starts," October 26, 1958, University of Guam's Richard F. Taitano Micronesian Area Research Center.

62. Stuart L. Udall, *America's Day Begins in Guam . . . U.S.A.* (Washington, DC: Office of Territories, 1967) 6–7.

63. Gillem, *America Town*, xv.

64. Robert Trumbull, "Congress Delays Guam Rebuilding," *New York Times*, February 19, 1946.

65. Robert Trumbull was born in Chicago in 1912 and served as a journalist for the *New York Times* covering Asia, the Middle East, and the Pacific. He covered important events such as

the day Pakistan became independent and interviewed people such as Ho Chi Minh. For more on Trumbull's life, refer to *New York Times*, "Robert Trumbull Dies at 80; Reported on War for Times," October 13, 1992, B6, accessed August 1, 2020, https://www.nytimes.com/1992/10/13/obituaries/robert-trumbull-dies-at-80-reported-on-war-for-times.html.

66. US Air Force, *Guam: Key to the Pacific*, 7.

67. Wing Public Information Office, *Destination Guam* (Guam: Andersen Air Force Base, 1950), 22, University of Guam, Richard F. Taitano Micronesian Area Research Center.

68. US Air Force, *Guam: Key to the Pacific*, 16.

69. Lizabeth Cohen, *A Consumers' Republic: The Politics of Mass Consumption in Postwar America* (New York: Vintage Books, 2003), 7.

70. Paul Carano, *Guam: Andersen Air Force Base* (Guam: Andersen Air Force Base, 1950), 19. University of Guam, Richard F. Taitano Micronesian Area Research Center.

71. For more on military, femininity, and gendered social norms, refer to Cynthia Enloe, *Bananas, Beaches and Bases: Making Feminist Sense of International Politics* (Berkeley: University of California Press, 2000).

72. In 1946 the navy opened the Admiral Nimitz eighteen-hole golf course, which was for military use only. This golf course was built on land that was condemned in the postwar era and did not allow local civilian use until 1997.

73. Vernon T. Bull, Letter to U.S. Navy in Washington D.C., November 13, 1947, RG 313, US National Archives and Records Administration, San Bruno, CA.

74. Ronald Levitt, "In Behalf of the Gooney Birds," *Our Navy*, July 1953, 11, Navy Vertical File, Nieves M. Flores Memorial Library, Hagåtña, Guåhan.

75. Christen Tsuyuko Sasaki, "Threads of Empire: Militourism and the Aloha Wear Industry in Hawai'i," *American Quarterly* 68, no. 3 (2016): 652.

76. Teresia Teaiwa, "Reading Paul Gauguin's *Noa Noa* with Epeli Hau'ofa's *Kisses in the Nederends*: Militourism, Feminism, and the 'Polynesian' Body" in *Inside Out: Literature, Cultural Politics, and Identity in the New Pacific*, eds. Vilsoni Hereniko and Rob Wilson (Lanham, MD: Rowman & Littlefield, 1999), 251. For more on militarism and tourism in the Pacific, refer to Vernadette Vicuña Gonzalez, *Securing Paradise: Tourism and Militarism in Hawai'i and the Philippines* (Durham, NC: Duke University Press, 2013); and Christine Taitano DeLisle, "Destination Chamorro Culture: Notes on Realignment, Rebranding, and Post-9/11 Militourism in Guam," *American Quarterly* 68, no. 3 (2016), 563–572.

77. *Industrial Miners Gazette*, "Places to See on Guam," September 10, 1949, vol. 10, no. 5, 3, RG 313 Naval Government Unit, US National Archives, San Bruno, CA.

78. Vernadette Vicuña Gonzalez and Jana K. Lipman, "Introduction: Tours of Duty and Tours of Leisure," *American Quarterly* 68, no. 3 (2016): 511.

79. *Pacific Area Travel Association*, "Pacific News," March 17, 1967.

80. US Air Force, *Guam: Key to the Pacific*, 20.

81. Udall, *America's Day Begins*, 8.

82. *Life*, "Guam: U.S. Makes," 74.

83. US Air Force, *Guam: Key to the Pacific*, 20.

84. US Air Force, 20.

85. Carano, *Guam: Andersen Air*, 15.

86. *Christian Science Monitor*, "Guam Dissatisfied," December 2, 1946, Navy Vertical File, Nieves M. Flores Memorial Library, Hagåtña, Guåhan.

87. Ford Q. Elvidge, "I Ruled Uncle Sam's Problem Child," *Saturday Evening Post*, December 1, 1956, Ford Elvidge Vertical File, Nieves M. Flores Memorial Library, Hagåtña, Guåhan.

3. The Civilian Military Workers of Guåhan

1. Wesley Attewell, "The Lifelines of Empire: Logistics as Infrastructural Power in Occupied South Vietnam," *American Quarterly* 72, no. 4 (2020), 909.

2. Adam Moore, *Empire's Labor: The Global Army that Supports U.S. Wars* (Ithaca: NY: Cornell University Press, 2019), 4.

3. Robert F. Rogers, *Destiny's Landfall: A History of Guam* (Honolulu: University of Hawai'i Press, 1995), 217–218.

4. Pacificweb, "Guam," Pacificweb.org, accessed May 15, 2014, http://www.pacificweb.org/DOCS/guam/NewUploads_11_07/Guam%201950.pdf; Paul Carano and Pedro C. Sanchez, *A Complete History of Guam* (Rutland, VT: Charles E. Tuttle, 1966), 329; Vicente M. Diaz, "'Fight Boys, til the Last . . .': Islandstyle Football and the Remasculinization of Indigeneity in the Militarized American Pacific Islands," in *Pacific Diaspora: Island Peoples in the United States and across the Pacific,* eds. Paul Spickard, Joanne L. Rondilla, and Debbie Hippolite Wright (Honolulu: University of Hawai'i Press, 2002), 175; and Rogers, *Destiny's Landfall,* 217. The CHamoru population of Guåhan was 22,177 in 1940, 27,124 in 1950, 34,762 in 1960, and 59,860 in 2015.

5. Andrew Friedman, "US Empire, World War 2 and the Racialising of Labour," *Race and Class* 58, no. 4 (2017), 23. For more on empire, labor, and race, refer to Moore, *Empire's Labor*; Daniel E. Bender and Jana K. Lipman, eds., *Making the Empire Work: Labor and United States Imperialism* (New York: New York University Press, 2015); Paul Kramer, *Blood of Government: Race, Empire, the United States and the Philippines* (Chapel Hill: University of North Carolina Press, 2006); Paul Spickard, *Almost All Aliens: Immigration, Race, and Colonialism in American History and Identity* (New York: Routledge, 2007); and Eric T. L. Love, *Empire over Race: Racism and U.S. Imperialism, 1865–1900* (Chapel Hill: University of North Carolina Press, 2004).

6. Valerie Yap, "From Transient Migration to Homemaking: Filipino Immigrants in Guam," in *The Age of Asian Migration: Continuity, Diversity, and Susceptibility,* vol. 2, eds. Yuk Wah Chan, Heidi Fung, and Grazyna Szymańska-Matusiewicz (Newcastle: Cambridge Scholars Publishing, 2015), 157.

7. JoAnna Poblete, *Islanders in the Empire: Filipino and Puerto Rican Laborers in Hawai'i* (Urbana: University of Illinois Press), 3.

8. For more on the systematic exploitation of labor, refer to Iyko Day, *Alien Capital: Asian Racialization and the Logic of Settler Colonial Capitalism* (Durham, NC: Duke University Press, 2016); Julie Greene, *The Canal Builders: Making America's Empire at the Panama Canal* (New York: Penguin Press, 2009); Jana K. Lipman, *Guantánamo: A Working-Class History between Empire and Revolution* (Berkeley: University of California Press, 2009); and Jason M. Colby, *The Business of Empire: United Fruit, Race, and U.S. Expansion in Central America* (Ithaca, NY: Cornell University Press, 2011).

9. Simeon Man, *Soldiering through Empire: Race and the Making of the Decolonizing Pacific* (Oakland: University of California Press, 2018), 10.

10. For more on this history of Seabee operations in the Pacific during World War II, refer to D. Harry Hammer, *Lion Six* (Annapolis, MD: United States Naval Institute, 1947).

11. Suzanne Falgout, Lin Poyer, and Laurence M. Carucci, *Memories of War: Micronesians in the Pacific War* (Honolulu: University of Hawai'i Press, 2008), 189 and 197. As I discuss in chapter 5, CHamorus were forced to clear these fields under Japanese occupation during World War II. The Japanese military used them as airfields during World War II until the US military recaptured the island and had the airfields paved.

12. Office of Naval Intelligence, "Strategic Study of Guam ONI-99," February 1, 1944, Nieves M. Flores Memorial Library, Hagåtña, Guåhan, 288.

13. Victor F. Bleasdale, "Monthly Report," March 1, 1946, RG 313, US National Archives and Records Administration, College Park, MD.

14. For more on pre–World War II US education in Guåhan, refer to Anne Perez Hattori, *Colonial Dis-Ease: U.S. Navy Health Policies and the Chamorros of Guam, 1898–1941*; Christine Taitano DeLisle, *Placental Politics: CHamoru Women, White Womanhood, and Indigeneity under U.S. Colonialism in Guam* (Chapel Hill: University of North Carolina Press, 2021); Alfred P. Flores, "US Colonial Education in Guam, 1899–1950," in *Oxford Research Encyclopedias of American History* (March 2019), https://doi.org/10.1093/acrefore/9780199329175.013.512; and Robert A. Underwood, "American Education and the Acculturation of the Chamorros of Guam" (PhD diss., University of Southern California, 1987).

15. For more on CHamoru women and US military health policies, refer to DeLisle, *Placental Politics*; and Hattori, *Colonial Dis-Ease*. For more on the exploitation of women as launderers in US militarized spaces, refer to Cynthia Enloe, *Bananas, Beaches and Bases: Making Feminist Sense of International Politics* (Berkeley: University of California Press, 2000), 136–140.

16. David Hanlon, *Remaking Micronesia: Discourses over Development in a Pacific Territory, 1944–1982* (Honolulu: University of Hawai'i Press, 1998), 41. For more on Western and Indigenous notions of time, refer to Frederick Cooper, *Colonialism in Question: Theory, Knowledge, History* (Berkeley: University of California Press, 2005); and Vine Deloria Jr., *God Is Red: A Native View of Religion* (Golden, CO: Fulcrum Publishing, 1992).

17. "Domestics—Employment of," September 4, 1944, RG 313, US National Archives and Records Administration, San Bruno, CA.

18. On Filipino house servants, refer to Yến Lê Espiritu, *Home Bound: Filipino American Lives across Cultures, Communities, and Countries* (Berkeley: University of California Press, 2003). On Mexican servants, refer to Kevin Adams, *Class and Race in the Frontier Army: Military Life in the West, 1870–1890* (Norman: University of Oklahoma Press, 2009); and Mario T. García, *Desert Immigrants: The Mexicans of El Paso, 1880–1920* (New Haven, CT: Yale University Press, 1981).

19. For more on imprisonment during World War II, refer to Keith L. Camacho, *Sacred Men: Law, Torture, and Retribution in Guam* (Durham, NC: Duke University Press, 2019); and Juliet Nebolon, "Settler-Military Camps: Internment and Prisoner of War Camps across the Pacific Islands during World War II," *Journal of Asian American Studies* 24, no. 2 (June 2021): 299–336.

20. D. D. Gurley, "POW Labor—Request for," November 3, 1945, RG 313, US National Archives and Records Administration, San Bruno, CA.

21. J. M. Arthur, "Memorandum: Prisoner of War Labor, Availability of," September 11, 1945, RG 313, US National Archives and Records Administration, San Bruno, CA.

22. Rogers, *Destiny's Landfall*, 194.

23. *Christian Science Monitor*, "Many Japs on Guam Are Still in Hiding," February 18, 1946, Vertical File, Nieves M. Flores Memorial Library, Hagåtña, Guåhan.

24. *Christian Science Monitor*, "Many Japs on Guam."

25. L. D. Herrle, "Augmentation of Native Labor on Guam for Employment by the Navy," March 4, 1946, RG 313, US National Archives and Records Administration, College Park, MD. While there are no records that document if CHamorus were able to negotiate that the Chinese workers be deported, it can be inferred that some of them did support this policy since several CHamoru politicians backed the US military's "local hire and alien displacement program," which began in 1957. In theory, the military was supposed to make a concerted effort to hire local workers. CHamorus and military officials believed this program would phase out the hiring of Filipinos. However, this would not be the case, especially with the recruitment of several thousand Filipinos to help in the reconstruction of the island due to severe damage wrought by Typhoon Karen in 1962.

26. Herrle, "Augmentation of Native Labor."

27. On the perceptions of Chinese workers in the nineteenth century, refer to Manu Karuka, *Empire's Tracks: Indigenous Nations, Chinese Workers, and the Transcontinental Railroad* (Oakland: University of California Press, 2019); and Alexander Saxton, *Indispensable Enemy: Labor and the Anti-Chinese Movement in California* (Berkeley: University of California Press, 1975).

28. Cletus E. Daniel, *Bitter Harvest: A History of California Farmworkers, 1870–1941* (Berkeley: University of California Press, 1981), 27.

29. Herrle, "Augmentation of Native Labor."

30. Poblete, *Islanders in the Empire*, 94.

31. The Johnson-Reed Act, or Immigration Act, of 1924 established quotas that limited the number of people who could immigrate to the United States based on the country of origin. For more on the Johnson-Reed Act, refer to Mae M. Ngai, *Impossible Subjects: Illegal Aliens and the Making of Modern America* (Princeton, NJ: Princeton University Press, 2004).

32. For more on US empire, labor, and corporations, refer to Karuka, *Empire's Tracks*; Bender and Lipman, *Making the Empire Work*; Greene, *The Canal Builders*; Catherine A. Lutz, *Homefront: A Military City and the American Twentieth Century* (Boston: Beacon Press, 2002); and Enloe, *Bananas, Beaches and Bases*.

33. Republic of the Philippines, "Exchange of Notes Constituting an Agreement between the Republic of the Philippines and the United States of America," May 1947, Department of Foreign Affairs Archives. Hereafter cited as "Exchange of Notes."

34. Republic of the Philippines, "Exchange of Notes." Information regarding the exchange rate between the US dollar and the Philippine peso (PHP) in 1947 is scant. However, based on Oanda Data Services (www.oanda.com), the current exchange rate as of December 6, 2022 is 1 US Dollar to approximately 55 PHP.

35. COMNAVMARIANAS, "Filipinos on Guam," January 1956, RG 38, US National Archives and Records Administration, College Park, MD.

36. For more on the McCarran-Walter Act of 1952, refer to Jane Hong, *Opening the Gates to Asia: A Transpacific History of How America Repealed Asian Exclusion* (Chapel Hill: University of North Carolina Press, 2019); and Ngai, *Impossible Subjects*.

37. In the mid-1950s, Marianas Stevedoring (MASDELCO) became a subsidiary company of LUSTEVECO in Guåhan. Thus, some people on Guåhan refer to the company as Luzon Stevedoring or Marianas Stevedoring/MASDELCO.

38. For more on the US military presence in the Philippines and its legacies, refer to Christopher Capozzola, *Bound by War: How the United States and the Philippines Built America's First Pacific Century* (New York: Basic Books, 2020); and Victoria Reyes, *Global Borderlands: Fantasy, Violence, and Empire in Subic Bay, Philippines* (Stanford, CA: Stanford University Press, 2019).

39. *Time*, "Philippines: Barging Ahead," August 25, 1967, accessed May 2, 2014, http://www.time.com/time/magazine/article/0,9171,841076,00.html.

40. Other postwar construction companies included Black Construction, Guam Dredging Company, J. H. Pomery Company, Pacific Islands Engineers, Perez Brothers, and the Vinnell Corporation.

41. *Manila Times*, "Filipino Employe[e]s of US Navy at Guam Contented, Says Union Chief," February 6, 1947, Lopez Museum and Library, Pasig City, Philippines.

42. Kevin Escudero, "Federal Immigration Laws and U.S. Empire: Tracing Immigration Lawmaking in the Mariana Islands," *Amerasia Journal* 46, no. 1 (2020), 65.

43. KBR, "History of KBR."

44. These uneven hiring practices resulted in several investigations in the 1980s of private construction companies in Guåhan for their preference to hire H-2 workers over workers from the island. This conflict over the preference for H-2 workers persists today.

45. Though racially segregated schools and hospitals existed in pre–World War II Guåhan, this was one of the earliest moments in which a large private company such as BPM was permitted to perpetuate racial segregation on the island.

46. US House Sub-Committee on Interior and Insular Affairs, December 1, 1954, 2nd GL Public Hearing Vertical File, Nieves M. Flores Memorial Library, Hagåtña, Guåhan.

47. Eugene Morgan, *So You Want to Go to Guam* (New York: Vantage Press, 1951), 84.

48. Guam Humanities Council, *A Journey Home: Camp Roxas and Filipino American History in Guam* (Hagåtña: GHC, 2009), 4.

49. Jorge V. Sibal, ed., *Changes and Challenges: 60 Years of Struggles Towards Decent Work* (Diliman: University of the Philippines, 2008), 2. For more on the economic and labor organizing of Iloilo, refer to Henry Florida, *Iloilo in the 20th Century: An Economic History* (Iloilo City: University of the Philippines, 1997), 78.

50. For more on US military bases and Filipino workers, refer to Brian McAllister Linn, *Guardians of Empire: The U.S. Army and the Pacific, 1902–1940* (Chapel Hill: University of North Carolina Press, 1999); and Reyes, *Global Borderlands*.

51. From the late 1940s to 1962, Guåhan was under a military security clearance program that required all people entering or leaving the island to obtain permission from US Naval Command.

52. For more on Clark Air Force Base, refer to Vernadette Vicuña Gonzalez, *Securing Paradise: Tourism and Militarism in Hawai'i and the Philippines* (Durham, NC: Duke University Press, 2013); and Reyes, *Global Borderlands*.

53. Gorgonio Cabot, interview with author, April 22, 2013, Hagåtña, Guåhan. Hereafter cited as G. Cabot interview, April 22, 2013.

54. Lipman, *Guantánamo*, 39.

55. For more on the Bracero Program and medical examinations, refer to Ronald L. Mize, *The Invisible Workers of the U.S.-Mexico Bracero Program* (Lanham, MD: Lexington Books, 2016).

56. C. A. Pownall, "Rules and Regulations for Labor Contracts," October 14, 1946, RG 313, US National Archives and Records Administration, San Bruno, CA.

57. Pownall, "Rules and Regulations."

58. Pownall.

59. Catherine Ceniza Choy, *Empire of Care: Nursing and Migration in Filipino American History* (Durham, NC: Duke University Press, 2003), 21. For more on American colonial perceptions of Filipinos during the early twentieth century, refer to Warwick Anderson, *Colonial Pathologies: American Tropical Medicine, Race, and Hygiene in the Philippines* (Durham, NC: Duke University Press, 2006).

60. J. N. Myers, "Examination of Native Civilians for Employment," July 31, 1946, RG 313, US National Archives and Records Administration, San Bruno, CA.

61. For more on the medical protection of white Americans in Guåhan, refer to Hattori, *Colonial Dis-Ease*.

62. The need for Filipino workers in Guåhan was immense enough that some Filipinos worked in the underground economy of immigrant smuggling. The *Manila Times* reported that a ring of smugglers had been sneaking Filipinos into Guåhan via military air transport and US ships. These smugglers received $30 to $100 for transportation and an additional $20 to $50 monthly during each Filipino's residency on the island. The creation of this underground immigration

industry demonstrates that Filipino labor was in high demand and that Filipino men were determined to obtain admittance into Guåhan. For more, refer to the *Manila Times*, "Guam Smuggling Ring Broken Up," June 9, 1950, Lopez Museum and Library, Pasig City, Philippines.

63. Guam Humanities Council, "A Journey Home," 21.

64. Guam Humanities Council, 21.

65. Guam Humanities Council, 21.

66. Rhacel Salazar Parreñas, "Asian Immigrant Women and Global Restructuring, 1970s–1990s," in *Asian/Pacific Islander American Women: A Historical Anthology*, eds. Shirley Hune and Gail M. Nomura (New York: New York University Press, 2003), 272.

67. Delfina Cataluna and Pilar Malilay, interview with Bernie Provido Schumann and Burt Sardoma Jr., May 28, 2009. Interview is courtesy of *Under the American Sun*, Camp Roxas film project.

68. For more on American notions of race and slavery in the Asia-Pacific region, refer to Alfred W. McCoy and Francisco Scarano, eds., *Colonial Crucible: Empire in the Making of the Modern American State* (Madison: University of Wisconsin Press, 2009); Kramer, *The Blood of Government*; Michael Salman, *The Embarrassment of Slavery: Controversies over Bondage and Nationalism in the American Colonial Philippines* (Berkeley: University of California Press, 2001).

69. US Civil Service Commission, "Application for Federal Employment," July 26, 1947, RG 313, US National Archives and Records Administration, San Bruno, CA.

70. Rogers, *Destiny's Landfall*, 217.

71. Morgan, *So You Want to Go to Guam*, 12.

72. G. Cabot interview, April 22, 2013.

73. Carano and Sanchez, *A Complete History of Guam*, 328.

74. Bruce L. Campbell, "The Filipino Community of Guam, 1945–1975" (Master's thesis: University of Hawai'i at Mānoa, 1987), 31.

75. V. Williams, "Additional Press Articles on Alleged Exploitation of Philippine Laborers in Guam," April 1, 1954, RG 85, US National Archives and Records Administration, College Park, MD, 2.

76. US Department of Labor, "History of Federal Minimum Wage Rates under the Fair Labor Standards Act, 1938–2009, accessed June 10, 2014, http://www.dol.gov/whd/minwage/chart.htm.

77. *Manila Times*, "Disclaim Guam Wage Discrimination," January 28, 1948, Lopez Museum and Library, Pasig City, Philippines.

78. On racist wage scales and ethnic antagonism in Hawai'i, refer to Ronald Takaki, *Pau Hana: Plantation Life and Labor in Hawaii* (Honolulu: University of Hawai'i Press, 1983).

79. Morgan, *So You Want to Go to Guam*, 21.

80. *Manila Times*, "2 Filipino Workers on Guam Interred," January 21, 1948, Lopez Museum and Library, Pasig City, Philippines.

81. *Daily Mirror*, "Filipino Electrician Dies in Guam Mishap," June 26, 1959, Lopez Museum and Library, Pasig City, Philippines.

82. J. B. Dunn, "Out-Patient Treatments of Civilian Employees to Brown Pacific Maxon Co.," June 5, July 7, and August 2, 1947, RG 313, US National Archives and Records Administration, San Bruno, CA.

83. Williams, "Additional Press Articles," 2.

84. Antonia and Sam Mabini, interview with author, April 28, 2013, Tomhom, Guåhan. Hereafter cited as A. and S. Mabini interview, April 28, 2013.

85. Mayo Clinic, "Asbestosis," accessed August 30, 2010, https://www.mayoclinic.org/diseases-conditions/asbestosis/symptoms-causes/syc-20354637.

86. I will reference BPM Camp #1, Camp #2, and Camp Quezon together as "BPM camps."

87. Guam Humanities Council, "A Journey Home," 13.

88. Hugh Carey, ed., *The Constructionaire*, October 31, 1951; and Hugh Carey, ed., *The Constructionaire*, November 3, 1951, Nieves M. Flores Memorial Library, Hagåtña, Guåhan.

89. Sanford M. Jacoby, *Modern Manors: Welfare Capitalism since the New Deal* (Princeton, NJ: Princeton University Press, 1997), 4. Welfare capitalism had its origins in Europe, and by the nineteenth century it had become a major corporate strategy in the United States. Besides deterring the growth of unions and government, it was a paternalistic relationship in which corporate executives and owners believed that they were obligated to take care of their employees in return of maximum worker efficiency.

90. Brown-Pacific-Maxon, *The Constructionaire* 6, no. 20, November 22, 1950, Nieves M. Flores Memorial Library, Hagåtña, Guåhan.

91. Guam Humanities Council, "A Journey Home," 19.

92. Lizabeth Cohen, *Making a New Deal: Industrial Workers in Chicago, 1919–1939*, 2nd ed. (New York: Cambridge University Press, 2008), 176–177.

93. Brown-Pacific-Maxon, *The Constructionaire* 6, no. 3, September 23, 1950, Nieves M. Flores Memorial Library, Hagåtña, Guåhan; and Guam Humanities Council, "A Journey Home," 14–18.

94. For more on company strategies to control workers through benevolent paternalism, refer to Takai, *Pau Hana*.

95. Guam Humanities Council, "A Journey Home," 12.

96. Jose and Olivia Savares, interview with author, June 5, 2013, Dédidu, Guåhan.

97. R. W. Jones, "Weekly Sanitation Report," October 10, 1949, RG 313, US National Archives and Records Administration, San Bruno, CA.

98. Guam Humanities Council, "A Journey Home," 10.

99. L. Eugene Wolfe, "Report of Field Trip to Pacific Islands," October 31, 1947, RG 313, US National Archives and Records Administration, San Bruno, CA.

100. Dorothea Minor Baker, "Letter to Governor C. A. Pownall," August 10, 1949, RG 313, US National Archives and Records Administration, San Bruno, CA.

101. Sid White, "Disparity in Pay Cited: Failure of Gov't to Secure Better Conditions Scored," *Manila Times*, September 10, 1956, Lopez Museum and Library, Pasig City, Philippines.

102. H. V. Hopkins, "Louie Levine, Resignation of," December 16, 1948, RG 313, US National Archives and Records Administration, San Bruno, CA.

103. L. E. Schmidt, "Security at Camp Asan," March 14, 1949, RG 313, US National Archives and Records Administration, San Bruno, CA.

104. A. J. Carrillo, "Security of Our Housing Areas, Report on," June 3, 1949, RG 313, US National Archives, San Bruno, CA.

105. *Guam News*, "Guam Police List Weapons, Drugs Found at Roxas," February 7, 1950, RG 126, US National Archives and Records Administration, College Park, MD.

106. *Guam News*, "Guam Police List Weapons."

107. Jonathan K. Okamura, *Ethnicity and Inequality in Hawai'i* (Philadelphia: Temple University Press, 2008), 156.

108. *Daily Mirror*, "Guam Filipinos Refuse Contracts, Sent Home," March 17, 1955, Lopez Museum and Library, Pasig City, Philippines.

109. E. F. Van Buskirk Jr., "Entry, Re-Entry, Repatriation and Deportation of Filipinos," January 16, 1958, RG 38, US National Archives, College Park, MD.

110. Hong, *Opening the Gates to Asia*, 112.

111. US Deputy Chief of Naval Operations Guam, "Filipino Labor Situation on Guam," July 11, 1952, RG 38, US National Archives and Records Administration, College Park, MD.

112. W. L. Eifrig, "U.S. Office of Naval Intelligence Information Report," April 23, 1954, RG 38, US National Archives and Records Administration, College Park, MD.

113. J. G. Bogdan, "U.S. Office of Naval Intelligence Information Report," April 19, 1954, RG 38, US National Archives and Records Administration, College Park, MD.

114. Bayani Mangibin, interview with author, May 2, 2013, Hagåtña, Guåhan. Hereafter cited as B. Mangibin interview, May 2, 2013.

115. Victorino P. Paredes, "Consulate of the Philippines," May 12, 1958, National Library of the Philippines, Manila, Philippines.

116. Generally, Filipino men were reported missing because they had not sent remittances to their families in the Philippines or they had not responded to families' letters in a timely manner. Reportedly, some Filipino men married CHamoru women and abandoned their families in the Philippines, which was a concern for the Philippine government.

117. Paredes, "Consulate of the Philippines."

118. Robyn Magalit Rodriguez, *Migrants for Export: How the Philippine State Brokers Labor to the World* (Minneapolis: University of Minnesota Press, 2010), xiv.

119. *Daily Mirror*, "Buck Floor Pay in U.S. Bases," February 24, 1956, 1, and "House Okays Guam Protest: U.S. State Department Backs Bill against P.I. Labor, Report," March 9, 1956, 1, Lopez Museum and Library, Pasig City, Philippines.

120. JoAnna Poblete-Cross, "Bridging Indigenous and Immigrant Struggles: A Case Study of American Samoa," *American Quarterly* 62, no. 3 (2010): 502.

121. Other notable twentieth-century social movements include the International Longshore and Warehousemen's Union (ILWU) of 1934 (Hawai'i), the Mau in the early 1900s (Sāmoa), the Oahu Sugar Strike of 1920 (Hawai'i), and the Polynesian Panthers in 1971 (Aotearoa, New Zealand).

122. *Daily Mirror*, "Speaker Presses Get-Tough Policy on Guam Solon Team," March 27, 1956, Lopez Museum and Library, Pasig City, Philippines.

123. *Manila Times*, "PI Workers in Guam Hit," April 13, 1956, Lopez Museum and Library, Pasig City, Philippines.

124. For more on Filipino worker resistance, refer to Dorothy B. Fujita-Rony, *American Workers, Colonial Power: Philippine Seattle and the Transpacific West, 1919–1941* (Berkeley: University of California Press, 2003), 19.

125. *Manila Times*, "PI Gov't Will Protest Guam Wage Bill in US," February 19, 1956, Lopez Museum and Library, Pasig City, Philippines; and Cesar Salenga, "PI Opposition Mounts against U.S. Labor Bill," March 31, 1956, Lopez Museum and Library, Pasig City, Philippines.

126. Salenga, "PI Opposition Mounts."

127. *Manila Times*, "Better Deal for Guam Folk," April 15, 1956, Lopez Museum and Library, Pasig City, Philippines.

128. *Manila Times*, "PI Workers in Guam Hit," April 13, 1956, Lopez Museum and Library, Pasig City, Philippines.

129. The PTUC was one of the four new labor federations that were created in the 1950s, after the Philippine Department of Labor cancelled the registration of the Congress of Labor Organizations (CLO) and arrested its leaders for being Communists. For more on the history of Philippine labor unions, refer to Jorge V. Sibal, "Milestones: The Philippines and the ILO Partnership 1948–2008," in *Changes and Challenges: 60 Years of Struggle Towards Decent Work*, ed. Jorge V. Sibal (Diliman: University of the Philippines, 2008).

130. *Daily Mirror*, "PTUC Seeks AFL-CIO Aid on Guam Wage Bill," February 20, 1956, Lopez Museum and Library, Pasig City, Philippines.

131. Salenga, "PI Opposition Mounts."

132. *Manila Times*, "Asian Group Backs PI on Floor Wage," April 15, 1956, Lopez Museum and Library, Pasig City, Philippines. In 1949 several trade unions broke off from the World Trade Union Federation based on claims that Communists dominated it. These anti-Communist organizations formed the ICFTU in the early 1950s; it was primarily composed of labor organizations located in Western Europe and the United States.

133. *Daily Mirror*, "Junk U.S.-P.I. Guam Labor Deal, 3 House Probers Urge," April 4, 1956, Lopez Museum and Library, Pasig City, Philippines.

134. *Daily Mirror*, "Deny U.S. Wage Rates for P.I. Bases Labor," June 20, 1956, Lopez Museum and Library, Pasig City, Philippines.

135. *Daily Mirror*, "AFL-CIO Support P.I. Bid on Overseas Labor Wages," February 29, 1956, Lopez Museum and Library, Pasig City, Philippines.

136. For more on the connection between labor and US foreign policy, refer to Beth Sims, *Workers of the World Undermined: American Labor's Role in U.S. Foreign Policy* (Boston: South End Press, 1992).

137. *Manila Times*, "Solons Assure Guam Workers, Hear Plaints," April 4, 1956, Lopez Museum and Library, Pasig City, Philippines.

4. Militarized Intimacies

1. Barbara and Eddie De La Cruz, interview with author, April 24, 2013, Hagåtña, Guåhan. Hereafter cited as De La Cruz interview, April 24, 2013.

2. Nicolyn Woodcock, "Narratives of Intimacy in Asian American Literature," in *Oxford Research Encyclopedia* (August 30, 2019), 1, DOI: 10.1093/acrefore/9780190201098.013.1173. For more on militarized intimacies, refer to Nicolyn V. Woodcock, "Militarized Intimacies: War, Family, and Transpacific Asian American Literature (PhD diss., Miami University, 2019).

3. Nayan Shah, *Stranger Intimacy: Contesting Race, Sexuality, and the Law in the North American West* (Berkeley: University of California Press, 2011), 8.

4. Shah, *Stranger Intimacy*, 2.

5. Moon-Ho Jung, *Menace to Empire: Anticolonial Solidarities and the Transpacific Origins of the US Security State* (Oakland: University of California Press, 2022), 9. For more on Asian and Asian American anticommunism and US government surveillance, refer to Seema Sohi, *Echoes of Mutiny: Race, Surveillance, and Indian Anticolonialism in North America* (New York: Oxford University Press, 2014).

6. For more on the US military's definition of subversion, refer to David Kilcullen, *The Accidental Guerrilla: Fighting Small Wars in the Midst of a Big One* (New York: Oxford University Press, 2011).

7. Mary L. Dudziak, *Cold War Civil Rights: Race and the Image of American Democracy* (Princeton, NJ: Princeton University Press, 2000), 11.

8. Judith A. Bennett and Angela Wanhalla, "Introduction: A New Net Goes Fishing," in *Mothers' Darlings of the South Pacific: The Children of Indigenous Women and U.S. Servicemen, World War II*, eds. Judith A. Bennett and Angela Wanhalla (Honolulu: University of Hawai'i Press, 2016), 14.

9. Rick Baldoz, "'Comrade Carlos Bulosan': U.S. State Surveillance and the Cold War Suppression of Filipino Radicals," *Asia-Pacific Journal* 33, no. 3 (2014), http://www.japanfocus.org/-Rick-Baldoz/4165.

10. Colleen Woods, *Freedom Incorporated: Anticommunism and Philippine Independence in the Age of Decolonization* (Ithaca, NY: Cornell University Press, 2020), 11. For more on US-Philippine relations, war, and military service refer to Christopher Capozzola, *Bound by War: How the United States and the Philippines Built America's First Pacific Century* (New York: Basic Books, 2020).

11. Robert F. Rogers, *Destiny's Landfall: A History of Guam* (Honolulu: University of Hawaiʻi Press, 1995), 218.

12. Alfred W. McCoy, *Policing America's Empire: The United States, the Philippines and the Rise of the Surveillance State* (Madison: University of Wisconsin Press, 2009), 104–105. For more on the racialization of Filipinos as subversive, refer to Rick Baldoz, *The Third Asiatic Invasion: Migration and Empire in Filipino America, 1898–1946* (New York: New York University Press, 2011); and Dylan Rodríguez, *Suspended Apocalypse: White Supremacy, Genocide, and the Filipino Condition* (Minneapolis: University of Minnesota Press, 2010).

13. For more on Filipino anticolonial thought, refer to Augusto Fauni Espiritu, *Five Faces of Exile: The Nation and Filipino American Intellectuals* (Stanford, CA: Stanford University Press, 2005).

14. W. B. Ammon, "Clearance Procedure for Entry into Guam," February 27, 1956, RG 38, US National Archives and Records Administration, College Park, MD.

15. G. M. Adams, "Information Report: Office of Naval Intelligence," June 9, 1956, RG 38, US National Archives and Records Administration, College Park, MD. In the early 1950s the ONI determined that 200–300 Filipinos were able to settle on Guåhan because they had obtained permanent residency while living on Hawaiʻi.

16. Admin CINCPACFLT, Memo to COMNAVMARIANAS, September 21, 1956, RG 38, US National Archives and Records Administration, College Park, MD.

17. Sucheng Chan, *Asian Americans: An Interpretive History* (New York: Twayne Publishers, 1991), 187. For more on Asian Americans as perpetual foreigners, refer to Shelley Sang-Hee Lee, *A New History of Asian America* (New York: Routledge, 2013); Erika Lee, *The Making of Asian America: A History* (New York: Simon & Schuster, 2015); and Ronald Takaki, *Strangers from a Different Shore: A History of Asian Americans* (New York: Little, Brown, 1998).

18. Rogers, *Destiny's Landfall*, 236.

19. Victorino P. Paredes, "Consulate of the Philippines Post Report," May 12, 1958, Philippine National Library.

20. *Filipiniana*, "Representations Made during Visit of Filipino Solons," April 1956, RG 38, US National Archives and Records Administration, College Park, MD.

21. The Office of Naval Intelligence dates back to the 1880s, under the supervision of co-creator Lieutenant Theodorous Bailey Myers Mason. Initially, the ONI was primarily concerned with collecting information from other nations that had more advanced naval technology in hopes of modernizing the US Navy. By World War I the ONI had expanded to work with other state departments. In World War II the ONI began gathering intelligence on other nations and participated in counterintelligence activities during the Cold War. For more on the ONI, refer to Jeffery M. Dorwat, *The Office of Naval Intelligence: The Birth of America's First Intelligence Agency, 1865–1918* (Annapolis, MD: Naval Institute Press, 1979); and Office of Naval Intelligence, "Proud ONI History," Accessed August 21, 2010, http://www.oni.navy.mil/This_is_ONI/Proud_History.html

22. James Forrestal, "Naval Intelligence Functions and Responsibilities," November 1, 1945, RG 313, US National Archives and Records Administration, San Bruno, CA.

23. C. Hawkins, "Loyalty Record Check of Employees as of 30 September 1947," December 28, 1949, RG 313, US National Archives and Records Administration, San Bruno, CA.

24. E. K. Shanahan, "Warning Regarding the Request for Information from Non-Official Agencies," September 16, 1949, RG 313, US National Archives and Records Administration, San Bruno, CA; and John L. Sullivan, "Removal of Employees Involving Reasonable Doubt as to Loyalty; Subversive Activity; and Membership in un-American Groups," January 14, 1947, RG 313, US National Archives and Records Administration, San Bruno, CA. For more on cultures of surveillance, refer to Michel Foucault, *Discipline and Punish: The Birth of the Prison* (New York: Vintage Books, 1995); and Jürgen Habermas, *The Structural Transformation of the Public Sphere: An Inquiry into a Category of Bourgeois Society* (Cambridge, MA: MIT Press, 1991).

25. G. M. Adams, "Information Report: Office of Naval Intelligence," April 27, 1956. RG 38, US National Archives and Records Administration, College Park, MD.

26. Adams, "Information Report," April 27, 1956.

27. C. J. Endres, "Information Report: Office of Naval Intelligence," November 1, 1957, RG 38, US National Archives and Records Administration, College Park, MD.

28. Adams, "Information Report," April 27, 1956.

29. Peyton Harrison, "Civilian Morale on Guam; Monthly Summary Report On," December 26, 1944, RG 313, US National Archives and Records Administration, College Park, MD.

30. Pete Taitingfong Rosario and Louie Furtado wrote the song "Uncle Sam Please Come Back to Guam" during the Japanese occupation of Guåhan. The lyrics of the song are, in part: "Eight of December 1941, people went crazy, right here in Guam, oh, Mr. Sam, Sam, My Dear Uncle Sam, won't you please, come back to Guam." For more on CHamoru loyalty and patriotism, refer to Keith L. Camacho, *Cultures of Commemoration: The Politics of War, Memory, and History in the Mariana Islands* (Honolulu: University of Hawai'i Press, 2011); Vicente M. Diaz, "Deliberating 'Liberation Day': Identity, History, Memory, and War in Guam," in *Perilous Memories: The Asia Pacific War(s)*, eds. T. T. Fujitani, Geoffrey White, and Lisa Yoneyama (Durham, NC: Duke University Press, 2001), 155–180; and Michael Lujan Bevacqua, "These May or May Not Be Americans: The Patriotic Myth and the Hijacking of Chamorro History on Guam," (Master's thesis, University of Guam, 2004).

31. W. B. Ammun, "Repatriation of Filipino Contract Laborer Employees on Guam; Additional Information Concerning," April 19, 1956, RG 38, US National Archives and Records Administration, College Park, MD.

32. De La Cruz interview, April 24, 2013.

33. Tessa Ong Winkelmann, "Rethinking the Sexual Geography of American Empire in the Philippines: Interracial Intimacies in Mindanao and the Cordilleras, 1898–1921," in *Gendering the Trans-Pacific World: Diaspora, Empire, and Race*, eds. Catherine Ceniza Choy and Judy Tzu-Chun Wu (Leiden: Brill, 2017), 40. DOI: 10.1163/9789004336100_005.

34. Rudy P. Guevarra Jr., *Becoming Mexipino: Multiethnic Identities and Communities in San Diego* (New Brunswick, NJ: Rutgers University Press, 2012), 6.

35. Julita Santos Walin, interview with author, May 6, 2013, Hagåtña, Guåhan. Hereafter cited as J. Walin interview, May 6, 2013.

36. J. Walin interview, May 6, 2013.

37. Joaquin Flores Lujan, interview with author, May 6, 2013, Mangilao, Guåhan. Hereafter cited as J. Lujan interview, May 6, 2013.

38. Felix B. Stump, "Repatriation of Filipino Contract Laborer Employees on Guam; Additional Information Concerning," June 12, 1956, RG 38, US National Archives and Records Administration, College Park, MD.

39. Jose C. Abcede, "Guam Policy Explained: US Naval Commander Says Navy out to Keep 'Guam for Guamanians,' Cites Strategy Needs," *Manila Times*, October 12, 1956.

40. Jose and Olivia Savares, interview with author, June 5, 2013, in Dédidu, Guåhan. Hereafter cited as J. and O. Savares interview, June 5, 2013.

41. Joe E. Quinata, interview with author, June 20, 2012, in Los Angeles, CA. Hereafter cited as J. Quinata interview, June 20, 2012.

42. Jose Ulloa Garrido, interview with author, May 17, 2013, Tutuhan, Guåhan. Hereafter cited as J. Garrido interview, May 17, 2013.

43. Vicente M. Diaz, *Repositioning the Missionary: Rewriting the Histories of Colonialism, Native Catholicism, and Indigeneity in Guam* (Honolulu: University of Hawai'i Press, 2010), 140.

44. Linda is a pseudonym.

45. Sandra is a pseudonym.

46. Sandra, interview with author, July 8, 2018, Hagåtña, Guåhan.

47. Christine Taitano DeLisle, *Placental Politics: CHamoru Women, White Womanhood, and Indigeneity under U.S. Colonialism in Guam* (Chapel Hill: University of North Carolina Press, 2021), 26; and Anne Perez Hattori, "Textbook Tells: Gender, Race, and Decolonizing Guam History Textbooks in the 21st Century," *AlterNative* 14, no. 2 (2018), 176.

48. Laura Marie Torres Souder, *Daughters of the Island: Contemporary Chamorro Women Organizers on Guam* (Lanham, MD: University Press of America, 1992), 50.

49. DeLisle, *Placental Politics*, 24; and Souder, *Daughters of the Island*, 47.

50. DeLisle, 4.

51. For more on taxi-dance clubs in the continental United States, refer to Linda M. Espana-Maram, *Creating Masculinity in Los Angeles's Little Manila: Working-Class Filipinos and Popular Culture, 1920s–1950s* (New York: Columbia University Press, 2006); and Takaki, *Strangers from a Different Shore.*

52. John Luces, interview with author, July 11, 2018, Hågat, Guåhan. Hereafter cited as J. Luces interview, July 11, 2018.

53. James Perez Viernes, "Louie Gombar," Guampedia.com, accessed September 5, 2020, http://www.guampedia.com/louie-gombar/.

54. J. Luces interview, July 11, 2018.

55. The establishment of these clubs dates to the 1920s. Filipino male laborers who worked throughout California attended dance halls where they would purchase tickets that guaranteed them an opportunity to dance with hostesses, who were usually white American women.

56. Guam Legislature, "Taxi-dance Hearing," January 16, 1954, Senators' Speeches Vertical File, Nieves M. Flores Memorial Library, Hagåtña, Guåhan. The first name of Siguenza is unknown.

57. Guam Legislature, "Taxi-dance Hearing." Johnston communicated part of her testimony in the CHamoru language.

58. V. Williams, "Information Report: Office of Naval Intelligence," April 12, 1954, RG 38, US National Archives and Records Administration, College Park, MD.

59. Omar L. Harrington, "Minutes of Armed Forces Disciplinary Control Board Meeting," March 25, 1954, RG 313, US National Archives and Records Administration, San Bruno, CA.

60. Mrs. Paul D. Shriver, "Letter to the Guam Legislature," December 8, 1953, Guam Legislature Vertical Files 1950s, Nieves M. Flores Memorial Library, Hagåtña, Guåhan.

61. J. Luces interview, July 11, 2018.

62. Francis Lester "Scotty" Moylan was a white American local businessman who came to Guam in 1946 by way of Hawai'i. The US War Department asked Moylan to establish local business services to aid in the military expansion of Guåhan. Among his businesses were camera film development, general merchandise stores, car dealerships, and car insurance. For more on Moylan

refer to *Marianas Business Journal*, "Obituary—Francis Lester "Scotty" Moylan," August 30, 2010, http://mbjguam.com/2010/08/30/obituary-francis-lester-aeoescottyae%C2%9D-moylan/.

63. Fred Moylan, "Letter to the Congress of Guam," January 4, 1954, Guåhan Legislature Vertical File, Nieves M. Flores Memorial Library, Hagåtña, Guåhan.

64. Rick Baldoz, *The Third Asiatic Invasion: Empire and Migration in Filipino America, 1898–1946* (New York: New York University Press, 2011), 14.

65. T. A. Darling, "Letter to A. B. Wonpat," January 14, 1954, Guam Legislature Vertical File, Nieves M. Flores Memorial Library, Hagåtña, Guåhan.

66. Ford Q. Elvidge served as the governor of Guåhan from 1953 to 1956.

67. Anita M. Elvidge, *Guam Interlude* (Privately printed, 1972), 120. It is unknown which "leading" Guam legislators were involved or supported taxi-dance clubs.

68. Mrs. Paul D. Shriver, "Guam Women's Club to Guam Legislature," December 8, 1953, Guam Legislature Vertical File, Nieves M. Flores Memorial Library, Hagåtña, Guåhan.

69. Vicariate Union of Holy Name Societies, "Petition to the Second Guam Legislature," January 4, 1954, Guam Legislature Vertical File, Nieves M. Flores Memorial Library, Hagåtña, Guåhan.

70. For more on the US military's endorsement of brothels near bases, refer to Grace M. Cho, *Haunting the Korean Diaspora: Shame, Secrecy, and the Forgotten War* (Minneapolis: University of Minnesota Press, 2008); and Katharine H. S. Moon, *Sex among Allies: Military Prostitution in U.S.-Korea Relations* (New York: Columbia University Press, 1997).

71. Naval Government of Guam, "Monthly Report for November 1946," November 30, 1946, RG 313, US National Archives and Records Administration, College Park, MD.

72. Duane Decker, "Nobody Came Formal," *Leatherneck*, May 1945, 46; and *Life*, "Speaking of Pictures . . . Marines Find Pin-Ups and Glamour on Guam," June 18, 1945, 12–14. While it is not fully clear if African American soldiers were allowed to attend these dances or if they had their own racially segregated dances, they were likely not included in these spaces until the US military was desegregated via Executive Order 9981 in July 1948.

73. DeLisle, *Placental Politics*, 26.

74. Alys Even Weinbaum, Lynn M. Thomas, Priti Ramamurthy, Uta G. Poiger, Madeleine Y. Dong, and Tani E. Barlow, "The Modern Girl as Heuristic Device: Collaboration, Connective Comparison, Multidirectional Citation," in *The Modern Girl around the World: Consumption, Modernity, and Globalization*, eds. Alys Even Weinbaum, Lynn M. Thomas, Priti Ramamurthy, Uta G. Poiger, Madeleine Y. Dong, and Tani E. Barlow (Durham, NC: Duke University Press, 2008), 1.

75. For more on sexual relationships of American servicemen in US-occupied places, refer to Moon, *Military Prostitution in U.S.-Korea*; and Ji-Yeon Yuh, "Imagined Community: Sisterhood and Resistance among Korean Military Brides in America, 1950–1996," in *Asian/Pacific Islander American Women: A Historical Anthology*, eds. Shirley Hune and Gail M. Nomura (New York: New York University Press, 2003), 221–236.

76. *Life*, "Speaking of Pictures," 12–14.

77. M. T. Hinson, "Letter to Island Commander of Guam," January 19, 1946, RG 313, US National Archives and Records Administration, San Bruno, CA.

78. Bennett and Wanhalla, "Introduction," 18.

79. Edward Leiss, "Letter to Island Commander Guam," February 25, 1946, RG 313, US National Archives and Records Administration, San Bruno, CA.

80. Edward Leiss, "Telegram to American Consul," April 5, 1947, RG 313, US National Archives and Records Administration, San Bruno, CA.

81. Felix B. Stump, "Command Responsibility in Representing the United States," June 24, 1954, RG 313, US National Archives and Records Administration, San Bruno, CA.

82. For more on the US military's Cold War reputation, refer to Michael H. Hunt, *The American Ascendancy: How the United States Gained and Wielded Global Dominance* (Chapel Hill: University of North Carolina Press, 2007); and Peter L. Hays, Brenda J. Vallance, and Alan R. Van Tassel, eds., *American Defense Policy* (Baltimore: John Hopkins University Press, 1997).

83. R. H. Fogler, "Negotiations between U.S. Government and Philippines Government Regarding Wage Rates and Conditions of Employment Applicable to Alien Filipinos Employed by Military or Military Contractors at Military Bases in Guam and the Philippines," February 27, 1956, RG 38, US National Archives and Records Administration, College Park, MD.

84. M. B. McNeely, "Report of Arrest—Case of Monico Vellar and Gregorio Velasco," April 6, 1948, RG 313, US National Archives and Records Administration, San Bruno, CA.

85. G. R. Newton, "Placing of Certain Public Places out of Bounds to All Service Personnel," November 25, 1947, RG 313, US National Archives and Records Administration, San Bruno, CA.

86. For more on roads in Guåhan, refer to Christine Taitano DeLisle and Vicente M. Diaz, "Itinerant Indigeneities: Navigating Guåhan's Treacherous Roads through CHamoru Feminist Pathways," in *Allotment Stories: Indigenous Land Relations under Settler Siege*, eds. Daniel Heath Justice and Jean M. O'Brien (Minneapolis: University of Minnesota Press, 2021), 145–163.

87. C. A. Pownall, "General Order 25–47: Liberty and Shore Leave on Guam," June 13, 1947, RG 313, US National Archives and Records Administration, San Bruno, CA.

88. A. J. Carrillo, "Incident Report: Criminal Investigation Section," June 8, 1949, RG 313, US National Archives and Records Administration, San Bruno, CA.

89. Carrillo, "Incident Report." The word "flip" is a derogatory term used to describe a person of Filipino descent.

90. Keith L. Camacho, "Homomilitarism: The Same-Sex Erotics of the US Empire in Guam and Hawai'i," *Radical History Review* 123 (2015), 146.

91. Detailed information regarding the punishment of US military servicemen for committing acts of violence is not always available. This information was likely recorded but is not housed at the US National Archives.

92. C. Hawkins, "Alleged Offenses of Civilian Guards Employed by the J&G Motor Company," October 25, 1949, RG 313, US National Archives and Records Administration, San Bruno, CA.

93. John C. Fischer, "Report of Judiciary Department for Quarter Ending 31 December 1949," RG 38, US National Archives and Records Administration, College Park, MD.

94. Violent incidents were recorded but they were not framed or documented as "interracial" or "violent." While some records did mention the racial or ethnic background of the people involved, this was done with great inconsistency. Tracking the number of interracial violent crimes on the island was also difficult because CHamorus and Filipinos share some Spanish surnames.

95. C. A. Pownall, "Executive Order #21–46," October 30, 1946, RG 313, US National Archives and Records Administration, San Bruno, CA.

96. C. A. Pownall, "Passes to Visit Native Communities and Homes of Guamanians, Issuance of," May 21, 1947, RG 313, US National Archives and Records Administration, San Bruno, CA.

97. Guam Congress, "House of Assembly, Twenty-Fourth Regular Session," August 13, 1949, RG 126, US National Archives and Records Administration, College Park, MD.

98. Guam Congress, "House of Assembly."

99. Guam Congress.

100. Robert J. Barnes and Howard D. Fischer, "Interrogation Reports of Joseph Cruz and Regina San Cruz," March 31, 1948, RG 313, US National Archives and Records Administration, San Bruno, CA.

101. Michael P. Bogdanovich, "Specifications of Offenses," September 18, 1946, RG 313, US National Archives and Records Administration, San Bruno, CA.

102. J. B. Dunn, "Recommendation for Trial by General Court-Martial in the Case of Gardner, Wilbur "W," Seaman First Class, U.S. Navy," September 24, 1947, RG 313, US National Archives and Records Administration, San Bruno, CA.

103. Lauren Robin Derby, "Imperial Secrets: Vampires and Nationhood in Puerto Rico," in *A Religion of Fools?: Superstition in Historical and Comparative Perspective*, ed. Steven A. Smith and Alan Knight (Oxford: Past and Present supplement, 2008), 290–312. For more on rumors, refer to Vicente L. Rafael, *White Love and Other Events in Filipino History* (Durham, NC: Duke University Press, 2000).

104. For more on sexual violence against Native American women, refer to Andrea Smith, *Conquest: Sexual Violence and American Indian Genocide* (Cambridge, MA: South End Press, 2005).

105. *Guam Gazette*, "Capital Offense Committed on Guamanian Woman," October 3, 1945, Vertical File, Nieves M. Flores Memorial Library, Hagåtña, Guåhan.

106. *Guam Gazette*, "Capital Offense Committed."

107. *Guam Gazette*, "Rape Attempt Frustrated," October 29, 1945, Vertical File, Nieves M. Flores Memorial Library, Hagåtña, Guåhan.

108. *Guam Gazette*, "Police Investigating Double Homicide Committed in Barrigada," October 16, 1945, Vertical File, Nieves M. Flores Memorial Library, Hagåtña, Guåhan.

109. *Manila Times*, "Manilan Held for Stabbing in Guam," August 19, 1957, Vertical File, Lopez Museum and Library.

110. *Manila Times*, "Filipino Kills Guam Official," September 17, 1960, Vertical File, Lopez Museum and Library.

111. Dan Kimball, "Letter to Governor Skinner," December 13, 1949, RG 313, US National Archives and Records Administration, San Bruno, CA.

112. Yến Lê Espiritu, *Body Counts: The Vietnam War and Militarized Refuge(es)* (Oakland: University of California Press, 2014), 21.

113. I found very little evidence that statistically tabulated interracial marriages in Guåhan from 1946 to 1962. While some government records did track the number of marriages that occurred on the island, they did not track if these marriages were interracial. Newspapers and newsletters such as the *Constructionaire* did provide some marriage announcements, but this information was not consistent and did not always disclose the racial or ethnic backgrounds of the couples. This is especially challenging since CHamorus and Filipinos share some Spanish surnames.

114. Richard Barrett Lowe, "Regarding Security Regulations," April 24, 1957, Vertical File, Nieves M. Flores Memorial Library, Hagåtña, Guåhan.

115. Richard Barrett Lowe, "Letter to the Speaker of the Guam Legislature," April 2, 1958, Vertical File, Nieves M. Flores Memorial Library, Hagåtña, Guåhan.

5. From Breadbasket to Naval Air Station

1. Sylvia M. Flores and Katherine Bordallo Aguon, *The Official Chamorro-English Dictionary* (Hagåtña: Department of Chamorro Affairs: 2009), 376.

2. Flores and Aguon, *The Official Chamorro-English Dictionary*, 208. There are other villages in Guåhan that are named after body parts. For example, Mongmong, To'to, and Maite'

make up one village. Mongmong means "pound," in reference to Pontan's heartbeat. And as was noted earlier, Hagåtña is believed to come from the word *haga*, meaning "blood" in reference to Pontan's blood. For more on village names and body parts, refer to the Commission on CHamoru Language and the Teaching of the History and Culture of the Indigenous People of Guåhan, https://kumisionchamoru.guam.gov and the Guåhan Visitors Bureau https://guam .stripes.com/travel/yes-its-true-some-guam-villages-named-after-body-parts.

3. Vicente Palacious Crawford, interview with author, April 11, 2013, Pågu Bay, Guåhan.

4. Chloe B. Babauta, "Guam's Capital, People Changed Forever after War," *Pacific Daily News*. July 22, 2018.

5. E. Benavente interview, May 4, 2013.

6. E. Benavente interview, May 4, 2013.

7. Antonio Artero Sablan, interview with author, April 17, 2013, Hagåtña, Guåhan. Hereafter cited as A. Sablan interview, April 17, 2013.

8. *Champulado* is a chocolate rice pudding that is served warm or cold. *Fina'denne'* is a spicy sauce used as a condiment that is comprised mainly of soy sauce, vinegar, lemon, and chili peppers. *Kelaguen* is shredded coconut that is combined with chopped chicken, meat, or seafood that is combined with lemon juice and hot pepper. *Tinaktak* is a coconut cream–based dish that is usually combined with finely chopped chicken.

9. Madeleine Z. Bordallo, "Nihi Ta Hasso, Unhappy Labor—A History of the Tiyan Airfield, Guam," July 31, 2009, https://www.govinfo.gov/content/pkg/CRECB-2009-pt15/pdf /CRECB-2009-pt15-Pg20559.pdf.

10. The term *militourist* derives from the late I-Kiribati and African American scholar Teresia K. Teaiwa's "militourism," which describes how the tourist industry conceals militarism. For more on militourism, refer to Teresia Teaiwa, "Reading Paul Gauguin's *Noa Noa* with Epeli Hau'ofa's *Kiss in the Nederends*: Militourism, Feminism, and the 'Polynesian' Body," in *Inside Out: Literature, Cultural Politics, and Identity in the New Pacific*, ed. Vilsoni Hereniko and Rob Wilson (Lanham, MD: Rowman & Littlefield, 1999), 249–264.

11. Piti and Sumai were the two main gateways for military and civilian settlers to enter Guåhan in the prewar era. In particular, Sumai was considered the commercial center of the island due to the presence of the Pan American Company, which operated clippers out of the village.

12. Anthony Leon Guerrero, "The Economic Development of Guam," in *Kinalamten Pulitikåt: Siñenten I Chamorro/Issues in Guam's Political Development: The Chamorro Perspective* (Hagåtña: Political Status Education Coordinating Commission, 2002), 99.

13. Pacific Wrecks, "Agana Airfield," Pacificwrecks.com, accessed June 13, 2019, https:// www.pacificwrecks.com/airfields/marianas/agana/index.html.

14. Wakako Higuchi, "Japanese Occupation of Guam," Guampedia.com, accessed November 13, 2020, https://www.guampedia.com/japanese-occupation-of-guam/.

15. Francisco Leon Guerrero Castro, interview with the Guam War Claims Review Commission, Hagåtña, December 9, 2003, http://guamwarsurvivorstory.com/index.php/francisco -leon-guerrero-castro.

16. Ben Blaz, *Bisita Guam: Let Us Remember Nihi Ta Hasso* (Mangilao: University of Guam Micronesian Area Research Center, 2008), 93. For more on the experiences of CHamoru elders during World War II, refer to Shannon J. Murphy, "WWII: Oral War Histories of the Chamorro People," Guampedia.com, accessed December 7, 2020, https://www.guampedia.com/wwii -oral-war-histories-of-the-chamorro-people/.

17. Kathleen R. W. Owings, ed., "The War Years on Guam: Narratives of the Chamorro Experience," vol. 1 (Mangilao: University of Guam Micronesian Area Research Center, 1981), 2–3.

18. Owings, "The War Years," 2–3.

19. Blaz, *Bisita Guam*, 95.

20. Blaz, 95–96.

21. Anne Stoler, "Intimidations of Empire: Predicaments of the Tactile and Unseen," in *Haunted by Empire: Geographies of Intimacy in North American History*, ed. Ann Laura Stoler (Durham, NC: Duke University Press, 2006), 1.

22. John C. Benavente, interview with author, April 14, 2013, Dédidu, Guåhan. Hereafter cited as J. Benavente interview, April 14, 2013.

23. D. Colt Denfeld, "'To Be Specific, It's Our Pacific': U.S. Base Selection in the Pacific from World War II to the Late 1990s," in *Farms, Firms, and Runways: Perspectives on U.S. Military Bases in the Western Pacific*, ed. L. Eve Armentrout Ma (Chicago: Imprint Publications, 2001), 50.

24. G. E. Fischer, "Acquisition Costs and Area of Naval Air Station, Agaña," April 29, 1954, RG 313, Box 315083, US National Archives and Records Administration, San Bruno, CA.

25. Fischer, "Acquisition Costs and Area."

26. "Narrative of Naval Air Station, Agaña," October 7, 1949, RG 313, Box 57, 2, and 4, US National Archives and Records Administration, San Bruno, CA.

27. Barbara and Eddie De La Cruz, interview with author, April 24, 2013, Hagåtña, Guåhan. Hereafter cited as B. and E. De La Cruz interview, April 24, 2013.

28. Gorgonio Cabot, interview with author, April 22, 2013, Hagåtña, Guåhan. Hereafter cited as G. Cabot interview, April 22, 2013.

29. J. B. Dunn, "Details of Clarification of Contract Work," September 4, 1947, RG 313, 315020 Box 20, p. 2, US National Archives and Records Administration, San Bruno, CA.

30. M. D. Smith, "Population Report; Submission of," March 6, 1951, RG 313-58-3320, Box V6986, US National Archives and Records Administration, San Bruno, CA.

31. Vincent F. Casey, "Visit of VADM Ralph E. Wilson; Facts in Connection with Briefing of," October 29, 1957, RG 64-A-744, Box 1, US National Archives and Records Administration, San Bruno, CA.

32. Michael R. Clement Jr., "First Pan American Flights," Guampedia.com, accessed June 15, 2019, https://www.guampedia.com/first-pan-american-flights/.

33. "Narrative of Naval Air Station," October 7, 1949.

34. Casey, "Visit of VADM Ralph E. Wilson."

35. R&R is also sometimes referred to as rest and recuperation or rest and recreation.

36. E. C. Chapman, D. L. Sodrel, and H. W. Fuchs III, eds., *Glimpses of Guam 1962* (Tokyo: Toppan Printing Company, 1962), 22.

37. *New York Times*, "Guam a Rear Base for U.S. in Pacific: Most of Air Force Retaliation Power Is Concentrated on Marianas Islands," August 21, 1955, 7, ProQuest Historical Newspapers.

38. For more on US military bases, consumerism, and America towns, refer to Mark L. Gillem, *America Town: Building the Outposts of Empire* (Minneapolis: University of Minnesota Press, 2007).

39. Lauren Hirshberg, *Suburban Empire: Cold War Militarization in the US Pacific* (Oakland: University of California Press, 2022), 4.

40. June V. Campbell, "Welcome to Guam Booklet," July 26, 1952, RG 313, 315078, Box 7, US National Archives and Records Administration, San Bruno, CA.

41. For more on the cultural appropriation of aloha, refer to Stephanie Nohelani Teves, *Defiant Indigeneity: The Politics of Hawaiian Performance* (Chapel Hill: University of North Carolina Press, 2018).

42. Hope Cristobal, interview with author, April 17, 2013, Tamuneng, Guåhan. Hereafter cited as H. Cristobal interview, April 17, 2013.

43. H. H. Meadows, "Mrs. Jane Parsons, Injury Report of," July 17, 1954, RG 313, 315083, Box 83, US National Archives and Records Administration, San Bruno, CA.

44. Meadows, "Mrs. Jane Parsons."

45. Ruth Wilson Gilmore, *Golden Gulag: Prisons, Surplus, Crisis, and Opposition in Globalizing California* (Berkeley: University of California Press, 2007), 28.

46. Joseph Gerson, "U.S. Foreign Military Bases and Military Colonialism: Personal and Analytical Perspectives," in *The Bases of Empire: The Global Struggle against U.S. Military Posts*, ed. Catherine Lutz (New York: New York University Press, 2009), 49.

47. NAS Fire Marshall, "Aircraft Crash Fire Report," March 7, 1947, RG 313, 315019, Box 19, p. 1, US National Archives and Records Administration, San Bruno, CA.

48. *Washington Post*, "77 Killed in Guam Plane Crash," September 19, 1960, A1, ProQuest Historical Newspapers.

49. *Chicago Daily Tribune*, "3 Die, 5 Survive in Navy Plane Crash on Guam," December 4, 1962, 18, ProQuest Historical Newspapers.

50. B. J. Bordallo, Guam Legislature, Resolution No. 160, 1954, p 1, Nieves M. Flores Memorial Library, Hagåtña, Guåhan.

51. Assistant Chief of Staff for Logistics, "Waiver for Construction on Leased Lands NAS Agaña, Guam," June 27, 1957, RG 64-A-744, Box 1, US National Archives and Records Administration, San Bruno, CA.

52. E. W. Armentrout Jr., "Dry Well Installation for Runway Surface Drainage, Naval Air Station, Agaña, Guam; Construction of," June 9, 1954, RG 313, 315083, Box 83, US National Archives and Records Administration, San Bruno, CA.

53. Catherine Punzalan Flores McCollum, interview with author, May 7, 2013, Hagåtña, Guåhan.

54. Robert A. Underwood, "Congressman Underwood Again Calls for Federal Survey of WWII Munitions and Chemical Dumps in Guam," October 3, 2000, http://www.cpeo.org/lists/military/2000/msg00552.html; and Robert A. Underwood, "Guam's Environmental Problems," December 1, 2020, https://www.govinfo.gov/content/pkg/CRECB-2000-pt14/html/CRECB-2000-pt14-Pg20349-2.htm.

55. Anthony Ramirez, interview with author, April 28, 2013, Barigåda, Guåhan.

56. Walter Simmons, "Guam on Guard: Guam," *Chicago Daily Tribune*, September 5, 1948, C5, ProQuest Historical Newspapers.

57. Simmons, "Guam on Guard."

58. *New York Times*, "Guam a Rear Base."

59. *Chicago Daily Tribune*, "One Year Makes Guam Greater than Singapore: Navy Tells of Gigantic Building," July 20, 1945, 4, ProQuest Historical Newspapers. Interestingly, M. E. Murphy also served as the commanding officer of Naval Operating Base in Guantánamo Bay beginning in 1950. For more on Murphy in Guantánamo Bay, refer to Allen Collier, "Rear Admiral Murphy Relieves Rear Admiral Bledsoe Today," *The Indian*, December 2, 1950, 1, accessed July 20, 2020, https://ufdcimages.uflib.ufl.edu/AA/00/03/12/77/00135/AA00031277_00135.pdf.

60. Jack Sher, "Change Here for Home!," *Los Angeles Times*, October 14, 1945, E4, ProQuest Historical Newspapers.

61. *New York Times*, "Symbol of Guam's Horn of Plenty Is Klaxon at U.S. Air Force Base," January 29, 1962, 76, ProQuest Historical Newspapers.

62. For more on nuclear testing in the Marshall Islands and Marshallese diaspora, refer to Teresia K. Teaiwa, "Bikinis and Other S/pacific N/oceans," in *Militarized Currents: Toward a Decolonized*

Future in Asia and the Pacific, eds. Setsu Shigematsu and Keith L. Camacho (Minneapolis: University of Minnesota Press, 2010), 15–32; Hirshberg, *Suburban Empire*; and Jessica A. Schwartz, *Radiation Sounds: Marshallese Music and Nuclear Silences* (Durham, NC: Duke University Press, 2021).

63. Catherine Lutz, "Introduction: Bases, Empire, and Global Response," in *The Bases of Empire: The Global Struggle against U.S. Military Posts,* ed. Catherine Lutz (New York: New York University Press, 2009), 20–21.

64. H. W. Baumuer, "Contractor Assistance in Correcting Serious Deficiencies in Secondary Electrical Distribution Systems, Naval Air Station, Agaña," May 20, 1947, RG 313, 315020, Box 20, US National Archives and Records Administration, San Bruno, CA.

65. H. V. Hopkins, "Road—Beginning at Route No. 8, Adjacent to Barrigada Village, and Running Thence Northerly through the Naval Air Station, Agaña, to Marine Drive,—Request for Authority to Close to Off-Station Through Traffic," March 14, 1949, RG 313, 315060, Box 60, US National Archives and Records Administration, San Bruno, CA.

66. Hopkins, "Road—Beginning."

67. Hopkins.

68. J.B. Dunn, "Maintenance on Island Highway No. 10 across NAS Agaña," January 12, 1948, RG 313, 315043, Box 43, US National Archives and Records Administration, San Bruno, CA.

69. Waite W. Worden, "Road Patrols on Route No. 10, NAS Agaña," March 25, 1949, RG 313, 315060, Box 60, US National Archives and Records Administration, San Bruno, CA.

70. H. V. Hopkins, "Re-routing of Island Highway Route No. 10," February 1, 1949, RG 313, 315060, Box 60, US National Archives and Records Administration, San Bruno, CA.

71. P. S. Tambling, "Highway, Route #10, through NAS Agaña—Request for Authority to Close to Off-Station Through Traffic," March 25, 1949, RG 313, 315060, Box 60, US National Archives and Records Administration, San Bruno, CA.

72. Tambling, "Highway, Route #10."

73. C. A. Pownall, "Highway, Route No. 10 through NAS, Agaña; Request for Authority to Close to Off-Station Through Traffic," April 8, 1949. RG 313, 315060 box 60, U.S. National Archives and Records Administration, San Bruno, CA.

74. James T. Sablan, "Letter to Captain G. M. Winne, USN, Chief of Staff," March 7, 1960, University of Guam, Richard F. Taitano Micronesian Area Research Center.

75. F. T. Ramirez, "Letter to Captain W. E. Gaillard, USN, Chief of Staff," October 19, 1961, University of Guam, Richard F. Taitano Micronesian Area Research Center.

76. Ramirez, "Letter to Captain."

77. Ramirez.

78. Ramirez.

79. Commander Naval Forces Marianas, "Encroachment of Private Construction on the Western Boundary of the Naval Air Station, Agaña," November 5, 1953, RG 313, 315078, Box 7, US National Archives and Records Administration, San Bruno, CA.

80. Commander Naval Forces Marianas, "Encroachment of Private Construction."

81. Commander Naval Forces Marianas.

82. S. Gazze, "Permission to Marry; Request for," July 6, 1953, RG 313, 315078, Box 7, US National Archives and Records Administration, San Bruno, CA.

83. H. Brent Jr., "Statement of Private First Class Donald E. Shoemaker (656958), (6400), USMC," October 13, 1949, RG 313, Box 315063, US National Archives and Records Administration, San Bruno, CA.

84. Brent, "Statement of Private First Class Donald E. Shoemaker"; H. Brent Jr., "Statement of Private First Class Ramson T. Tew, Jr. (663639), (6400), USMC," October 13, 1949, RG 313, Box 315063, U.S National Archives and Records Administration, San Bruno, CA.

85. H. Brent Jr., "Statement of Private First Class Robert D. Talley, (611527), (7000), USMC," October 13, 1949, RG 313, Box 315036, US National Archives and Records Administration, San Bruno, CA; H. Brent Jr., "Statement of Private First Class William B. Prince, (8993010), U.S. Marine Corps," October 13, 1949, RG 313, Box 315063, US National Archives and Records Administration, San Bruno, CA.

86. C. Hawkins, "Alleged Offenses of Civilian Guards Employed by the J&G Motor Company," October 25, 1949, RG 313, Box 315063, US National Archives and Records Administration, San Bruno, CA.

Conclusion

1. From 1944 to 1949 the US government had reestablished naval authority by reinstating a naval commander to also serve as the governor of Guam. However, the Guam Congress walkout of 1949 demonstrated the disdain and frustration that CHamorus had with military rule. In 1950 the US Congress passed the Guam Organic Act, which gave CHamorus limited citizenship and a civilian-run government. From 1949 to 1970 the president of the United States had the power to appoint the governor of Guam. This would end in 1971 with the election of Carlos Camacho, the first locally elected governor of the island.

2. Robert F. Rogers, *Destiny's Landfall: A History of Guam* (Honolulu: University of Hawai'i Press, 1995), 238.

3. For more on CHamoru diaspora, refer to Jesi Lujan Bennett, "I Sengsong San Diego": The Chamoru Cultural Festival and the Formation of a Chamoru Diasporic Community," *Pacific Arts* 22, no. 1 (March 2022): 114–129, https://doi.org/10.5070/PC222156844; Michael P. Perez, "Insiders Without, Outsiders Within: Chamorro Ambiguity and Diasporic Identities on the U.S. Mainland," in *The Challenges of Globalization: Cultures in Transition in the Pacific-Asia Region*, eds. Lan-Hung Nora Chiang, John Lidstone, and Rebecca A. Stephenson (Lanham, MD: University Press of America, 2004), 47–72; Jesi Lujan Bennett, "Migrating beyond the Mattingan: CHamoru Diasporic Routes, Indigenous Identities, and Public Exhibitions" (PhD diss., University of Hawai'i at Mānoa, 2021); and Jessica Ann Unpingco Solis, "Traditions and Transitions: Explorations of Chamorro Culture through the Rosary Practice" (master's thesis: University of California, Los Angeles, 2014).

4. Keith L. Camacho and Laurel A. Monnig, "Uncomfortable Fatigues: Chamorro Soldiers, Gendered Identities, and the Question of Decolonization in Guam," in *Militarized Currents: Toward a Decolonized Future in Asia and the Pacific*, eds. Setsu Shigematsu and Keith L. Camacho (Minneapolis: University of Minnesota Press, 2010), 157.

5. Clarissa David, "Chamorro Soldiers Killed in Vietnam War Honored in DC Rites," *Saipan Tribune*, accessed August 2, 2022, https://www.saipantribune.com/index.php/chamorro-soldiers-killed-in-vietnam-war-honored-in-dc-rites/.

6. Evyn Lê Espiritu Gandhi, *Archipelago of Resettlement: Vietnamese Refugee Settlers and Decolonization across Guam and Israel-Palestine* (Oakland: University of California Press, 2022), 79–80.

7. Jana K. Lipman, *In Camps: Vietnamese Refugees, Asylum Seekers, and Repatriates* (Oakland: University of California Press, 2020), 24.

8. Lipman, *In Camps*, 32.

9. For more on the repatriation of Vietnamese refugees to Vietnam, refer to Trụ Trần Đình, *Ship of Fate: Memoir of a Vietnamese Repatriate* (Honolulu: University of Hawai'i Press, 2017).

Bibliography

Archival Collections

College Park, Maryland
  US National Archives and Records Administration
  RG 38: Records of the Office of the Chief of Naval Operations
  RG 71: Records of the Bureau of Yards and Docks
  RG 80: General Records of the Department of the Navy, 1804–1983
  RG 85: Records of the Immigration and Naturalization Service
  RG 126: Records of the Office of Territories
  RG 342: Photographs of Activities, Facilities and Personnel
Hagåtña, Guåhan
  Nieves M. Flores Memorial Library
    Vertical Files Collection
Honolulu, Hawai‘i
  Hamilton Library, University of Hawai‘i at Mānoa
    Pacific Collection
Mangilao, Guåhan
  Richard F. Taitano Micronesian Area Research Center, University of Guam
    Vertical Files Collection
Manila, Republic of the Philippines
  Department of Foreign Affairs
  Department of Labor and Employment
  National Archives of the Philippines
Pasig, Republic of the Philippines
  Lopez Museum and Library
    Vertical Files Collection

Quezon City, Republic of the Philippines
    Ateneo de Manila University
        American Historical Collection
    University of the Philippines Diliman
        University Archives and Records Depository
San Bruno, California
    US National Archives and Records Administration
        RG 313: Records of Naval Operating Forces
Silver Spring, Maryland
    National Labor College
        George Meany Memorial Archives
Washington, DC
    Naval History and Heritage Command
    US National Archives and Records Administration

Oral History Interviews

Amuan, Faye and Rodolfo. Interview with author. May 15, 2013. Hagåtña, Guåhan.
Benavente, Ed. Interview with author. May 4, 2013. Mangilao, Guåhan.
Benavente, John C. Interview with author. April 14, 2013. Dédidu, Guåhan.
Bordallo, Madeleine Z. Interview with author. May 27, 2013. Tomhom, Guåhan.
Cabot, Gorgonio. Interview with author. April 22, 2013. Hagåtña, Guåhan.
Castro, Francisco Leon Guerrero. Interview with the Guam War Claims Review
    Commission. December 9, 2003. Hagåtña, Guåhan. http://guamwarsurvivorstory
    .com/index.php/francisco-leon-guerrero-castro.
Cataluna, Delfina and Pilar Malilay. Interview with Bernie Provido Schumann and
    Burt Sardoma Jr. May 28, 2009. Interview is courtesy of *Under the American Sun*,
    Camp Roxas film project.
Crawford, Vicente Palacious. Interview with author. April 11, 2013. Pågu Bay, Guåhan.
Cristobal, Hope. Interview with author. April 17, 2013. Tamuneng, Guåhan.
De La Cruz, Barbara and Eddie. Interview with author. April 24, 2013. Hagåtña,
    Guåhan.
Diaz, Dolores. Interview with author. May 4, 2013. Tiyan, Guåhan.
Flores-Quitugua, Lourdes. Interview with author. November 30, 2009. Long
    Beach, CA.
Garrido, Jose Ulloa. Interview with author. May 17, 2013. Tutuhan, Guåhan.
Kaae, Leonard K. Interview with author. April 26, 2013. Tamuneng, Guåhan.
Long, Thomas A. Interview with author. February 8, 2011. Valley Center, CA.
Luces, John. Interview with author. July 11, 2018. Hågat, Guåhan.
Lujan, Joaquin Flores. Interview with author. May 6, 2013. Mangilao, Guåhan.
Mabini, Antonia and Sam. Interview with author. April 28, 2013. Tomhom, Guåhan.
Madrano, Cipriano. Interview with author. June 6, 2013. Dédidu, Guåhan.
Mangibin, Bayani. Interview with author. May 2, 2013. Hagåtña, Guåhan.

McCollum, Catherine Punzalan Flores. Interview with author. May 7, 2013. Hagåtña, Guåhan.

Perez, Joaquin Pangelinan. Interview with author. May 6, 2013. Hagåtña, Guåhan.

Quinata, Joe E. Interview with author. June 24, 2012, Los Angeles, CA.

———. Interview with author. June 20, 2012. Los Angeles, CA.

Ramirez, Anthony. Interview with author. April 28, 2013. Barigåda, Guåhan.

———. Personal communication. August 3, 2009. Barigåda, Guåhan.

Sablan, Antonio Artero. Interview with author. April 17, 2013. Hagåtña, Guåhan.

San Agustin, Joe T. Interview with author. May 5, 2013. Dédidu, Guåhan.

Sandra (pseudonym). Interview with author. July 8, 2018. Hagåtña, Guåhan.

Savares, Jose and Olivia. Interview with author. June 5, 2013. Dédidu, Guåhan.

Snipes, Connie Blaz. Interview with author. May 24, 2013. Dédidu, Guåhan.

Taitano, Carlos P. Personal communication. October 10, 2008. Los Angeles, CA.

Underwood, Robert A. Interview with author. April 22, 2013. Mangilao, Guåhan.

Unpingco, John S. Interview with author. May 29, 2013. Assan, Guåhan.

Walin, Julita Santos. Interview with author. May 6, 2013. Hagåtña, Guåhan.

Primary Sources

Abcede, Jose C. "Guam Policy Explained: US Naval Commander Says Navy out to Keep 'Guam for Guamanians,' Cites Strategy Needs." *Manila Times*, October 12, 1956.

Adams, G. M. "Information Report: Office of Naval Intelligence." April 27, 1956. RG 38, US National Archives and Records Administration, College Park, MD.

———. "Information Report: Office of Naval Intelligence." June 9, 1956, RG 38, US National Archives and Records Administration, College Park, MD.

Admin CINCPACFLT. "Memo to COMNAVMARIANAS." September 21, 1956. RG 38, US National Archives and Records Administration, College Park, MD.

Ammun, W. B. "Clearance Procedure for Entry into Guam." February 27, 1956. RG 38, US National Archives and Records Administration, College Park, MD.

———. "Repatriation of Filipino Contract Laborer Employees on Guam; Additional Information Concerning." April 19, 1956. RG 38, US National Archives and Records Administration, College Park, MD.

Armentrout Jr., E. W. "Dry Well Installation for Runway Surface Drainage, Naval Air Station, Agaña, Guam; Construction of." June 9, 1954. RG 313, 315083, Box 83, US National Archives and Records Administration, San Bruno, CA.

Arthur, J. M. "Memorandum: Prisoner of War Labor, Availability of." September 11, 1945. RG 313, US National Archives and Records Administration, San Bruno, CA.

Assistant Chief of Staff for Logistics. "Waiver for Construction on Leased Lands NAS Agaña, Guam." June 27, 1957. RG 64-A-744, Box 1, US National Archives and Records Administration, San Bruno, CA.

Babauta, Chloe B. "Guam's Capital, People Changed Forever after War." *Pacific Daily News.* July 22, 2018.

Baker, Dorothea Minor. "Letter to Governor C. A. Pownall." August 10, 1949. RG 313, US National Archives and Records Administration, San Bruno, CA.

Barnes, Robert J., and Howard D. Fischer. "Interrogation Reports of Joseph Cruz and Regina San Cruz." March 31, 1948. RG 313, US National Archives and Records Administration, San Bruno, CA.

Baumuer, H. W. "Contractor Assistance in Correcting Serious Deficiencies in Secondary Electrical Distribution Systems, Naval Air Station, Agaña." May 20, 1947. RG 313, 315020, Box 20, US National Archives and Records Administration, San Bruno, CA.

Beane, J. F. *From Forecastle to Cabin*. New York: Editor Publishing Co., 1905.

Beaty, Janice J. *Discovering Guam: A Guide to Its Towns, Trails and Tenants*. Tokyo: Faith Book Store, 1968.

Beers, Henry P. *American Naval Occupation and Government of Guam, 1898–1902*. Washington, DC: Navy Department, 1944.

Blaz, Ben. *Bisita Guam: Let Us Remember Nihi Ta Hasso*. Mangilao: University of Guam Micronesian Area Research Center, 2008.

Bleasdale, Victor F. "Monthly Report." March 1, 1946. RG 313, US National Archives and Records Administration, College Park, MD.

Bogdan, J. G. "U.S. Office of Naval Intelligence Information Report." April 19, 1954. RG 38, US National Archives and Records Administration, College Park, MD.

Bogdanovich, Michael P. "Specifications of Offenses." September 18, 1946. RG 313, US National Archives and Records Administration, San Bruno, CA.

Bordallo, B. J. "Guam Legislature, Resolution No. 160." 1954. Nieves M. Flores Memorial Library.

Brent, H., Jr. "Statement of Private First Class Donald E. Shoemaker (656958), (6400), USMC." October 13, 1949. RG 313, Box 315063, US National Archives and Records Administration, San Bruno, CA.

——. "Statement of Private First Class Ramson T. Tew, Jr. (663639), (6400), USMC." October 13, 1949. RG 313, Box 315063, US National Archives and Records Administration, San Bruno, CA.

——. "Statement of Private First Class Robert D. Talley, (611527), (7000), USMC." October 13, 1949. RG 313, Box 315036, US National Archives and Records Administration, San Bruno, CA.

——. "Statement of Private First Class William B. Prince, (8993010), U.S. Marine Corps." October 13, 1949. RG 313, Box 315063, US National Archives and Records Administration, San Bruno, CA.

Brown-Pacific-Maxon. *The Constructionaire* 6, no. 3, September 23, 1950. Nieves M. Flores Memorial Library, Hagåtña, Guåhan.

——. *The Constructionaire* 6, no. 20, November 22, 1950. Nieves M. Flores Memorial Library, Hagåtña, Guåhan.

Bull, Vernon T. "Letter to U.S. Navy in Washington D.C." November 13, 1947. RG 313, US National Archives and Records Administration, San Bruno, CA.

Campbell, June V. "Welcome to Guam Booklet." July 26, 1952. RG 313, 315078, Box 7, US National Archives and Records Administration, San Bruno, CA.

Carano, Paul. *Guam: Andersen Air Force Base*. Guam: Andersen Air Force Base, 1950.

Carey, Hugh, ed. *The Constructionaire*, November 3, 1951. Nieves M. Flores Memorial Library, Hagåtña, Guåhan.

———. *The Constructionaire*, October 31, 1951. Nieves M. Flores Memorial Library, Hagåtña, Guåhan.

Carrillo, A. J. "Incident Report: Criminal Investigation Section." June 8, 1949. RG 313, US National Archives and Records Administration, San Bruno, CA.

———. "Security of Our Housing Areas, Report on," June 3, 1949. RG 313, US National Archives, San Bruno, CA.

Carter, Rosa Roberto. "Education in Guam to 1950: Island and Personal History." In *Guam History: Perspectives*, vol. 1, edited by Lee D. Carter, William L. Wuerch, and Rosa Roberto Carter, 181–218. Mangilao: University of Guam Micronesian Area Research Center, 1998.

Casey, Vincent F. "Visit of VADM Ralph E. Wilson; Facts in Connection with Briefing of." October 29, 1957. RG 64-A-744, Box 1, US National Archives and Records Administration, San Bruno, CA.

Channell, Mary Augusta. "A Bit of Guam Life." *The Independent*, 1902.

Chapman, E. C., D. L. Sodrel, and H. W. Fuchs III, eds. *Glimpses of Guam 1962*. Tokyo: Toppan Printing Company, 1962. University of Guam Micronesian Area Research Center.

Chicago Daily Tribune. "One Year Makes Guam Greater than Singapore: Navy Tells of Gigantic Building." July 20, 1945, 4. ProQuest Historical Newspapers.

———. "3 Die, 5 Survive in Navy Plane Crash on Guam." December 4, 1962, 18. ProQuest Historical Newspapers.

Christian Science Monitor. "Guam Dissatisfied." December 2, 1946. Vertical File, Nieves M. Flores Memorial Library, Hagåtña, Guåhan.

———. "Many Japs on Guam Are Still in Hiding." February 18, 1946. Vertical File, Nieves M. Flores Memorial Library, Hagåtña, Guåhan.

Collier, Allen. "Rear Admiral Murphy Relieves Rear Admiral Bledsoe Today." *The Indian*, December 2, 1950, 1. Accessed July 20, 2020. https://ufdcimages.uflib.ufl.edu/AA/00/03/12/77/00135/AA00031277_00135.pdf.

Collier, John. *From Every Zenith: A Memoir; and Some Essays on Life and Thought*. Thousand Oaks, CA: Sage Books, 1963.

———. "Guam Citizens," *Washington Post*, December 4, 1946, 6

Commander Naval Forces Marianas. "Encroachment of Private Construction on the Western Boundary of the Naval Air Station, Agaña." November 5, 1953. RG 313, 315078, Box 7, US National Archives and Records Administration, San Bruno, CA.

COMNAVMARIANAS. "Filipinos on Guam." January 1956. RG 38, US National Archives and Records Administration, College Park, MD.

Coote, Robert K. *A Report on the Land-Use Condition and Land Problems on Guam*. Washington, DC: US Department of the Interior, 1950.

Coulter, Doloris. "Editor's Note." *Guam Echo*, June 30, 1948.

Cox, L. M., E. J. Dorn, K. C. McIntosh, M. G. Cook, and Allen H. White. *The Island of Guam*. Washington, DC: Government Printing Office, 1926.

Daily Mirror. "AFL-CIO Support P.I. Bid on Overseas Labor Wages." February 29, 1956. Lopez Museum and Library, Pasig City, Philippines.

——. "Buck Floor Pay in U.S. Bases," February 24, 1956, 1. Lopez Museum and Library, Pasig City, Philippines.

——. "Deny U.S. Wage Rates for P.I. Bases Labor." June 20, 1956. Lopez Museum and Library, Pasig City, Philippines.

——. "Filipino Electrician Dies in Guam Mishap." June 26, 1959. Lopez Museum and Library, Pasig City, Philippines.

——. "Guam Filipinos Refuse Contracts, Sent Home." March 17, 1955. Lopez Museum and Library, Pasig City, Philippines.

——. "House Okays Guam Protest: U.S. State Department Backs Bill Against P.I. Labor, Report," March 9, 1956, 1. Lopez Museum and Library, Pasig City, Philippines.

——. "Junk U.S.-P.I. Guam Labor Deal, 3 House Probers Urge." April 4, 1956. Lopez Museum and Library, Pasig City, Philippines.

——. "PTUC Seeks AFL-CIO Aid on Guam Wage Bill." February 20, 1956. Lopez Museum and Library, Pasig City, Philippines.

——. "Speaker Presses Get-Tough Policy on Guam Solon Team." March 27, 1956. Lopez Museum and Library, Pasig City, Philippines.

Darling, T. A. "Letter to A. B. Wonpat." January 14, 1954. Guam Legislature Vertical File, Nieves M. Flores Memorial Library, Hagåtña, Guåhan.

Decker, Duane. "Nobody Came Formal." May 1945. *Leatherneck* magazine.

De Leon, Jose P. "Reoccupation of Privately-owned Home, Request for." July 29, 1946. RG 313, US National Archives and Records Administration, San Bruno, CA.

"Domestics—Employment of." September 4, 1944. RG 313, US National Archives and Records Administration, San Bruno, CA.

Dunn, J. B. "Details of Clarification of Contract Work." September 4, 1947. RG 313, 315020, Box 20, p. 2, US National Archives and Records Administration, San Bruno, CA.

——. "Maintenance on Island Highway No. 10 across NAS Agaña." January 12, 1948. RG 313,315043, Box 43, US National Archives and Records Administration, San Bruno, CA.

——. "Out-Patient Treatments of Civilian Employees to Brown Pacific Maxon Co." June 5, July 7, and August 2, 1947. RG 313, US National Archives and Records Administration, San Bruno, CA.

——. "Recommendation for Trial by General Court-Martial in the Case of Gardner, Wilbur W. Seaman First Class, U.S. Navy." September 24, 1947. RG 313, US National Archives and Records Administration, San Bruno, CA.

Dyer, George L. "The Present Condition of Guam." *The Independent*, April 20, 1905. Guam History Vertical File, Nieves M. Flores Memorial Library, Hagåtña, Guåhan.

Eifrig, W. L. "U.S. Office of Naval Intelligence Information Report." April 23, 1954. RG 38, US National Archives and Records Administration, College Park, MD.

Elvidge, Anita M. *Guam Interlude.* Privately printed, 1972.

Elvidge, Ford Q. "I Ruled Uncle Sam's Problem Child." *Saturday Evening Post*, December 1, 1956. Ford Elvidge Vertical File, Nieves M. Flores Memorial Library, Hagåtña, Guåhan.

Endres, C. J. "Information Report: Office of Naval Intelligence." November 1, 1957. RG 38, US National Archives and Records Administration, College Park, MD.

Federal Land Taking Questionnaire of Ciriaco C. Sanchez. April 10, 1974. Federal Land Taking, Vertical File, Nieves M. Flores Memorial Library, Hagåtña, Guåhan.

Federal Land Taking Questionnaire of Delfina Cruz. April 10, 1974. Federal Land Taking, Vertical File, Nieves M. Flores Memorial Library, Hagåtña, Guåhan.

Federal Land Taking Questionnaire of Francisco S. Santos. April 11, 1974. Federal Land Taking, Vertical File, Nieves M. Flores Memorial Library, Hagåtña, Guåhan.

Federal Land Taking Questionnaire of Felicita Santos San Nicolas. April 10, 1974. Federal Land Taking, Vertical File, Nieves M. Flores Memorial Library, Hagåtña, Guåhan.

Federal Land Taking Questionnaire of Galo Lujan Salas. April 10, 1974. Federal Land Taking Vertical File, Nieves M. Flores Memorial Library, Hagåtña, Guåhan.

Federal Land Taking Questionnaire of Urelia Anderson Francisco. April 10/11, 1974. Federal Land Taking, Vertical File, Nieves M. Flores Memorial Library, Hagåtña, Guåhan.

Filipiniana. "Representations Made during Visit of Filipino Solons." April 1956. RG 38, US National Archives and Records Administration, College Park, MD.

Fischer, G. E. "Acquisition Costs and Area of Naval Air Station, Agaña." April 29, 1954. RG 313, Box 315083, US National Archives and Records Administration, San Bruno, CA.

Fischer, John C. "Report of Judiciary Department for Quarter Ending 31 December 1949." RG 38, US National Archives and Records Administration, College Park, MD.

——. "Statement of Chief Justice of Guam for Secretary John T. Koehler Concerning the Status and Situation of the Land Acquisition Program on Guam Insofar as the Courts Are Involved." January 8, 1950. RG 38, US National Archives and Records Administration, College Park, MD.

Fogler, R. H. "Negotiations between U.S. Government and Philippines Government Regarding Wage Rates and Conditions of Employment Applicable to Alien Filipinos Employed by Military or Military Contractors at Military Bases in Guam and the Philippines." February 27, 1956. RG 38, US National Archives and Records Administration, College Park, MD.

Forrestal, James. "Naval Intelligence Functions and Responsibilities." November 1, 1945. RG 313, US National Archives and Records Administration, San Bruno, CA.

Gazze, S. "Permission to Marry; Request for." July 6, 1953. RG 313, 315078, Box 7, US National Archives and Records Administration, San Bruno, CA.

Guam Congress. "House of Assembly, Twenty-Fourth Regular Session." August 13, 1949. RG 126, US National Archives and Records Administration, College Park, MD.

——. "Senate Subcommittee on Territories of the Senate, Committee on Interior and Insular Affairs. S. 1215." 11th Legislature, August 4, 1971. Federal Land Taking, Vertical File, Nieves M. Flores Memorial Library, Hagåtña, Guåhan.

Guam Gazette. "Capital Offense Committed on Guamanian Woman." October 3, 1945. Vertical File, Nieves M. Flores Memorial Library, Hagåtña, Guåhan.

——. "Police Investigating Double Homicide Committed in Barrigada." October 16, 1945. Vertical File, Nieves M. Flores Memorial Library, Hagåtña, Guåhan.

——. "Rape Attempt Frustrated." October 29, 1945. Vertical File, Nieves M. Flores Memorial Library, Hagåtña, Guåhan.

Guam Legislature. "Taxi-dance Hearing." January 16, 1954. Senators' Speeches Vertical File, Nieves M. Flores Memorial Library, Hagåtña, Guåhan.

Guam News. "Guam Police List Weapons, Drugs Found at Roxas." February 7, 1950. RG 126, US National Archives and Records Administration, College Park, MD.

Gurley, D. D. "POW Labor—Request for." November 3, 1945. RG 313, US National Archives and Records Administration, San Bruno, CA.

Harrison, Peyton. "Civilian Morale on Guam; Monthly Summary Report On." December 26, 1944. RG 313, US National Archives and Records Administration, College Park, MD.

Harrington, Omar L. "Minutes of Armed Forces Disciplinary Control Board Meeting." March 25, 1954. RG 313, US National Archives and Records Administration, San Bruno, CA.

Hawkins, C. "Alleged Offenses of Civilian Guards Employed by the J&G Motor Company." October 25, 1949. RG 313, Box 315063, US National Archives and Records Administration, San Bruno, CA.

——. "Loyalty Record Check of Employees as of 30 September 1947." December 28, 1949. RG 313, US National Archives and Records Administration, San Bruno, CA.

Henson, Maria Rosa. *Comfort Woman: A Filipina's Story of Prostitution and Slavery under the Japanese Military.* Lanham, MD: Rowman & Littlefield, 1999.

Herrle, L. D. "Augmentation of Native Labor on Guam for Employment by the Navy." March 4, 1946. RG 313, US National Archives and Records Administration, College Park, MD.

Hinson, M. T. "Letter to Island Commander of Guam." January 19, 1946. RG 313, US National Archives and Records Administration, San Bruno, CA.

Hopkins, Ernest M., Maurice J. Tobin, and Knowles A. Ryerson. "Hopkins Committee Report on the Civil Governments of Guam and American Samoa." March 25, 1947. Hopkins Report Vertical File, Nieves M. Flores Memorial Library, Hagåtña, Guåhan.

Hopkins, H. V. "Louie Levine, Resignation of." December 16, 1948. RG 313, US National Archives and Records Administration, San Bruno, CA.

——. "Re-routing of Island Highway Route No. 10." February 1, 1949. RG 313, 315060, Box 60, US National Archives and Records Administration, San Bruno, CA.

——. "Road—Beginning at Route No. 8, adjacent to Barrigada Village, and Running Thence Northerly through the Naval Air Station, Agaña, to Marine Drive—Request for Authority to Close to Off-Station Through Traffic." March 14, 1949. RG 313, 315060, Box 60, US National Archives and Records Administration, San Bruno, CA.

Jones, R. W. "Weekly Sanitation Report." October 10, 1949. RG 313, US National Archives and Records Administration, San Bruno, CA.

Kimball, Dan. "Letter to Governor Skinner." December 13, 1949. RG 313, US National Archives and Records Administration, San Bruno, CA.

Koehler, John T. "Guam Land Acquisition Program." April 18, 1950. RG 38, US National Archives and Records Administration, College Park, MD.

Land and Claims Commission, Guam, to the Chief of Naval Operations. "Scope of Program and Request for Personnel—Report on." December 18, 1945. RG 38, US National Archives and Records Administration, College Park, MD.

Larson, Henry L. "The Story of Guam." *Navy News*. January 5, 1946. Guam History Vertical File, Nieves M. Flores Memorial Library, Hagåtña, Guåhan.

Leiss, Edward. "Letter to Island Commander Guam." February 25, 1946. RG 313, US National Archives and Records Administration, San Bruno, CA.

——. "Telegram to American Consul." April 5, 1947. RG 313, US National Archives and Records Administration, San Bruno, CA.

Levitt, Ronald. "In Behalf of the Gooney Birds," *Our Navy*. July 1953, 11. Navy Vertical File, Nieves M. Flores Memorial Library, Hagåtña, Guåhan.

Life. "Guam: U.S. Makes Little Island into Mighty Base." July 2, 1945.

——. "Speaking of Pictures . . . Marines Find Pin-Ups and Glamour on Guam." June 18, 1945.

Lowe, Richard Barrett. "Letter to the Speaker of the Guam Legislature." April 2, 1958. Vertical File, Nieves M. Flores Memorial Library, Hagåtña, Guåhan.

——. "Regarding Security Regulations." April 24, 1957. Vertical File, Nieves M. Flores Memorial Library, Hagåtña, Guåhan.

Manila Times. "Asian Group Backs PI on Floor Wage." April 15, 1956. Lopez Museum and Library, Pasig City, Philippines.

——. "Better Deal for Guam Folk." April 15, 1956. Lopez Museum and Library, Pasig City, Philippines.

——. "Disclaim Guam Wage Discrimination." January 28, 1948. Lopez Museum and Library, Pasig City, Philippines.

——. "Filipino Employe[e]s of US Navy at Guam Contented, Says Union Chief." February 6, 1947. Lopez Museum and Library, Pasig City, Philippines.

——. "Filipino Kills Guam Official." September 17, 1960. Vertical File, Lopez Museum and Library.

——. "Guam Smuggling Ring Broken Up." June 9, 1950. Lopez Museum and Library, Pasig City, Philippines.

——. "Manilan Held for Stabbing in Guam." August 19, 1957. Vertical File, Lopez Museum and Library, Pasig City, Philippines.

——. "PI Workers in Guam Hit." April 13, 1956. Lopez Museum and Library, Pasig City, Philippines.

——. "PI Workers in Guam Hit." April 13, 1956. Lopez Museum and Library, Pasig City, Philippines.

——. "PI Gov't Will Protest Guam Wage Bill in US." February 19, 1956. Lopez Museum and Library, Pasig City, Philippines.

——. "Solons Assure Guam Workers, Hear Plaints." April 4, 1956. Lopez Museum and Library, Pasig City, Philippines.

——. "2 Filipino Workers on Guam Interred." January 21, 1948. Lopez Museum and Library, Pasig City, Philippines.

Martin, Harold H. "Heart Trouble in Paradise." *Saturday Evening Post.* November 1, 1947.

Navy News. "Island Rebuilding to Include Modern Homes for Guamanians." February 10, 1946. Vertical File, Nieves M. Flores Memorial Library, Hagåtña, Guåhan.

McNeely, M. B. "Report of Arrest—Case of Monico Vellar and Gregorio Velasco." April 6, 1948. RG 313, US National Archives and Records Administration, San Bruno, CA.

Meadows, H. H. "Mrs. Jane Parsons, Injury Report of." July 17, 1954. RG 313, 315083, Box 83, US National Archives and Records Administration, San Bruno, CA.

Morgan, Eugene. *So You Want to Go to Guam.* New York: Vantage Press, 1951.

Moylan, Fred. "Letter to the Congress of Guam." January 4, 1954. Guåhan Legislature Vertical File, Nieves M. Flores Memorial Library, Hagåtña, Guåhan.

Myers, J. N. "Examination of Native Civilians for Employment." July 31, 1946. RG 313, US National Archives and Records Administration, San Bruno, CA.

"Narrative of Naval Air Station, Agaña." October 7, 1949. RG 313, Box 57, 2, and 4, US National Archives and Records Administration, San Bruno, CA.

NAS Fire Marshall. "Aircraft Crash Fire Report." March 7, 1947. RG 313, 315019, Box 19, p. 1, US National Archives and Records Administration, San Bruno, CA.

Naval Government of Guam. "Monthly Report for November 1946." November 30, 1946. RG 313, US National Archives and Records Administration, College Park, MD.

Newton, G. R. "Placing of Certain Public Places out of Bounds to All Service Personnel." November 25, 1947. RG 313, US National Archives and Records Administration, San Bruno, CA.

New York Times. "Forgotten Guam." February 20, 1946.

——. "Guam Converted into Big Fortress." December 6, 1944.

——. "Guam Is Declared New Pearl Harbor." April 22, 1945.

——. "Guam a Rear Base for U.S. in Pacific: Most of Air Force Retaliation Power Is Concentrated on Marianas Islands." August 21, 1955, 7. ProQuest Historical Newspapers.

——. "Robert Trumbull Dies at 80; Reported on War for Times." October 13, 1992, B6. Accessed August 1, 2020. https://www.nytimes.com/1992/10/13/obituaries/robert-trumbull-dies-at-80-reported-on-war-for-times.html.

——. "Symbol of Guam's Horn of Plenty Is Klaxon at U.S. Air Force Base." January 29, 1962, 76. ProQuest Historical Newspapers.

Office of Naval Intelligence. "Strategic Study of Guam ONI-99." February 1, 1944. Nieves M. Flores Memorial Library, Hagåtña, Guåhan.

Owings, Kathleen R. W., ed. "The War Years on Guam: Narratives of the Chamorro Experience," vol. 1. Mangilao: University of Guam Micronesian Area Research Center, 1981.

Pacific Area Travel Association. "Pacific News." March 17, 1967.

Paredes, Victorino P. "Consulate of the Philippines." May 12, 1958. National Library of the Philippines, Manila, Philippines.

Peiper, Mark-Alexander. "Guam Survivor Recalls WWII Forced March." *Pacific Daily News.* June 22, 2004. http://166.122.164.43/archive/2004/june/06-22-17.htm.

Pownall, C. A. "Availability of Guamanians for Consultation and Evidence." December 28, 1946. RG 313, US National Archives and Records Administration, San Bruno, CA.

——. "Executive Order #21–46." October 30, 1946. RG 313, US National Archives and Records Administration, San Bruno, CA.

——. "General Order 25–47: Liberty and Shore Leave on Guam." June 13, 1947. RG 313, US National Archives and Records Administration, San Bruno, CA.

——. "Highway, Route No. 10 through NAS, Agaña; Request for Authority to Close to Off-Station Through Traffic." April 8, 1949. RG 313-315060, Box 60, US National Archives and Records Administration, San Bruno, CA.

——. "Passes to Visit Native Communities and Homes of Guamanians, Issuance of." May 21, 1947. RG 313, US National Archives and Records Administration, San Bruno, CA.

——. "Rules and Regulations for Labor Contracts." October 14, 1946. RG 313, US National Archives and Records Administration, San Bruno, CA.

Public Relations Newsletter. "Community Relations Stressed by UnderSecNav." November 18, 1949, vol. 1, no. 37. RG 313 Naval Government Unit, US National Archives and Records Administration, San Bruno, CA.

Ramirez, F. T. "Letter to Captain W. E. Gaillard, USN, Chief of Staff." October 19, 1961. University of Guam, Richard F. Taitano Micronesian Area Research Center.

Rauber, Louis J. "Guam Land and Claims Commission and Guam Land Transfer Board." September 24, 1948. RG 313, US National Archives and Records Administration, San Bruno, CA.

Republic of the Philippines. "Exchange of Notes Constituting an Agreement between the Republic of the Philippines and the United States of America." May 1947. Department of Foreign Affairs Archives.

Sablan, James T. "Letter to Captain G. M. Winne, USN, Chief of Staff." March 7, 1960. University of Guam, Richard F. Taitano Micronesian Area Research Center.

Salenga, Cesar. "PI Opposition Mounts against U.S. Labor Bill." March 31, 1956. Lopez Museum and Library, Pasig City, Philippines.

Salisbury, K. B. "Reoccupation of Privately-owned Home—Request for." August 15, 1946. RG 313, US National Archives and Records Administration, San Bruno, CA.

Sanchez, Simon A. "Resolution Adopted by the Guam Congress on 1 May 1948." May 10, 1948. Land Taking (Federal) Vertical File, Nieves M. Flores Memorial Library, Hagåtña, Guåhan.

Schmidt, L. E. "Security at Camp Asan." March 14, 1949. RG 313, US National Archives and Records Administration, San Bruno, CA.

Schwartz, Harold. "Policy Regarding Disposition of Government-owned Property Remaining on Lands Released for Guamanian Uses." January 23, 1948. RG 313, US National Archives and Records Administration, San Bruno, CA.

Shanahan, E. K. "Warning Regarding the Request for Information from Non-Official Agencies." September 16, 1949. RG 313, US National Archives and Records Administration, San Bruno, CA.

Sher, Jack. "Change Here for Home!" *Los Angeles Times.* October 14, 1945, E4. ProQuest Historical Newspapers.

Shriver, Mrs. Paul D. "Guam Women's Club to Guam Legislature." December 8, 1953. Guam Legislature Vertical File, Nieves M. Flores Memorial Library, Hagåtña, Guåhan.

——. "Letter to the Guam Legislature." December 8, 1953. Guam Legislature Vertical Files 1950s, Nieves M. Flores Memorial Library, Hagåtña, Guåhan.

Simmons, Walter. "Guam on Guard: Guam." *Chicago Daily Tribune.* September 5, 1948, C5. ProQuest Historical Newspapers.

Smith, M. D. "Population Report; Submission of." March 6, 1951. RG 313-58-3320, Box V6986, US National Archives and Records Administration, San Bruno, CA.

Stump, Felix B. "Command Responsibility in Representing the United States." June 24, 1954. RG 313, US National Archives and Records Administration, San Bruno, CA.

——. "Repatriation of Filipino Contract Laborer Employees on Guam; Additional Information Concerning." June 12, 1956. RG 38, US National Archives and Records Administration, College Park, MD.

Sullivan, John L. "Removal of Employees Involving Reasonable Doubt as to Loyalty; Subversive Activity; and Membership in un-American Groups." January 14, 1947. RG 313, US National Archives and Records Administration, San Bruno, CA.

Sullivan, Walter. "Guam Mushrooms into a Metropolis." *New York Times.* November 30, 1948.

Tambling, P. S. "Highway, Route #10, through NAS Agaña—Request for Authority to Close to Off-Station Through Traffic." March 25, 1949. RG 313-315060, Box 60, US National Archives and Records Administration, San Bruno, CA.

Territorial Sun. "$20 Million Capehart Project Starts." October 26, 1958. University of Guam's Richard F. Taitano Micronesian Area Research Center.

Torres, Jose M. *The Massacre at Atåte.* Mangilao: University of Guam Press, 2021.

Trần Đình, Trụ. *Ship of Fate: Memoir of a Vietnamese Repatriate*, translated by Bac Hoai Tran and Jana K. Lipman. Honolulu: University of Hawai'i Press, 2017.

Trumbull, Robert. "Congress Delays Guam Rebuilding." *New York Times.* February 19, 1946.

Udall, Stuart L. *America's Day Begins in Guam . . . U.S.A.* Washington, DC: Office of Territories, 1967.

US Air Force. *Guam: Key to the Pacific.* Guam: Andersen Air Force Base, 1947.

US Civil Service Commission. "Application for Federal Employment." July 26, 1947. RG 313, US National Archives and Records Administration, San Bruno, CA.

US Deputy Chief of Naval Operations Guam. "Filipino Labor Situation on Guam." July 11, 1952. RG 38, US National Archives and Records Administration, College Park, MD.

US House Sub-Committee on Interior and Insular Affairs. "2nd GL Public Hearing." December 1, 1954. Vertical File, Nieves M. Flores Memorial Library, Hagåtña, Guåhan.

US House Sub-Committee on Public Lands. November 22, 1949. RG 38, US National Archives and Records Administration, College Park, MD.

Buskirk, E. F., Jr. "Entry, Re-Entry, Repatriation and Deportation of Filipinos." January 16, 1958. RG 38, US National Archives and Records Administration, College Park, MD.

Vicariate Union of Holy Name Societies. "Petition to the Second Guam Legislature." January 4, 1954. Guam Legislature Vertical File, Nieves M. Flores Memorial Library, Hagåtña, Guåhan.

Washington Post. "77 Killed in Guam Plane Crash." September 19, 1960, A1. ProQuest Historical Newspapers.

Watson, L. J. "Status of Investigations of Land and Claims Commission. Proposed Issuance of T.A.D. Orders to OinC to Confer with Office of CNO." August 20, 1945. RG 38, US National Archives and Records Administration, College Park, MD.

White, Sid. "Disparity in Pay Cited: Failure of Gov't to Secure Better Conditions Scored." *Manila Times.* September 10, 1956. Lopez Museum and Library, Pasig City, Philippines.

Williams, V. "Additional Press Articles on Alleged Exploitation of Philippine Laborers in Guam." April 1, 1954. RG 85, US National Archives and Records Administration, College Park, MD.

———. "Information Report: Office of Naval Intelligence." April 12, 1954. RG 38, US National Archives and Records Administration, College Park, MD.

Wing Public Information Office. *Destination Guam.* Guam: Andersen Air Force Base, 1950. University of Guam, Richard F. Taitano Micronesian Area Research Center.

Wolfe, L. Eugene. "Report of Field Trip to Pacific Islands." October 31, 1947. RG 313, US National Archives and Records Administration, San Bruno, CA.

Worden, Waite. "Road Patrols on Route No. 10, NAS Agaña." March 25, 1949. RG 313, 315060, Box 60, US National Archives and Records Administration, San Bruno, CA.

Secondary Sources

Adams, Kevin. *Class and Race in the Frontier Army: Military Life in the West, 1870–1890.* Norman: University of Oklahoma Press, 2009.

Anderson, Warwick. *Colonial Pathologies: American Tropical Medicine, Race, and Hygiene in the Philippines.* Durham, NC: Duke University Press, 2006.

Attewell, Nadine, and Wesley Attewell. "Between Asia and Empire: Infrastructures of Encounter in the Archive of War." *Inter-Asia Cultural Studies* 20, no. 2 (2019): 162–179.

Attewell, Wesley. "The Lifelines of Empire: Logistics as Infrastructural Power in Occupied South Vietnam." *American Quarterly* 72, no. 4 (2020): 909–935.

Ayala, Cesar J., and Jose L. Bolivar. *Battleship Vieques: Puerto Rico from World War II to the Korean War.* Princeton, NJ: Markus Wiener Publishers, 2011.

Baldoz, Rick. "'Comrade Carlos Bulosan': U.S. State Surveillance and the Cold War Suppression of Filipino Radicals." *Asia-Pacific Journal* 33, no. 3 (2014). http://www.japanfocus.org/-Rick-Baldoz/4165.

——. *The Third Asiatic Invasion: Migration and Empire in Filipino America, 1898–1946.* New York: New York University Press, 2011.

Ballendorf, Dirk Anthony. "Guam Military Action in World War II." In *Guam History: Perspectives*, vol. 1, edited by Lee D. Carter, William L. Wuerch, and Rosa Roberto Carter, 219–238. Mangilao: University of Guam Micronesian Area Research Center, 1998.

Bender, Daniel E., and Jana K. Lipman, eds. *Making the Empire Work: Labor and United States Imperialism.* New York: New York University Press, 2015.

Bennett, Jesi Lujan. "'I Sengsong San Diego': The Chamoru Cultural Festival and the Formation of a Chamoru Diasporic Community." *Pacific Arts* 22, no. 1 (March 2022): 114–129. https://doi.org/10.5070/PC222156844.

——. "Migrating beyond the Mattingan: CHamoru Diasporic Routes, Indigenous Identities, and Public Exhibitions." PhD diss., University of Hawai'i at Mānoa, 2021.

Bennett, Judith A., and Angela Wanhalla. "Introduction: A New Net Goes Fishing." In *Mothers' Darlings of the South Pacific: The Children of Indigenous Women and U.S. Servicemen, World War II*, edited by Judith A. Bennett and Angela Wanhalla, 1–30. Honolulu: University of Hawai'i Press, 2016.

Bevacqua, Michael Lujan. "These May or May Not Be Americans: The Patriotic Myth and the Hijacking of Chamorro History on Guam." Master's thesis, University of Guam, 2004.

Bogliolo, Luis Paulo. "Rethinking Military Necessity in the Law of Armed Conflict." *SSRN Electronic Journal* (Brasilia: University of Brazil, 2012), n.p. doi: 10.2139/ssrn.2201129.

Brown, Jennifer S. H., and Elizabeth Vibert. *Reading beyond Words: Contexts for Native History.* Toronto: University of Toronto Press, 2003.

Byrd, Jodi A. *The Transit of Empire: Indigenous Critiques of Colonialism.* Minneapolis: University of Minnesota Press, 2011.

Camacho, Keith L. *Cultures of Commemoration: The Politics of War, Memory, and History in the Mariana Islands.* Honolulu: University of Hawai'i Press, 2011.

——. "Homomilitarism: The Same-Sex Erotics of the US Empire in Guam and Hawai'i." *Radical History Review* 123 (2015): 144–175.

———. "The Politics of Indigenous Collaboration: The Role of Chamorro Interpreters in Japan's Pacific Empire, 1914–45." *Journal of Pacific History* 43, no. 2 (2008): 207–222.

———. *Sacred Men: Law, Torture, and Retribution in Guam.* Durham, NC: Duke University Press, 2019.

Camacho, Keith L., and Laurel A. Monnig. "Uncomfortable Fatigues: Chamorro Soldiers, Gendered Identities, and the Question of Decolonization in Guam." In *Militarized Currents: Toward a Decolonized Future in Asia and the Pacific*, edited by Setsu Shigematsu and Keith L. Camacho, 147–180. Minneapolis: University of Minnesota Press, 2010.

Campbell, Bruce L. "The Filipino Community of Guam, 1945–1975." Master's thesis, University of Hawai'i at Mānoa, 1987.

Capozzola, Christopher. *Bound by War: How the United States and the Philippines Built America's First Pacific Century.* New York: Basic Books, 2020.

Carano, Paul, and Pedro C. Sanchez. *A Complete History of Guam.* Rutland, VT: Charles E. Tuttle, 1964.

Carson, Mike T., Anthony Tamayo Jr., Victoria-Lola M. Leon Guerrero, Brett Storie, Monique Storie, and Mary E. Camacho. *Lina'la': Portraits of Life at Litekyan.* Mangilao: University of Guam Richard Flores Taitano Micronesian Area Research Center, 2018.

Choy, Catherine Ceniza. *Empire of Care: Nursing and Migration in Filipino American History.* Durham, NC: Duke University Press, 2003.

Chan, Sucheng. *Asian Americans: An Interpretive History.* New York: Twayne Publishers, 1991.

Cho, Grace M. *Haunting the Korean Diaspora: Shame, Secrecy, and the Forgotten War.* Minneapolis: University of Minnesota Press, 2008.

Choy, Catherine Ceniza. *Empire of Care: Nursing and Migration in Filipino American History.* Durham, NC: Duke University Press, 2003.

Cogan, Doloris Coulter. *We Fought the Navy and Won: Guam's Quest for Democracy.* Honolulu: University of Hawai'i Press, 2008.

Cohen, Lizabeth. *A Consumers' Republic: The Politics of Mass Consumption in Postwar America.* New York: Vintage Books, 2003.

———. *Making a New Deal: Industrial Workers in Chicago, 1919–1939*, 2nd ed.. New York: Cambridge University Press, 2008.

Colby, Jason M. *The Business of Empire: United Fruit, Race, and U.S. Expansion in Central America.* Ithaca, NY: Cornell University Press, 2011.

Cooper, Frederick. *Colonialism in Question: Theory, Knowledge, History.* Berkeley: University of California Press, 2005.

Cowen, Deborah. "Following the Infrastructures of Empire: Notes on Cities, Settler Colonialism, and Method." *Urban Geography* 41, no. 4 (2019): 469–486.

Crocombe, Ron. *Asia in the Pacific Islands: Replacing the West.* Suva, Fiji: IPS Publications, 2007.

Cunningham, Lawrence J. *Ancient Chamorro Society.* Honolulu: Bess Press, 1992.

Dalisay, Francis. "Social Control in an American Pacific Island: Guam's Local Newspaper Reports on Liberation." *Journal of Communication and Inquiry* 33, no. 3 (July 2009): 239–257.

Daniel, Cletus E. *Bitter Harvest: A History of California Farmworkers, 1870–1941.* Berkeley: University of California Press, 1981.

Davis, Sasha. *The Empires' Edge: Militarization, Resistance, and Transcending Hegemony in the Pacific.* Athens: University of Georgia Press, 2015.

Day, Iyko. *Alien Capital: Asian Racialization and the Logic of Settler Colonial Capitalism.* Durham, NC: Duke University Press, 2016.

DeLisle, Christine Taitano. "Destination Chamorro Culture: Notes on Realignment, Rebranding, and Post-9/11 Militourism in Guam,." *American Quarterly* 68, no. 3 (2016): 563–572.

——. "A History of Chamorro Nurse-Midwives in Guam and a 'Placental Politics' for Indigenous Feminisms." *Intersections: Gender and Sexuality in Asia and the Pacific* 37 (2015): n.p. http://intersections.anu.edu.au/issue37/delisle.htm.

——. *Placental Politics: CHamoru Women, White Womanhood, and Indigeneity under U.S. Colonialism in Guam.* Chapel Hill: University of North Carolina Press, 2021.

DeLisle, Christine Taitano, and Vicente M. Diaz. "Itinerant Indigeneities: Navigating Guåhan's Treacherous Roads through CHamoru Feminist Pathways." In *Allotment Stories: Indigenous Land Relations under Settler Siege*, edited by Daniel Heath Justice and Jean M. O'Brien, 145–163. Minneapolis: University of Minnesota Press, 2021.

Deloria, Vine, Jr. *God Is Red: A Native View of Religion.* Golden, CO: Fulcrum Publishing, 1992.

DeLoughrey, Elizabeth M. "Heliotropes: Solar Ecologies and Pacific Radiations." In *Postcolonial Ecologies: Literatures of the Environment*, edited by Elizabeth M. DeLoughrey and George B. Handley, 235–253. New York: Oxford University Press, 2011.

——. "The Myth of Isolates: Ecosystem Ecologies in the Nuclear Pacific." *Cultural Geographies* 20, no. 2 (2012): 167–184.

Denfeld, D. Colt. "'To Be Specific, It's Our Pacific': Base Selection in the Pacific from World War II to the Late 1990s." *Farms, Firms, and Runways: Perspectives on U.S. Military Bases in the Western Pacific*, edited by L. Eve Armentrout Ma, 49–64. Chicago: Imprint Publications, 2001.

Derby, Lauren Robin. "Imperial Secrets: Vampires and Nationhood in Puerto Rico." In *A Religion of Fools?: Superstition in Historical and Comparative Perspective*, edited by Steven A. Smith and Alan Knight, 290–312. Oxford: Past and Present supplement, 2008.

Diaz, Vicente M. "Deliberating 'Liberation Day': Identity, History, Memory, and War in Guam." In *Perilous Memories: The Asia Pacific War(s)*, edited by T. T. Fujitani, Geoffrey White, and Lisa Yoneyama, 155–180. Durham, NC: Duke University Press, 2001.

——. "'Fight Boys, til the Last . . .': Islandstyle Football and the Remasculinization of Indigeneity in the Militarized American Pacific Islands." In *Pacific Diaspora: Island Peoples in the United States and across the Pacific*, edited by Paul Spickard, Joanne L. Rondilla, and Debbie Hippolite Wright, 169–194. Honolulu: University of Hawai'i Press, 2002.

——. *Repositioning the Missionary: Rewriting the Histories of Colonialism, Native Catholicism, and Indigeneity in Guam.* Honolulu: University of Hawai'i Press, 2010.

Dorwat, Jeffery M. *The Office of Naval Intelligence: The Birth of America's First Intelligence Agency, 1865–1918*. Annapolis, MD: Naval Institute Press, 1979.

Dower, John W. *War without Mercy: Race and Power in the Pacific War*. New York: Pantheon, 1987.

Dudziak, Mary L. *Cold War Civil Rights: Race and the Image of American Democracy*. Princeton, NJ: Princeton University Press, 2000.

Dunbar-Ortiz, Roxanne. *An Indigenous Peoples' History of the United States*. Boston: Beacon Press, 2014.

Ekbladh, David. *The Great American Mission: Modernization and the Construction of an American World Order*. Princeton, NJ: Princeton University Press, 2010.

Enloe, Cynthia. *Bananas, Beaches and Bases: Making Feminist Sense of International Politics*. Berkeley: University of California Press, 2000.

———. *Maneuvers: The International Politics of Militarizing Women's Lives*. Berkeley: University of California Press, 2000.

Eperjesi, John R. "Basing the Pacific: Exceptional Spaces of the Wilkes Exploring Expedition, 1838–1842." *Amerasia Journal* 37, no. 3 (2011): 1–17.

Escudero, Kevin. "Federal Immigration Laws and U.S. Empire: Tracing Immigration Lawmaking in the Mariana Islands." *Amerasia Journal* 46, no. 1 (2020): 63–78.

Espana-Maram, Linda M. *Creating Masculinity in Los Angeles's Little Manila: Working-Class Filipinos and Popular Culture, 1920s–1950s*. New York: Columbia University Press, 2006.

Espiritu, Augusto. *Five Faces of Exile: The Nation and Filipino American Intellectuals*. Stanford, CA: Stanford University Press, 2005.

———. "Inter-Imperial Relations, the Pacific, and Asian American History." *Pacific Historical Review* 83, no. 2 (2014): 238–254.

Espiritu Gandhi, Evyn Lê. *Archipelago of Resettlement: Vietnamese Refugee Settlers and Decolonization across Guam and Israel-Palestine*. Oakland: University of California Press, 2022.

Espiritu, Yến Lê. *Body Counts: The Vietnam War and Militarized Refuge(es)*. Oakland: University of California Press, 2014.

———. *Home Bound: Filipino American Lives across Cultures, Communities, and Countries*. Berkeley: University of California Press, 2003.

Falgout, Suzanne, Lin Poyer, and Laurence M. Carucci. *Memories of War: Micronesians in the Pacific War*. Honolulu: University of Hawai'i Press, 2008.

Farish, Matthew. *The Contours of America's Cold War*. Minneapolis: University of Minnesota Press, 2010.

Farrell, Don A. *Tinian and the Bomb: Project Alberta and Operation Centerboard*. Tinian: Micronesian Productions, 2018.

Flores, Alfred P. "US Colonial Education in Guam, 1899–1950." In *Oxford Research Encyclopedias of American History*. March 26, 2019. https://doi.org/10.1093/acrefore/9780199329175.013.512.

Flores, Judy Selk. *Estorian Inalahan: History of a Spanish Era Village in Guam*. Hagåtña: Irensia Publications, 2011.

Flores, Sylvia M., and Katherine Bordallo Aguon. *The Official Chamorro-English Dictionary*. Hagåtña: Department of Chamorro Affairs, 2009.

Florida, Henry. *Iloilo in the 20th Century: An Economic History*. Iloilo City: University of the Philippines, 1997.

Forbes, Mark. "Military." In *Kinalamten Pulitikåt: Siñenten I Chamorro/Issues in Guam's Political Development: The Chamorro Perspective*. Hagåtña: Political Status Education Coordinating Commission, 2002: 39–44.

Foucault, Michel. *Discipline and Punish: The Birth of the Prison*. New York: Vintage Books, 1995.

Friedman, Andrew. "US Empire, World War 2, and the Racialising of Labour." *Race and Class* 58, no. 4 (2017), 23–38.

Fujikane, Candace, and Jonathan Y. Okamura. "Introduction." In *Asian Settler Colonialism: From Local Governance to the Habits of Everyday Life in Hawai'i*, edited by Candace Fujikane and Jonathan Y. Okamura, 1–42. Honolulu: University of Hawai'i Press, 2008.

Fujitani, T. *Race for Empire: Koreans as Japanese and Japanese as Americans during World War II*. Berkeley: University of California Press, 2013.

Fujita-Rony, Dorothy B. *American Workers, Colonial Power: Philippine Seattle and the Transpacific West, 1919–1941*. Berkeley: University of California Press, 2003.

Gaddis, John Lewis. *The Cold War: A New History*. New York: Penguin Books, 2005.

Garcia, Mario T. *Desert Immigrants: The Mexicans of El Paso, 1880–1920*. New Haven, CT: Yale University Press, 1981.

Garrison, Rebekah. "Settler Responsibility: Respatialising Dissent in 'America' beyond Continental Borders." *Shima* 13, no. 2 (2019): 56–75.

Gerson, Joseph. "U.S. Foreign Military Bases and Military Colonialism: Personal and Analytical Perspectives." In *The Bases of Empire: The Global Struggle against U.S. Military Posts*, edited by Catherine Lutz, 47–70. New York: New York University Press, 2009.

Gillem, Mark L. *America Town: Building the Outposts of Empire*. Minneapolis: University of Minnesota Press, 2007.

Gilmore, Ruth Wilson. *Golden Gulag: Prisons, Surplus, Crisis, and Opposition in Globalizing California*. Berkeley: University of California Press, 2007.

Go, Julian. "Modes of Rule in America's Overseas Empire: The Philippines, Puerto Rico, Guam and Samoa." In *The Louisiana Purchase and American Expansion*, edited by Sanford Levinson and Bartholomew Sparrow, 209–229. Lanham, MD: Rowen & Littlefield, 2005.

——. "The New Sociology of Empire and Colonialism." *Sociology Compass* 3, no. 5 (2009): 775–788.

Gonzalez, Vernadette Vicuña. *Securing Paradise: Tourism and Militarism in Hawai'i and the Philippines*. Durham, NC: Duke University Press, 2013.

Gonzalez, Vernadette Vicuña, and Jana K. Lipman. "Introduction: Tours of Duty and Tours of Leisure." *American Quarterly* 68, no. 3 (2016): 507–522.

Greenberg, Amy S. *Manifest Destiny and American Territorial Expansion: A Brief History with Documents*. New York: Bedford/St. Martin's, 2011.

Guam Humanities Council *A Journey Home: Camp Roxas and Filipino American History in Guam.* Hagåtña: Humanities Guåhan, 2009.

Greene, Julie. *The Canal Builders: Making America's Empire at the Panama Canal.* New York: Penguin, 2009.

Guerrero, Anthony Leon. "The Economic Development of Guam." In *Kinalamten Pulitikåt: Siñenten I Chamorro/Issues in Guam's Political Development: The Chamorro Perspective,* 83–101. Hagåtña: Political Status Education Coordinating Commission, 2002.

Guevarra, Rudy P., Jr. *Becoming Mexipino: Multiethnic Identities and Communities in San Diego.* New Brunswick, NJ: Rutgers University Press, 2012.

Habermas, Jürgen. *The Structural Transformation of the Public Sphere: An Inquiry into a Category of Bourgeois Society.* Cambridge, MA: MIT Press, 1991.

Hammer, D. Harry. *Lion Six.* Annapolis, MD: United States Naval Institute, 1947.

Hanlon, David. *Remaking Micronesia: Discourses over Development in a Pacific Territory, 1944–1982.* Honolulu: University of Hawai'i Press, 1998.

Hattori, Anne Perez. *Colonial Dis-Ease: US Navy Health Policies and the Chamorros of Guam, 1898–1941.* Honolulu: University of Hawai'i Press, 2004.

——. "Guardians of Our Soil: Indigenous Responses to Post–World War II Military Land Appropriation on Guam." In *Farms, Firms, and Runways: Perspectives on U.S. Military Bases in the Western Pacific,* edited by L. Eve Armentrout Ma, 186–202. Chicago: Imprint Publications, 2001.

——. "Righting Civil Wrongs: Guam Congress Walkout of 1949." In *Kinalamten Pulitikåt: Siñenten I Chamorro/Issues in Guam's Political Development: The Chamorro Perspective,* 57–69. Hagåtña: Political Status Education Coordinating Commission, 2002.

——. "Textbook Tells: Gender, Race, and Decolonizing Guam History Textbooks in the 21st Century." *AlterNative* 14, no. 2 (2018): 173–184.

Hayashi, Nobuo. "Military Necessity as Normative Indifference." *Georgetown Journal of International Law* 44 (2013): 675–782. https://www.law.georgetown.edu/academics/law-journals/gjil/recent/upload/zsx00213000675.PDF.

Hays, Peter L., Brenda J. Vallance, and Alan R. Van Tassel, eds. *American Defense Policy.* Baltimore: Johns Hopkins University Press, 1997.

Hernández, Kelly Lytle. *City of Inmates: Conquest, Rebellion, and the Rise of Human Caging in Los Angeles, 1771–1965.* Chapel Hill: University of North Carolina Press, 2017.

Higuchi, Wakako. *The Japanese Administration of Guam, 1941–1944.* Jefferson, NC: MacFarland & Company, 2013.

Herring, George C. *From Colony to Superpower: U.S. Foreign Relations since 1776.* New York: Oxford University Press, 2008.

High, Steven. *Base Colonies in the Western Hemisphere, 1940–1967.* New York: Palgrave Macmillan, 2009.

Hirshberg, Lauren. "Home Land (In)security: The Labor of U.S. Cold War Military Empire in the Marshall Islands." In *Making the Empire Work: Labor and United States Imperialism,* edited by Daniel E. Bender and Jana K. Lipman, 335–356. New York: New York University Press, 2015.

——. "Nuclear Families: (Re)producing 1950s Suburban America in the Marshall Islands." *OAH Magazine of History* 26, no. 4 (2012): 1–5.

——. *Suburban Empire: Cold War Militarization in the US Pacific*. Oakland: University of California Press, 2022.

Holmes, Leslie. *Communism: A Very Short Introduction*. Oxford: Oxford University Press, 2009.

Hong, Jane. *Opening the Gates to Asia: A Transpacific History of How America Repealed Asian Exclusion*. Chapel Hill: University of North Carolina Press, 2019.

Hunt, Michael H. *The American Ascendancy: How the United States Gained and Wielded Global Dominance*. Chapel Hill: University of North Carolina Press, 2007.

Immerwahr, Daniel. *How to Hide an Empire: A History of the Greater United States*. New York: Farrar, Straus and Giroux, 2019.

Jacobson, Matthew Frye. *Barbarian Virtues: The United States Encounters Foreign Peoples at Home and Abroad 1876–1917*. New York: Hill & Wang, 2000.

Jacoby, Sanford M. *Modern Manors: Welfare Capitalism since the New Deal*. Princeton, NJ: Princeton University Press, 1997.

Johnson, Chalmers. *Blowback: The Costs and Consequences of American Empire*. New York: Metropolitan Books, 2000.

——. *The Sorrows of Empire: Militarism, Secrecy, and the End of the Republic*. New York: Henry Holt, 2004.

Jung, Moon-Ho. *Menace to Empire: Anticolonial Solidarities and the Transpacific Origins of the US Security State*. Oakland: University of California Press, 2022.

Kajihiro, Kyle. "The Militarizing of Hawai'i: Occupation: Accommodation, and Resistance." In *Asian Settler Colonialism: From Local Governance to the Habits of Everyday Life*, edited by Candace Fujikane and Jonathan Y. Okamura, 170–194. Honolulu: University of Hawai'i Press, 2008.

Karuka, Manu. *Empire's Tracks: Indigenous Nations, Chinese Workers, and the Transcontinental Railroad*. Oakland: University of California Press, 2019.

Kasperbauer, Carmen Artero. "The Chamorro Culture." In *Kinalamten Pulitikåt: Siñenten I Chamorro/Issues in Guam's Political Development: The Chamorro Perspective*, 26–38. Hagåtña: Political Status Education Coordinating Commission, 2002.

Kauanui, J. Kēhaulani, and Patrick Wolfe. "Settler Colonialism Then and Now: A Conversation between J. Kēhaulani Kauanui and Patrick Wolfe." *Politica & Societa* 2 (2012): 235–258.

Khalili, Laleh. "The Infrastructural Power of the Military: The Geoeconomic Role of the US Army Corps of Engineers in the Arabian Peninsula." *European Journal of International Relations* 24, no. 4 (2017): 911–933.

Kilcullen, David. *The Accidental Guerrilla: Fighting Small Wars in the Midst of a Big One*. New York: Oxford University Press, 2011.

Klein, Christina. *Cold War Orientalism: Asia in the Middlebrow Imagination, 1945–1961*. Berkeley: University of California Press, 2003.

Kramer, Paul. *Blood of Government: Race, Empire, the United States and the Philippines*. Chapel Hill: University of North Carolina Press, 2006.

Lafeber, Walter. *The New Empire: An Interpretation of American Expansion, 1860–1898*. Ithaca, NY: Cornell University Press, 1998.

Lee, Erika. *The Making of Asian America: A History*. New York: Simon & Schuster, 2015.

Lee, Shelley Sang-Hee. *A New History of Asian America*. New York: Routledge, 2013.

Lewis, Tom. *Divided Highways: Building the Interstate Highways, Transforming American Life*. Ithaca, NY: Cornell University Press, 2013.

Lindstrom, Lamont. *Cargo Cult: Strange Stories of Desire from Melanesia and Beyond*. Honolulu: University of Hawai'i Press, 1993.

Linn, Brian McAllister. *Guardians of Empire: The U.S. Army and the Pacific, 1902–1940*. Chapel Hill: University of North Carolina Press, 1999.

Lipman, Jana K. *In Camps: Vietnamese Refugees, Asylum Seekers, and Repatriates*. Oakland: University of California Press, 2020.

——. *Guantánamo: A Working-Class History between Empire and Revolution*. Berkeley: University of California Press, 2009.

——. "'A Precedent Worth Setting . . .': Military Humanitarianism—The U.S. Military and the 1975 Vietnamese Evacuation." *Journal of Military History* 79 (January 2015): 151–179.

Love, Eric T. L. *Empire over Race: Racism and U.S. Imperialism, 1865–1900*. Chapel Hill: University of North Carolina Press, 2004.

Lujan, Pilar C. "The Role of Education in the Preservation of the Indigenous Language of Guam." In *Kinalamten Pulitikåt: Siñenten I Chamorro/Issues in Guam's Political Development: The Chamorro Perspective*, 17–25. Hagåtña: Political Status Education Coordinating Commission, 2002.

Lutz, Catherine. *Homefront: An American City and the American Twentieth Century*. Boston: Beacon Press, 2002.

——. "Introduction: Bases, Empire, and Global Response." In *The Bases of Empire: The Global Struggle against U.S. Military Posts*, edited by Catherine Lutz, 1–46. New York: New York University Press, 2009.

——. "US Military Bases on Guam in Global Perspective." *Asia-Pacific Journal: Japan Focus*. http://www.japanfocus.org/-catherine-lutz/3389.

Mahan, Alfred Thayer. *The Influence of Sea Power upon History, 1660–1783*. London: Sampson Low, Marston & Co., 1890.

Man, Simeon. *Soldiering through Empire: Race and the Making of the Decolonizing Pacific*. Oakland: University of California Press, 2018.

Matsuda, Matt K. *Pacific Worlds: A History of Seas, Peoples, and Cultures*. New York: Cambridge University Press, 2012.

Matsumoto, Valerie J. *Farming the Home Place: A Japanese American Community in California, 1919–1982*. New York: Cornell University Press, 1993.

McMahon, Robert J. *The Cold War: A Very Short Introduction*. Oxford: Oxford University Press, 2003.

McCoy, Alfred W. *Policing America's Empire: The United States, the Philippines and the Rise of the Surveillance State*. Madison: University of Wisconsin Press, 2009.

McCoy, Alfred W., and Francisco Scarano, eds. *Colonial Crucible: Empire in the Making of the Modern American State*. Madison: University of Wisconsin Press, 2009.

Miller, Robert J. *Native America, Discovered and Conquered: Thomas Jefferson, Lewis and Clark, and Manifest Destiny*. Lincoln, NE: Bison Books, 2008.

Mize, Ronald L. *The Invisible Workers of the U.S.-Mexico Bracero Program.* Lanham, MD: Lexington Books, 2016.

Moon, Katharine H. S. *Sex among Allies: Military Prostitution in U.S.-Korea Relations.* New York: Columbia University Press, 1997.

Moore, Adam. *Empire's Labor: The Global Army that Supports U.S. Wars.* Ithaca, NY: Cornell University Press, 2019.

Nabokov, Peter. *A Forest of Time: American Indian Ways of History.* New York: Cambridge University Press, 2002.

Na'puti, Tiara R. "Disaster Militarism and Indigenous Responses to Super Typhoon Yutu in the Mariana Islands." *Environmental Communication* 16, no. 5 (2022): 612–629.

Na'puti, Tiara R., and Michael Lujan Bevacqua. "Militarization and Resistance from Guåhan: Protecting and Defending Pågat." *American Quarterly* 67, no. 3 (September 2015): 837–858.

Nebolon, Juliet. "'Life Given Straight from the Heart': Settler Militarism, Biopolitics, and the Public Health in Hawai'i during World War II." *American Quarterly* 69, no. 1 (2017): 23–45.

——. "Settler-Military Camps: Internment and Prisoner of War Camps across the Pacific Islands during World War II." *Journal of Asian American Studies* 24, no. 2 (June 2021): 299–336.

Ngai, Mae M. *Impossible Subjects: Illegal Aliens and the Making of Modern America.* Princeton, NJ: Princeton University Press, 2004.

Nguyen, Mimi Thi. *The Gift of Freedom: War, Debt, and Other Refugee Passages.* Durham, NC: Duke University Press, 2012.

Oberiano, Kristin. "Territorial Discontent: Chamorros, Filipinos, and the Making of the United States Empire on Guam." PhD diss., Harvard University, 2021.

Okamura, Jonathan K. *Ethnicity and Inequality in Hawai'i.* Philadelphia: Temple University Press, 2008.

Osorio, Jon Kamakawiwo'ole. "Memorializing Pu'uloa and Remembering Pearl Harbor." In *Militarized Currents: Toward a Decolonized Future in Asia and the Pacific*, edited by Setsu Shigematsu and Keith L. Camacho, 3–14. Minneapolis: University of Minnesota Press, 2010.

Paleri, Prabhakaran. *National Security: Imperatives and Challenges.* New Delhi: Tata McGraw-Hill, 2008.

Palomo, Tony. *An Island in Agony.* Washington, DC: Library of Congress, 1984.

Parreñas, Rhacel Salazar. "Asian Immigrant Women and Global Restructuring, 1970s–1990s." In *Asian/Pacific Islander American Women: A Historical Anthology*, edited by Shirley Hune and Gail M. Nomura, 271–285. New York: New York University Press, 2003.

Perez, Michael P. "Chamorro Resistance and Prospects for Sovereignty in Guam." In *Sovereignty Matters: Locations of Contestation and Possibility in Indigenous Struggles for Self-Determination*, edited by Joanne Barker, 169–190. Lincoln: University of Nebraska Press, 2005.

——. "Insiders Without, Outsiders Within: Chamorro Ambiguity and Diasporic Identities on the U.S. Mainland." In *The Challenges of Globalization: Cultures in Transition in the Pacific-Asia Region*, edited by Lan-Hung Nora Chiang, John Lidstone, and Rebecca A. Stephenson, 47–72. Lanham, MD: University Press of America, 2004.

Perez, Robert C. "Guantánamo and the Logic of Colonialism: The Deportation of Enemy Indians and Enemy Combatants to Cuba." *Radical Philosophy Review* 14, no. 1 (2011): 25–47.

Phillips, Michael F. "Land." In *Kinalamten Pulitikåt: Siñenten I Chamorro/Issues in Guam's Political Development: The Chamorro Perspective*, 2–16. Hagåtña: Political Status Education Coordinating Commission, 2002.

Poblete, JoAnna. *Islanders in the Empire: Filipino and Puerto Rican Laborers in Hawai'i*. Urbana: University of Illinois Press, 2014.

Poblete-Cross, JoAnna. "Bridging Indigenous and Immigrant Struggles: A Case Study of American Samoa." *American Quarterly* 62, no. 3 (2010): 501–522.

Political Status Education Coordinating Commission. "Public Proclamation of United States Sovereignty over Guam, August 10, 1899." In *Hale'-ta Hinasso': Tinige' Put Chamorro*, 21–22. Hagåtña: Political Status Education Coordinating Commission.

Quimby, Frank. "Fortress Guahan." *Journal of Pacific History* 46, no. 3 (2011): 357–380.

Rafael, Vicente L. *White Love and Other Events in Filipino History*. Durham, NC: Duke University Press, 2000.

Renda, Mary A. *Taking Haiti: Military Occupation and the Culture of U.S. Imperialism, 1915–1940*. Chapel Hill: University of North Carolina Press, 2001.

Reyes, Victoria. *Global Borderlands: Fantasy, Violence, and Empire in Subic Bay, Philippines*. Stanford, CA: Stanford University Press, 2019.

Rodríguez, Dylan. *Suspended Apocalypse: White Supremacy, Genocide, and the Filipino Condition*. Minneapolis: University of Minnesota Press, 2010.

Rodriguez, Robyn Magalit. *Migrants for Export: How the Philippine State Brokers Labor to the World*. Minneapolis: University of Minnesota Press, 2010.

Rogers, Robert F. *Destiny's Landfall: A History of Guam*. Honolulu: University of Hawai'i Press, 2011.

Salman, Michael. *The Embarrassment of Slavery: Controversies over Bondage and Nationalism in the American Colonial Philippines*. Berkeley: University of California Press, 2001.

Santos, Elyssa Juline. "Practicing Economy": Chamorro Agency and U.S. Colonial Agricultural Projects, 1898–1941." Master's thesis, University of Hawai'i at Mānoa, 2018.

Saranillio, Dean Itsuji. *Unsustainable Empire: Alternative Histories of Hawai'i Statehood*. Durham, NC: Duke University Press, 2018.

Sasaki, Christen T. "Emerging Nations, Emerging Empires: Inter-Imperial Intimacies and Competing Settler Colonialisms in Hawai'i." *Pacific Historical Review* 90, no. 1 (2021): 28–56.

——. "Threads of Empire: Militourism and the Aloha Wear Industry in Hawai'i." *American Quarterly* 68, no. 3 (2016): 643–667.

Saxton, Alexander. *Indispensable Enemy: Labor and the Anti-Chinese Movement in California*. Berkeley: University of California Press, 1975.

Schwartz, Jessica A. *Radiation Sounds: Marshallese Music and Nuclear Silences*. Durham, NC: Duke University Press, 2021.

Scott, James C. *Domination and the Arts of Resistance: Hidden Transcripts*. New Haven, CT: Yale University Press, 1990.

Shah, Nayan. *Stranger Intimacy: Contesting Race, Sexuality, and the Law in the North American West*. Berkeley: University of California Press, 2011.

Shigematsu, Setsu, and Keith L. Camacho. "Introduction: Militarized Currents, Decolonizing Futures." In *Militarized Currents: Toward a Decolonized Future in Asia and the Pacific*, edited by Setsu Shigematsu and Keith L. Camacho, xv–xlviii. Minneapolis: University of Minnesota Press, 2010.

Sibal, Jorge V. "Milestones: The Philippines and the ILO Partnership 1948–2008." In *Changes and Challenges: 60 Years of Struggle Towards Decent Work*, ed. Jorge V. Sibal. Diliman: University of the Philippines, 2008.

Sibal, Jorge V., ed. *Changes and Challenges: 60 Years of Struggles Towards Decent Work*. Diliman: University of the Philippines, 2008.

Simpson, Audra, and Andrea Smith. "Introduction." In *Theorizing Native Studies*, edited by Audra Simpson and Andrea Smith, 1–30. Durham, NC: Duke University Press, 2014.

Sims, Beth. *Workers of the World Undermined: American Labor's Role in U.S. Foreign Policy*. Boston: South End Press, 1992.

Smith, Andrea. *Conquest: Sexual Violence and American Indian Genocide*. Cambridge, MA: South End Press, 2005.

Sohi, Seema. *Echoes of Mutiny: Race, Surveillance, and Indian Anticolonialism in North America*. New York: Oxford University Press, 2014.

Solis, Jessica Ann Unpingco. "Traditions and Transitions: Explorations of Chamorro Culture through the Rosary Practice." Master's thesis, University of California, Los Angeles, 2014.

Souder, Laura Marie Torres. *Daughters of the Island: Contemporary Chamorro Women Organizers on Guam*. Lanham, MD: University Press of America, 1992.

Stephanson, Anders. *Manifest Destiny: American Expansionism and the Empire of Right*. New York: Hill & Wang, 1996.

Spickard, Paul. *Almost All Aliens: Immigration, Race, and Colonialism in American History and Identity*. New York: Routledge, 2007.

Stoler, Ann Laura, ed. *Haunted by Empire: Geographies of Intimacy in North American History*. Durham, NC: Duke University Press, 2006.

Stur, Heather Marie. "'Hiding behind the Humanitarian Label': Refugees, Repatriates, and the Rebuilding of America's Benevolent Image after the Vietnam War." *Diplomatic History* 39, no. 2 (April 2015): 223–244.

Swift, Earl. *The Big Roads: The Untold Stories of the Engineers, Visionaries, and Trailblazers who Created the American Superhighways*. New York: Mariner Books, 2012.

Takaki, Ronald. *Pau Hana: Plantation Life and Labor in Hawaii*. Honolulu: University of Hawai'i Press, 1983.

———. *Strangers from a Different Shore: A History of Asian Americans.* New York: Little, Brown, 1998.

Teaiwa, Teresia K. "Bikinis and Other S/pacific N/oceans." In *Militarized Currents: Toward a Decolonized Future in Asia and the Pacific,* edited by Setsu Shigematsu and Keith L. Camacho, 15–32. Minneapolis: University of Minnesota Press, 2010).

———. "Reading Paul Gauguin's *Noa Noa* with Epeli Hau'ofa's *Kiss in the Nederends:* Militourism, Feminism, and the 'Polynesian' Body." In *Inside Out: Literature, Cultural Politics, and Identity in the New Pacific,* edited by Vilsoni Hereniko and Rob Wilson, 249–264. Lanham, MD: Rowman & Littlefield, 1999.

Teves, Stephanie Nohelani. *Defiant Indigeneity: The Politics of Hawaiian Performance.* Chapel Hill: University of North Carolina Press, 2018.

Thomas, Nicholas. *Entangled Objects: Exchange, Material Culture, and Colonialism in the Pacific.* Cambridge, MA: Harvard University Press, 1991.

———. *Islanders: The Pacific in the Age of Empire.* New Haven, CT: Yale University Press, 2012.

Thompson, Laura M. "Crisis on Guam." *Far Eastern Quarterly* 6, no. 1 (November 1946): 5–11.

———. *Guam and Its People: With a Village Journal by Jesus C. Barcinas.* Princeton, NJ: Princeton University Press, 1947.

Thomson, Jay Earle. *Our Pacific Possessions.* New York: Charles Scribner's Sons, 1931.

Trask, Haunani-Kay. *From a Native Daughter: Colonialism and Sovereignty in Hawai'i.* Honolulu: University of Hawai'i Press, 1999.

Turner, Frederick Jackson. *The Significance of the Frontier in American History.* Eastford, CT: Martino Fine Books, 2014.

Underwood, Robert A. "American Education and the Acculturation of the Chamorros of Guam." PhD diss., University of Southern California, 1987.

Veracini, Lorenzo. "Natives Settlers Migrants." *Politica & Societa* 1, no. 2 (2012): 187–240.

Viernes, James Perez. "Fanhasso I Tao Tao Sumay: Displacement, Dispossession, and Survival in Guam." Master's thesis, University of Hawai'i at Mānoa, 2008.

Vine, David. *Base Nation: How the U.S. Military Bases abroad Harm America and the World.* New York: Skyhorse Publishing, 2015.

———. *The United States of War: A Global History of America's Endless Conflicts, from Columbus to the Islamic State.* Oakland: University of California Press, 2020.

Vizenor, Gerald. "Aesthetics of Survivance: Literary Theory and Practice." In *Survivance: Narrative of Native Presence,* edited by Gerald Vizenor, 1–24. Lincoln: University of Nebraska Press, 2008.

Warheit, Vanessa, dir. *The Insular Empire: America in the Mariana Islands.* Palo Alto, CA: Horse Opera Productions, 2009. DVD.

Weinbaum, Alys Even, Lynn M. Thomas, Priti Ramamurthy, Uta G. Poiger, Madeleine Y. Dong, and Tani E. Barlow. "The Modern Girl as Heuristic Device: Collaboration, Connective Comparison, Multidirectional Citation." In *The Modern Girl around the World: Consumption, Modernity, and Globalization,* edited by Alys Even Weinbaum, Lynn M. Thomas, Priti Ramamurthy, Uta G. Poiger, Madeleine Y. Dong, and Tani E. Barlow, 1–24. Durham, NC: Duke University Press, 2008.

Williams, Raymond. *Keywords: A Vocabulary of Culture and Society*. New York: Oxford University Press, 1983.

Winkelmann, Tessa Ong. "Rethinking the Sexual Geography of American Empire in the Philippines: Interracial Intimacies in Mindanao and the Cordilleras, 1898–1921." In *Gendering the Trans-Pacific World: Diaspora, Empire, and Race*, edited by Catherine Ceniza Choy and Judy Tzu-Chun Wu, 39–76. Leiden: Brill, 2017. DOI: 10.1163/9789004336100_005.

Wolfe, Patrick. "Settler Colonialism and the Elimination of the Native." *Journal of Genocide Research* 8, no. 4 (2006): 387–409.

Woodcock, Nicolyn. "Militarized Intimacies: War, Family, and Transpacific Asian American Literature." PhD diss., Miami University, 2019.

———. "Narratives of Intimacy in Asian American Literature." In *Oxford Research Encyclopedia*. August 30, 2019, 1. DOI: 10.1093/acrefore/9780190201098.013.1173.

Woods, Colleen. *Freedom Incorporated: Anticommunism and Philippine Independence in the Age of Decolonization*. Ithaca, NY: Cornell University Press, 2020.

Wu, Judy Tzu-Chun. "The Dead, the Living, and the Sacred: Patsy Mink, Antimilitarism, and Reimagining the Pacific World." *Meridians: Feminism, Race, Transnationalism* 18, no. 2 (October 2019): 304–331.

Yap, Valerie. "From Transient Migration to Homemaking: Filipino Immigrants in Guam." In *The Age of Asian Migration: Continuity, Diversity, and Susceptibility*, vol. 2, edited by Yuk Wah Chan, Heidi Fung, and Grazyna Szymańska-Matusiewicz, 157–174. Newcastle: Cambridge Scholars Publishing, 2015.

Yuh, Ji-Yeon. "Imagined Community: Sisterhood and Resistance among Korean Military Brides in America, 1950–1996." In *Asian/Pacific Islander American Women: A Historical Anthology*, edited by Shirley Hune and Gail M. Nomura, 221–236. New York: New York University Press, 2003.

Index

Page numbers in italics refer to figures.

Adams, G. M., 91–92
Acfalle, Alberto Babauta, 117–18
Admiral Nimitz Golf Course, 147n89, 147n93, 153n72
Aloha Committee of NAS Hagåtña, 121–22
Ammun, W. B., 93
Anderlini, Douglas Anthony, 131
Andersen Air Force Base, 8, 9, 128, 145n50; home construction at, 54, 60
Anderson, George, 78
anticommunism, 79, 84, 161n132; taxi-dance clubs and, 99–100. *See also* communism
Antonio B. Won Pat International Airport, 16, 114, 132, 134. *See also* NAS Hagåtña
Apapa (Apra) Harbor, 42, 43–44, 47, 51, 149n13; expansion of, 46, 133
archives, 12–13
Asia and Pacific Regional Organization (APRO), 84
assimilation, 38, 148n104; "benevolent," 8; of CHamorus, 21, 42–43; settler militarism and, 43
Attewell, Wesley, 61
Ayala, Cesar J., 29
Azada, Resurrecion A., 92–93

Baker, Dorothea Minor, 77
Baldoz, Rick, 89
Ballendorf, Dirk, 21
bases, military, 5–6, 8–9, 23; Andersen Air Force Base, 8, 9, 54, 60, 128, 145n50; displacement and, 152n55; militarization and, 6; modernization and, 51; postwar expansion of, 48, 151n43; settler colonialism and, 6; at Sumai, 8, 24, 35, 46; violence on, 6. *See also* NAS Hagåtña
Beane, J. F., 43–44
Beers, Henry, 43
Benavente, Ed, 33, 114, 115
Benavente, John C., 119
benevolence, discourse of, 43, 111; land taking and, 42, 136; militarization and, 13, 41–42, 48; modernization and, 48, 59–60; settler colonialism and, 133
Benito, Justino, 80, 91
Bennett, Judith A., 105
Bevacqua,, Michael Lujan, 10
Blaz, Ben, 16, 117–19, 141n1
Bolivar, Jose L., 29
Bordallo, Barbara, *103*
Bordallo, Madeline, 35

Brown-Pacific-Maxon (BPM): Filipino labor recruitment, 67–68, 120; Guam Wage Bill, support for, 82; hierarchized labor force, 70–71; labor pool for, 67–68; racial segregation and, 62, 73, 85, 157n45; welfare capitalism, use of, 73; white employees of, 120

Bull, Vernon T., 56–57

Byrd, Jodi, 7

Cabot, Gorgonio, 68–69, 120

Calvo, Ed, 131

Camacho, Carlos, 172n1

Camacho, Felix, 52

Camacho, Keith L., 6, 32, 52

Camp Roxas, 61, 70, 74–79, 86; armed workers in, 79; living conditions in, 76, 76–77, 77. See also company camps

capitalism, 2, 59; racialized labor and, 6, 64–65; taxi-dance clubs and, 100; welfare capitalism, 73, 75, 159n89; wage suppression and, 82–83, 90, 134

Carano, Paul, 58–59

Carrillo, A. J., 78–79

Carter, Rosa Roberto, 21

Castano, Angel, 80

Castro, Jose Borja, 111

CHamorus: assimilation of, 21, 42–43; citizenship of, 5, 17, 20, 87; definition of term, 137n3; displacement of, 28, 46, 52–53, 55, 63–64, 145n50, 152n55; dispossession of, 3, 28–29, 52–53, 59, 133, 136; land stewardship of, 17–19, 20, 22, 35, 39–40; racialization of, 14, 42, 64–65, 86, 88–89, 102; sexualization of, 42, 102, 104; US military, perceptions of, 28–32, 34, 151n33

champulado, 1, 137n2, 168n8

Channell, Mary Augusta, 43–44

citizenship: Aquino Ruling, 90; of CHamorus, 5, 17, 20, 87; of Filipino workers, 80, 90; Guam Organic Act and, 87, 94, 172n1; intermarriage and, 80, 95; lånchos and, 20; land taking and, 36–38; McCarran-Walter Act of 1952, 66, 80, 87; residency and, 66, 87, 90

collaboration: of Sa'ipan CHamorus, 22; in settler militarism, 32–33

Collier, John, 37, 148n99

colonialism, Japanese, 94; education under, 21

colonialism, Spanish, 94; land ownership under, 18–19; surveillance under, 7–8

colonialism, US, 94, 143n18; colonization of Guåhan, 2, 8, 39; Filipino labor and, 6–7; Filipino resistance to, 89–90. See also settler colonialism

comfort women, 144n36

communism: anticommunism, 79, 84, 99–100, 161n132; containment policy, 23, 106; labor unions and, 68, 79, 89, 161n132

company camps, 157n45; Camp Roxas, 61, 70, 74–79, 76, 77, 86; food quality in, 77–78; gender in, 74; living conditions in, 75–78, 76, 77; minstrel shows in, 73; segregation in, 62, 73–75, 85, 157n45; violence in, 78–79

Constructionaire, The (newsletter), 73, 167n113

containment, 23, 106

Corn, Charlie, 131

Coulter, Doloris, 36, 37–38

Cristobal, A. L., 130

Cristobal, Hope, 122

Cruz, A. C., 130

Cruz, Delfina, 30

Cruz, Joseph, 110

Cruz, Juan, 30

dances, 14, 96; enlisted men's, 101–2, 102, 103, 104, 112, 165n72; Filipino, 74, 91

Darling, T. A., 100

David, Francisco Bernardo, 111

Day, Iyko, 7

De La Cruz, Barbara (née Castro), 87–88, 89, 93–94, 112

De La Cruz, Eddie, 87–88, 89, 93–94, 112, 120

De Leon, Jose P., 33–34

DeLisle, Christine Taitano, 18, 42, 101–2

Diaz, Vicente M., 42

displacement: of CHamorus, 28, 46, 52–53, 55, 63–64, 145n50, 152n55; militarization and, 6–7, 8, 46, 52; military bases and, 152n55

dispossession: of CHamorus, 3, 28–29, 52–53, 59, 133, 136

Domondon, Anselma B., 80

education: under Japanese colonialism, 20; pre-WW II, 145n54; under settler militarism, 43; under US military, 63, 145n54

Efe, Maria, 22
Elvidge, Anita, 100–101
Elvidge, Ford Q., 59, 100–101
Endres, C. J., 92
Enloe, Cynthia, 5
Escudero, Kevin, 67

Fairbanks, Elizabeth, 44
Farmer, Roy, 110
Filipino Community of Guam (FCG), 91–93
Filipinos: citizenship of, 80, 90; community
    dances, 74, 91; Guam Wage Bill, resistance
    to, 83–85, 88, 89, 92; migration of, 62, 63,
    134; as perpetual foreigners, 90, 92; racial-
    ization of, 14, 86, 88–89, 92; stereotypes
    of, 87, 88; surveillance of, 89, 90–93; US
    colonialism, resistance to, 89–90. See also
    labor, Filipino
Filipinos for Guåhan, 136
Fischer, John C., 26
Fitzgerald, George, 111–12
Flores, Leon, Jr., 109
Flores, Pedro Martinez, 1–2, 135
Flores, Soledad Chargualaf, 1–2, 135
foreign policy, US: containment, 23, 106,
    Pivot to Asia, 2
Forrestal, James V., 27
Francisco, Urelia Anderson, 32
Fujikane, Candace, 6
Furtado, Louie, 163n30

Gandhi, Evyn Lê Espiritu, 135
Ganzon, Rodelpho, 80
Gardner, Wilbur, 111–12
Garrido, Joe Ulloa, 96
Gazze, S., 131
gender: in company camps, 74; consumerism
    and, 122; infrastructure and, 46;
    masculinity, 46, 74, 96; modernity and,
    45–46; NAS Hagåtña and, 122; in
    representations of US military, 46;
    suburbanization and, 56
Gillem, Mark L., 54
Gorospe, Teodoro, 71
Grimm, Edward M., 66
Guåhan: commercial growth in, 55; Filipino
    labor in, 6–7, 12, 14; Japanese occupation
    of, 8, 13, 15–16, 21–22, 116–19, 132,
    143nn30–31, 154n11; militarization of,
    3–4, 8–11, 9, 10, 88, 136; modernization

of, 5, 149n7; as nuclear site, 8, 125, 127–28;
    out-migration from, 13, 15, 135; place
    naming in, 18, 117, 141n2, 167n2; Spanish
    colonization of, 7–8; strategic importance
    of, 2, 41; suburbanization of, 13, 42,
    53–57, 135; as "tip of America's spear,"
    3–4, 9, 13, 126, 136; tourist economy of,
    3, 13, 57–58, 116, 135, 147n89; US coloni-
    zation of, 2, 8, 39; US occupation of, 12,
    13; US reoccupation of, 13, 22–24, 23, 24,
    49, 144n35, 145n50
Guam. See Guåhan
Guamanians: use of term, 137n3
Guam Congress, 36; protesting of naval
    governance, 38–39, 172n1
Guam Echo (newsletter), 38
Guam Land and Claims Commission (GLCC),
    16–17; employment of CHamorus, 32; land
    taking role, 5, 25–28, 31; settler militarism
    and, 39
Guam News, 79
Guam Organic Act of 1950, 16–17, 83, 110;
    CHamoru survival and, 17; citizenship
    and, 87, 94, 172n1; land taking under, 5,
    38–39, 94
Guamu Dai Ni airfield, 116–19, 132. See also
    NAS Hagåtña
Guam Wage Bill of 1956, 14, 62, 81–85,
    134; corporation support for, 82; Filipino
    resistance to, 83–85, 88, 89, 92; opposition
    to, 82–85, 89; organized labor opposition
    to, 83–84, 89, 92
Guam Women's Club, 99, 101
Guerrero, Frank Leon, 35
Guevarra, Rudy P., Jr., 94
Gumataotao, Joe, 93–94

Hagåtña, 149n13; bombardment of, 23, 25,
    26, 143n30; rebuilding of, 53. See also
    NAS Hagåtña
Hammers, Floyd C., 107–8
Hanlon, David, 49–50
Harrison, Peyton, 93
Hattori, Anne Perez, 28–29, 43
Hernandez, Jose, 83
Herrle, L. D., 64–65
Hicklin, Harrel LaVerne, 110
Hinson, M. T., 104–5
Hinson, William P., 104–5
Hirshberg, Lauren, 54, 121

homes, residential, 42, 44–45, 52, 127, 133, 152n58; at Andersen Air Force Base, 54, 60; modernization of, 44–45; at NAS Hagåtña, 122; suburbanization and, 122, 135. *See also* infrastructure
Hopkins, Ernest M., 27
Hopkins Report, 27–28, 146n58
Hora, Luis, 91

immigration laws, US: Chinese Exclusion Act of 1882, 65; Johnson-Reed Act of 1924, 65, 156n31; McCarran-Walter Act of 1952, 66, 80, 87. *See also* migration
ináfa'maolek, 1–2, 97
Independent Guåhan, 136
Indian Claims Commission, 27
Indian Reorganization Act of 1934 (IRA), 38, 148n104
infrastructure: Apapa Harbor, expansion of, 42, 133; gender and, 46; of Japanese occupation, 116–19; labor recruitment and, 66; modernization of, 48–49, 54; of occupation, 116–19; in periodicals, 53; race and, 46; residential homes, 42, 44–45, *45*, 52, 54, 127, 133, 152n58; roads, 42–44, 46–49, *50*, *51*, 63, 128–30, 133; settler colonialism and, 119
intermarriage, 85, 93–94, 131, 160n116; citizenship and, 80, 95; masculinity and, 96; naturalization and, 80; policing of, 95, 104–6; resistance to, 104–5; taxi-dance clubs and, 98; tracking of, 112, 167n113
International Confederation of Free Trade Unions (ICFTU), 84, 161n132
International Labor Organization (ILO), 84
interracial intimacies, 14, 87–88, 93–98, 134; enlisted men's dances and, 101–4; intermarriage, 80, 85, 93–95, 104–6, 112, 131, 160n116, 167n113; at NAS Hagåtña, 131; policing of, 3–5, 14, 95, 104–6, 112, 131; taxi-dance clubs, 98–101

Japanese occupation, 8, 13, 143nn30–31; forced labor under, 15, 16, 21–22, 116–19, 132, 154n11
Johnston, Agueda, 98
Jones, R. W., 75–76

Jung, Moon-Ho, 88

Kauanui, J. Kēhaulani, 5
Kennedy, John F., 134
kinship, Indigenous, 2
Kirwan, Michael J., 130
Koehler, John T., 26, 36
kostumbren CHamoru, 4; sex and, 96–100

labor: Asian, 6, 62; Chinese, 69, 70, 155n25; exploitation of, 14, 62, 64, 80–81; Fair Labor Standards Act (FLSA), 82; Guam Wage Bill, 62, 81–85; hierarchized, 61–63, 70–71, 134; migration and, 2, 5, 14, 62–63, 69, 86, 134; racialization of, 3, 6, 14, 62–65, 69, 79–80, 133, 157n44; US laborers, 14; wage discrimination, 83
labor, CHamoru, 32, 128, 134; forced, 15, 16, 21–22; training of, 62; US military employment, 62; wages, 71
labor, Filipino, 5, 155n25; archives of, 12–13; citizenship and, 80, 90; colonialism and, 7; company camps, 61, 62; criminalization of, 79; deportation of, 79–80, 87, 95–96, 134; exploitation of, 80–81; Filipina labor, 70, 74; in Guåhan, 6–7, 12, 14; Guam Wage Bill, opposition to, 82–83; migration of, 62, 68–69, 86, 134; at NAS Hagåtña, 120; pathologizing of, 68–69; racialization of, 69, 79, 80; recruitment of, 40, 61–62, 65–70, 75, 85, 120, 157n62; remittances of, 81, 99, 160n116; repatriation of, 72; smuggling of, 157n62; unionization of, 160n129; US military suspicions of, 89–90; wages, 62, 71
labor, forced: of CHamorus, 15, 16, 21–22, 116–19, 132, 154n11; of Japanese POWs, 64–65
labor, white American, 67, 70–71, 134; recruitment of, 62
labor movements, 82, 160n121
labor unions, 79–80, 160n129; AFL-CIO, 83–84; communism and, 68, 79, 85, 161n132; PCLU, 67; PTUC, 83
lånchos, 133, 137n1; CHamoru culture and, 1; citizenship and, 20; in Tiyan, 115–16, 119, 131; under US military rule, 19–20
låncho system, 13, 39

land: CHamoru relationship to, 1–2, 17, 33, 49; CHamoru stewardship of, 17–19, 20, 22, 39–40, 133; dispossession of, 3; human body as extension of, 18; Indigenous epistemologies of, 6; military occupation of, 13; ownership, 18–20, 39, 53; survival and, 33

land taking: benevolent discourse and, 42, 136; citizenship and, 36–38; under coercion, 5, 13, 16, 30–33; compensation for, 25–27, 28, 34–36, 145n56; corporate leasing, 148n95; GLCC and, 5, 25–28, 31; Guam Organic Act and, 5, 38–39, 94; under IRA, 148n104; liberation narrative and, 28–39, 32; Meritorious Claim Act of 1945, 25; militarization and, 17, 53, 59, 119; "military necessity" justification, 27, 55, 146n59; in Puerto Rico, 29; resistance to, 33–36; settler militarism and, 133; under Treaty of Paris, 19, 141n61; war on terror and, 11

Lapervse, Freddie J., 107–8

Larson, Henry L., 46–48, 51

Leary, Richard, 20

Legazpi, Miguel Lopez de, 7

Leiss, Edward, 105–6

Lemke, William, 29

Leon Guerrero, Justo Torre, 115

Levine, Louie, 78

Levitt, Ronald, 57

Liberation Day, 22

liberation of Guåhan narrative, 16–17, 21; CHamoru military enlistment and, 135; critiques of, 38; land taking and, 28–29, 32; modernization and, 51–52; settler militarism and, 39

Lim, Roseller, 80

Lo, Antonio E., 72

Low, Richard Barrett, 112–13

Luces, John, 98, 99

Lujan, Joaquin Flores, 95

Lujan, M. U., 130

Luzon Stevedoring (LUSTEVECO), 156n37; Camp Roxas, 61, 70, 74–77, 76, 77, 79, 86; company camps, 72–73; Filipino labor recruitment, 66–68, 70; Filipino workers, deportation of, 79–80; Guam Wage Bill, support for, 82; labor injuries, 71–72; welfare capitalism, use of, 73

Mabini, Larry, 72

Mabini, Sam, 72

Mahan, Alfred Thayer, 2

Mangibin, Bayani, 81

manifest destiny, 49

March to Manenggon, 22

Mariana Islands, 138n16

Marianas Stevedoring (MASDELCO), 71, 156n37

Marshall, Donald, 61, 66

Martin, Harold H., 48–49

masculinity, 46; intermarriage and, 96

Mason, Theodorous Bailey Myers, 21

Mason, Walter J., 84

Matsumoto, Valerie J., 11

McCarran-Walter Act of 1952, 66, 80, 87

McCollum, Catherine Punzalan Flores, 37, 124–25

McKinley, William, 19

Meany, George, 83

migration: CHamoru out-migration, 13, 15, 135; Chinese, 65; of Filipino labor, 62, 63, 68–69, 86, 134; labor and, 5, 14, 62–63, 69, 86; militarization and, 6–7

militarization: benevolence, discourse of, 13, 41–42, 48; benevolent paternalism, 48; criticism of, 59; displacement and, 6–7, 8, 46, 52; of Guåhan, 3–4, 8–11, 9, 10, 88, 136; land taking and, 17, 53, 59, 119; migration and, 6–7; military bases and, 6; modernity and, 41–42, 56–57, 59–60; modernization and, 13–14, 120; resistance to, 11; roads and, 50–51, 133; settler colonialism and, 3–6; suburbanization and, 121; of Tiyan, 118–19; violence and, 14, 111

militourism, 57, 58, 116, 168n10

modernity: gendered, 45; militarization and, 41–42, 56–57, 59–60; racialized, 45

modernization: benevolence discourse and, 48, 59–60; of Guåhan, 5, 149n7; of infrastructure, 48–49, 54; liberation narrative and, 51–52; militarization and, 13–14, 120; military bases and, 6; periodicals, representations of, 48–49, 53; of residential homes, 44–45; settler militarism and, 41

Moore, Adam, 61

Morgan, Eugene, 67

Moylan, Fred, 99–100, 164n62

Na'puti, Tiara R., 10
NAS Hagåtña, *118*; closure of, 115, 132; commercial flights at, 120–21; construction of, 15, 16, 114, 119–20, 134; environmental contamination at, 123, 124–25; gender and, 122; guest passes at, 130–31; land taking and, 119; origin as Guamu Dai Ni, 116–19; perceptions of, 125–28; periodical representations of, 125–26; plane crashes at, 123–24; residential homes at, 122; roads of, 128–30; as settler-colonial site, 114–15, 120–21; settler militarism, as culmination of, 115, 134; suburbanization of, 121–23; surveillance at, 128
Nebolon, Juliet, 3
North Korea, 2
nurses, Filipina, 74

Oberiano, Kristin, 39
occupation: infrastructure of, 116–19; Japanese, 8, 13, 15, 16, 21–22, 117–19, 132, 143nn30–31; US, 8–9, 12–13, 22–24, *23, 24*, 49, 144n35, 145n50
Office of Naval Intelligence (ONI), 101, 162n21; surveillance of Filipinos, 91–92
Okamura, Jonathan, 6
Operation New Life, 10, 135–36
oral history, 11–12

Pangelinan, John, 22
Parsons, Charles, 66
Pearl Harbor, 8, 43, 46
Pelengon, Elisa, 107–8
Perez, Emily, 105–6
Perez, Frank D., 35, 109
Perez, Joaquin A., 29, 130
Perez, Joaquin Pangelinan, 35
periodicals: consumerism and, 56; infrastructure articles in, 53; interracial romance in, 104, 105; militarization of Guåhan and, 41; modernization and, 48–49, 53; NAS Hagåtña, representations of, 125–26; tourism articles, 57
Philippine Consolidated Labor Union, (PCLU), 67
Philippine Trade Unions Council (PTUC), 83, 160n129
Philippine-American War, 90
Phillips, Michael F., 17
Poblete, JoAnna, 7, 82

Pontan and Fo'na, 18
Pownall, C. A., 32, 77, 107, 129–30
POWs, Japanese, 64–65
Prince, William B., 131
Prutehi, Litekyan, 136
Punzalan, Bernardo Delmundo, 37

Quinata, Joe E., 19, 33, 96

race: in Guåhan, 137n3; health requirements and, 69; hierarchized labor and, 5, 61–62, 134; in representations of US military, 46
racialization: of CHamorus, 14, 42, 64–65, 86, 88–89, 102; of CHamoru women, 102; of Filipinos, 14, 69, 79, 80, 86, 88–89, 92; of labor, 3, 6, 14, 62, 63–65, 69, 79–80, 133, 157n44; of Micronesians, 64; of military labor, 3, 6, 62, 63–65; of white Americans, 14, 88–89
racism: toward CHamoru women, 104–5; Jim Crow segregation, 73–75; minstrel shows, 73; stereotypes, 87, 88; white supremacy, 73. *See also* segregation
Ramirez, Anthony J., 125
Ramirez, F. T., 130
Ramirez, Tony, 51
Rauber, Louis J., 27
reducción, 7–8, 138n43
resistance, 136; to Guam Wage Bill, 82–85, 89, 92; to intermarriage, 104–5; to land taking, 33–36; to militarization, 11; to military power, 4; to US colonialism, 89–90
Rizal, Jose, 74
Rizal Beach, 74, *75*
roads, 42, 43–44, 46–49, *50, 51*; Marine Corps Drive, 49–53, 63; militarization and, 50–51, 133; at NAS Hagåtña, 128–30; violence on, 107–8
Romulo, Carlos P., 83
Rosario, Pete Taitingfong, 163n30

Sablan, Antonio Artero, 31, 116
Sablan, Benita Pereda, 131
Sablan, James T., 67, 130
Sa'ipan (Saipan), 138n16; interpreters in, 22; *reducción* policy in, 138n16
Salas, Galo Lujan, 35
Salvador, Serafin, 84, 91
San Agustin, Joe T., 30–31

Sanchez, Ciriaco C., 31
San Cruz, Regina, 110
San Nicolas, Felicita Santos, 30
Santos, Francisco S., 31–32
San Vitores, Diego Luis de, 7
Saranillio, Dean Itsuji, 7
Sarmago, Felix, 71
Savares, Jose, 74–75
Savares, Olivia Benavente, 95–96
Schwartz, Harold, 34
Seabees, 46, 47, 48, 50, 63; use of POW
    labor, 64–65
security clearance policy, 15, 55, 68, 95–96,
    112–13, 157n51
segregation: in company camps, 62, 73–75,
    85, 157n45; suburbanization and, 122; of
    US military, 165n72
settler colonialism, 136; Asian labor and, 6;
    benevolence discourse and, 133; labor and,
    6; militarization and, 3–6; military bases
    and, 6; NAS Hagåtña as site of, 114–15,
    120–21; settlers, defined, 7; Tiyan as gate-
    way to, 116, 121; violence and, 5–6
settler militarism, 3, 11; assimilation and,
    43; CHamoru collaboration with, 32–33;
    education under, 43; GLCC and, 39; Guam
    Organic Act and, 39; hierarchical labor
    system of, 61–63, 70–71, 85, 134; Japanese
    occupation infrastructure, use of, 119; land
    taking and, 133; liberation narrative and,
    39; military bases and, 6; modernization
    and, 41; naming of infrastructure, 52; NAS
    Hagåtña as culmination of, 115; private
    contractors, dependence upon, 69; racial-
    ized labor and, 65; suburbanization and,
    55–56; survival of, 4–5
sexualization: of CHamoru women, 42, 102,
    104
Shah, Nayan, 88
Shelton, Gayle, 111
Sher, Jack, 126
Shigematsu, Setsu, 6
Shoemaker, Donald E., 131–32
Simmons, Walter, 114
Snipes, Connie, 18, 33
Souder, Laura Marie Torres, 97
Spanish-American War, 8, 143n18
Squire, Allan T., 52
Stanford, Leland, 65
Stump, Felix, 106

suburbanization, 59–60, 152n58; consumer-
    ism and, 122; gender and, 56; of Guåhan,
    13, 42, 53–57, 135; homebuilding, 60,
    122, 135; militarization and, 121; NAS
    Hagåtña and, 121–23; segregation and,
    122; settler militarism and, 55–56
Sullivan, Walter, 53–54
Sumai (Sumay), 6, 44, 168n11; bombardment
    of, 52–53; land taking in, 53; military
    bases at, 8, 24, 35, 46
surveillance: of FCG, 91–93; of Filipinos,
    89, 90–93; at NAS Hagåtña, 128; under
    Spanish colonialism, 7–8
survival, CHamoru, 17, 136; land and, 33; of
    settler militarism, 4–5
survivance, 4

Taitano, Carlos P., 29, 109, 146n66
Talley, Robert D., 131
Tambling, P. S., 129
Taussig, Edward D., 19
taxi-dance clubs, 98–101, 164n55; anticom-
    munism and, 99–100; intermarriage and,
    98
Teaiwa, Teresia, 57, 168n10
Tew, Ramson T., Jr., 131–32
Thompson, Laura M., 37–38, 53, 148n99
Tini'an (Tinian), 8; reducción policy in,
    138n16
Tiyan, 15; bombardment of, 119; as bread-
    basket of Guåhan, 116; Guamu Dai Ni
    airfield, construction of, 116–19; lånchos,
    115–16, 119, 131; militarization of, 118–19;
    naming of, 18, 115, 141n2; pre-WW II,
    115–16, 122; as settler colonial gateway,
    116, 121
Tomhom (Tumon) Beach, 36, 147n89
tourism, 3, 13, 116, 135, 147n89; beaches,
    commodification of, 58; in periodicals, 57
Trask, Haunani-Kay, 5
Treaty of Paris (1898), 8, 143n18; land taking
    under, 19, 141n61
Trumbull, Robert, 54–55, 152n65
Trump, Donald J., 2
Typhoon Karen, 6, 15, 152n58, 155n25

Udall, Stuart, 54, 57
Umayan, Consul, 78
"Uncle Sam Please Come Back to Guam"
    (song), 93, 163n30

Underwood, James Holland, 36–37
Underwood, Robert A., 36, 148n96
Unpingco, John S., 19

Velasco, Gregorio, 107
Vellar, Monico, 107
Vietnam War, 9; CHamoru casualties, 15,
    135; CHamoru enlistment, 15; refugees,
    10, 135–36
village pass system, 109, 134
Vine, David, 4
violence: in company camps, 78–79; inter-
    racial, 89, 106–8, 110, 131, 166n94; milita-
    rized, 14, 111; on military bases, 6; roads
    as sites of, 107–8; settler colonialism and,
    5–6; sexual, 22, 110–11, 112, 144n36
Vizenor, Gerald, 4

Walin, Julita Santos, 94–95
Wanhalla, Angela, 105
war on terror, 11
We Are Guåhan, 136
welfare capitalism, 73, 75, 159n89
Winkelmann, Tessa Ong, 94
Winne, G. M., 130
Wolfe, L. Eugene, 76
Wolfe, Patrick, 5
Won Pat, Antonio B., 82
Woodcock, Nicolyn, 88
World War II: bombardment of Guåhan,
    52–53, 115–18; bombardment of Tiyan,
    115–18; Japanese occupation of Guåhan, 8,
    13, 15, 16, 21–22, 117–19, 132, 143nn30–31,
    154n11; military base construction during,
    3, 5–6